Baudelaire

and the Poetics of Modernity

Baudelaire

AND THE POETICS
OF MODERNITY

EDITED BY

Patricia A. Ward

with the assistance of
James S. Patty

VANDERBILT UNIVERSITY PRESS

Nashville

Library of Congress Cataloging-in-Publication Data

Baudelaire and the poetics of modernity / edited by Patricia A. Ward
with the assistance of James S. Patty.—1st ed.
p. cm.   Includes bibliographical references (p.) and index.
ISBN 0-8265-1377-8 (alk. paper)
1. Baudelaire, Charles, 1821–1867—Aesthetics. I. Ward,
Patricia A., 1940– II. Patty, James S. III. Title.
PQ2191.Z5 B358 2001
841'.8—dc21   00-010466

Photograph on p. iii reproduced with the permission
of M. Gérard Oberlé

Published by Vanderbilt University Press
Printed in the United States of America

for Claude Pichois,
director of the W. T. Bandy Center
for Baudelaire Studies at Vanderbilt University
from 1982 to 1998

Contents

viii

Preface

Baudelaire and his older contemporary, Gautier, were the writers who gave currency in France to the term *modernité*. In his most famous definition of the word in the section by that title in *Le Peintre de la vie moderne,* Baudelaire arrests the attention of his reader: "Modernity is the transitory, the fleeting, the contingent, half of art whose other half is the eternal and immutable" (*OC* 2:695). Lest we project onto that definition a twentieth-century sense of the quick pace of life which was ushered in by the speed of urbanization and technology of Baudelaire's own age, we should pay attention to the context of this, above all, aesthetic formulation. Keenly aware of the root of the word *moderne,* Baudelaire gives to this rather new variation its basic sense; he personifies it in its context of the actual and contingent. "There was a modernity for each ancient painter," he adds immediately and then goes on to say, "every epoch had its own bearing, its own look, and its own gesture" (695–96). Thus, in its original usage, "modernity" became a vehicle for expressing Baudelaire's unique sense of the painter's or poet's capacity via the imagination and a moral sensibility to capture the singular qualities of an age, but to formalize them aesthetically in ways that transcend those temporal boundaries.

Readers and critics have, of course, focused on the themes of Baudelaire's perception of his time, his rejection of received tradition, his ironic retention of the vocabulary of this tradition, and the urban qualities of his poetry. Consequently, "modernity" became for some synonymous with decadence, with poetry of the city, with the poet as *flâneur,* and with the sense of the anonymity of nineteenth-century crowds. This thematics of modernity, as well as an initial critical awareness of Baudelaire's reformulation of received aesthetic and theological categories, was eventually to be succeeded by a discussion of literary modernity, of Baudelaire's relationship to Mallarmé and his successors. More particularly, the questions of the nature of the self and of the representative quality of language, essential to the lyric in its early history, were viewed by critics as key to the development of the modern lyric that questioned them. Despite Mallarmé's complicated relationship to the poetry of Baudelaire, Baudelaire has been seen as opening the way to the depersonalization and nonreferentiality of the modern lyric, of which Mallarmé has been a prototype.

In reviewing these issues in his seminal essay "Lyric and Modernity," Paul de Man concludes that "the question of modernity reveals the paradoxical nature of a structure that makes lyric poetry into an enigma which never stops asking for the unreachable answer to its own riddle" (*Blindness and Insight* 186). Baudelaire gazed unflinchingly into the dilemmas of existence and of language, all within the context of memory and temporality. One thinks of a biblical expression, "Now we see into a glass, darkly" (1 Cor. 13:12), of which a more literal translation would be, "Now we see through a mirror into a dark saying, an enigma." Baudelaire looked deeply and clearly into the dark sayings, the enigmas, posed for him existentially and artistically, and he gazed upon them unflinchingly.

If in this volume we speak, then, of a "poetics" of modernity, we mean the conditions of the dark sayings or the enigmas of the Baudelairean text. The authors of these essays try to tease out the principles behind the rich paradoxes at the heart of Baudelaire's poetry and prose, of his literary and critical method. If Michel Brix, in the first essay, speaks of Baudelaire's secular Platonism and Michel Deguy, in the concluding essay, refers to his religious atheism, they do so to highlight the aesthetic questions of an enigmatic corpus. In different ways, often with a postmodernist vision, their colleagues broach the complexities and richness of the Baudelairean text which embodies again and again a loss of innocence of which he as a postromantic was so aware and we as postmodernists are continually reminded.

This volume came about as a result of a conference, "L'ère de Baudelaire," at Vanderbilt University in 1998, honoring the distinguished Baudelairean Claude Pichois upon his retirement. It honors him for providing a textual and biographical basis of immense historical and literary erudition for all contemporary discussion of Baudelaire. These essays are by his colleagues, friends, and students, as well as by a new generation of interpreters of Baudelaire. These are not the proceedings of the conference, but constitute essays inspired, in part, by it. They are offered as a homage, but also as a gift to a new generation of readers who will sense that Baudelaire, perhaps, lived and wrote their own enigmas.

Acknowledgments

Support for the publication of this book was provided by the W. T. Bandy Center for Baudelaire and Modern French Studies, the College of Arts and Science, and the University Research Council, all of Vanderbilt University, and by the Service Culturel de France.

Marc Froment-Meurice and Adelaide Russo provided assistance with this project. The staff of the Bandy Center, particularly Yvonne Boyer and Margaret Splane, have been most supportive. Josette Amsilli was responsible for the preparation of the manuscript, a particularly difficult task. Richard Espénant assisted in the compilation of the bibliography. Charles Backus and Paul Elledge of the Vanderbilt University Press encouraged and oversaw the actualization of the book.

The cover portrait of Charles Baudelaire by Nadar has been reproduced with the permission of Monsieur Gérard Oberlé. The National Gallery (London) gave permission to reproduce Manet's *La Musique aux Tuileries*. Monsieur Michel Deguy also approved the inclusion in this collection of the translation of his essay, which was originally published in French in 1994.

We are most grateful to all of the above and to the contributors and translators whose work constitutes this text.

A Note on Abbreviations
and Translations

References to the editions by Claude Pichois of the complete works and correspondence of Charles Baudelaire, published in the Bibliothèque de la Pléiade and cited in the bibliography at the end of this volume, are abbreviated as *OC* and *COR,* respectively.

This book is directed toward an English-speaking readership with a knowledge of French. Titles to Baudelaire's poetry and prose writings have been given in French because these are generally well known. Poetry in verse has been cited in French, followed by a prose translation. All prose poetry or critical writing has been translated into English. Unless otherwise indicated, the translations are those of the individual essayists.

PART I

Aesthetic Categories

Modern Beauty versus Platonist Beauty

Michel Brix

Translated by *Tony Campbell*

CRITICS are in agreement in acknowledging the preponderant influence exerted on French romanticism by the German writers known as the "romantiques d'Iéna," principally the brothers Friedrich and August-Wilhelm von Schlegel, Novalis, and the philosopher Schelling, associated around the publication of the *Athenaeum* (in six installments appearing between 1798 and 1800). The ideas of the romantics of Jena are close to Platonist doctrine. According to the compilers of the *Athenaeum,* art consists of "engraving on the tables of nature the thoughts of the divinity and the stylet of the creative spirit of forms" or in other terms, of forming "inside philosophy itself a tighter circle in which we see the eternal immediately in some kind of visible form" (from the translation of F. von Schlegel and Schelling in Lacoue-Labarthe and Nancy 1978, 225, 239). The second quotation is from the introduction to Schelling's *Philosophy of Art,* in which we also find the following words: "truth and beauty are only two different ways of considering the unique Absolute (Lacoue-Labarthe and Nancy 1978, 404). The Berlin *Lessons on Art and Literature* of August-Wilhelm von Schlegel adopt the premises that nature is a "hieroglyphic poem" and that beauty constitutes the symbolic representation of the infinite by the finite. One could multiply the quotations: Platonism or idealism defines the philosophical horizon of the romantics of Jena—those who took upon themselves the task of suppressing the "invisible partition which separates the real from the ideal world" (Lacoue-Labarthe and Nancy 1978,

1

342), so as to make Ideas perceptible, especially that which unites them all, the Idea of beauty.

The views of the members of the Jena circle were diffused in France by the treatise *De l'Allemagne* of Madame de Staël, a writer who was linked with the Schlegel brothers and used them as her main sources of information on German literature and thought. Madame de Staël also defends the thesis that there exist universal Beauty, Truth, and Good. If one believes the author of *De l'Allemagne,* the Germanic peoples would have a greater aptitude than others to feel and express innate ideas. Germans feel happy "in the ideal," their idealist metaphysic "has (as for the Greeks) at its origin the cult of beauty par excellence, which our soul alone can conceive and recognize"; being naturally drawn to Platonism, Germany has produced a poetry which constitutes "the terrestrial mirror of divinity" and expresses "the eternal and infinite" as the "secret alliance of our being" with the soul of nature (Staël 1968, 166, 187, 207, 232, 237).

In 1813 Madame de Staël's treatise (which had already appeared in 1810 but had been impounded by the Napoleonic government) invited French writers to renew themselves by dipping for inspiration into the well of Platonic or idealistic thought. A few years later, the author of *Corinne* would find a weighty ally in the person of Victor Cousin. A future intellectual guide of the university and of French philosophy under the July Monarchy, Cousin met Schelling in Munich in 1818, had the latter's work translated, corresponded regularly with him, and, above all, published from 1822 to 1840 the first complete French translations of the writings of Plato. Deputizing for Royer-Collard in the Sorbonne, Cousin gave, in 1818, a course in philosophy which was to be published with some modifications in 1853 and whose title leaves no doubt about its Platonist or idealist content, *Du Vrai, du Beau et du Bien.*[1] In this work the author announced the meeting, in the Beautiful, of divine infinity with the finiteness of the world of the senses and the human mind; the major role of the artist is as the discoverer and interpreter of the Beautiful, one called to awaken in sense objects the intuition of eternal realities. This "official" aesthetic of the French university was also preached by Théodore Jouffroy, whose *Cours d'esthétique* of 1826 was published in 1843.

Such doctrines have not remained without their echoes in literature, and Jacques Seebacher has written of Victor Hugo that "the greatest part of Victor Hugo's aesthetic is not original. Independent of any question of source, we find its model in Victor Cousin" (Seebacher 1993, 27). To the joint influence of the aesthetic and theories of the German writers united around the publication of the *Athenaeum* was added the propagation of the doctrines of the Enlightenment, all of which are based more or less on certain intuitions of the author of the *Banquet* (for instance, the system of correspondences expounded in Swedenborg's work).[2] During the first half of the nineteenth century, Platonism radiates more than ever in the writers and the poetry of French Romanticism, which, in order to unfold itself, was to lean for support on some of the main tenets of the aesthetic formulated by the Greek philosopher.

The triad of major ideas, at the center of which the Idea of the Beautiful shines with unrivaled brightness, determines the efforts of artists to provide an image for that Idea and to stimulate in the soul the feelings originating from Heaven which Beauty awakens. Nature is regarded as the sign or mirror of the divine; ideal forms come to be known in the world in a symbolic or written form; the visible and the invisible are linked together through analogies, which the human mind is invited to discover, so as to raise itself from the vision of the world below to grasp heavenly realities. The poet's is a quasi-spiritual ministry to uncover the divine message by decoding symbols. Shedding light on nature and human destiny, he becomes also the interpreter of the history of the world, which integrates as well into a grand design beyond history; the writer makes the divine work explicit and, so to say, makes real the link between the finite and the infinite.

The influence of Platonism or of idealism as filtered through German thought marks Hugo's writings very deeply, just as it influences those of Maurice de Guérin, Vigny, Ballanche, Lamartine, Madame de Staël, Quinet, Michelet, and the majority of humanitarian and socially concerned thinkers. Does this mean that, between the words *romanticism* and *Platonism* we can place an equal sign? I doubt it. The more it seems to be appropriate to search in numerous romantic works for the evidence of Platonic inspiration, the more it would be wrong to state that French romanticism should be attributed entirely to its Platonist inheritance. Some nineteenth-century writers—and not the least important—dared to question the "official" aesthetic system, derived partly from classicism and partly also from the romantics of Jena. There were not one but two romanticisms.

In this way, having made fun of Hugo's *Han d'Islande* and the mysticism of Vigny's *Eloa,* Stendhal is none the less author of the two editions of the romantic manifesto *Racine et Shakespeare*. But it is clear that, through-out that work, Stendhal does not defend the same aesthetic ideas as his two contemporaries. Thus he indicates in a letter to Louis Crozet of 28 September 1816 that the "dull Germans have seized the romantic system, have given it a name and have spoiled it" (Stendhal 1934, 370–71); the following 1 October, he went further in a new letter to Crozet and speaks of the "romantic system, spoiled by Schlegel's mysticism" (388).

There was, then, a romantic aesthetic which did not owe anything either to the Schlegels nor, above all, to the mysticism—by that we mean the Platonism or idealism—extolled by certain German thinkers. But, in order to express their originality, Stendhal and the writers who followed him had to shake off the guardianship of Plato, a guardianship even more burdensome and constraining than he had indicated in the *Phaedrus,* and, seemingly in a definitive manner, in what constituted art.

So the theory of ideal Beauty, unchangeable, permanent, eternal, transcending history—"sub specie aeternitatis"—antagonistic to all change, did not, in the nineteenth century, gain the allegiance of all romantic writers. Far from it. Even before the publication of the treatise *De l'Allemagne,* Chateaubriand had distanced himself from such a theory; in fact, the *Génie du christianisme* defended the idea that, corresponding to Greco-Roman polytheism and Christianity, there were two different aesthetics, products of the thought, the tastes and the aspirations of each age: from polytheism derives "the beautiful as a *physical* ideal" and from medieval Christianity, "the beautiful as a *moral ideal,* or what amounts to the same, the beautiful as an *ideal for characters*" (Chateaubriand 1978, 680–81). That was to open more than a gap in the Platonic system—a gap which others, with Stendhal in the front rank, would again not fail to widen. For instance, one finds at work in the treatise *De l'amour* Stendhal's keen sense of the relativity of aesthetic values: in the same way that one will not find *a* literary beauty, there is not *a* feminine beauty, there are as many feminine beauties as there are lovers and "each man has his *ideal beauty*" (Stendhal 1926, 137). The Beautiful is manifold and particular, linked to an individual set of circumstances and passions, subjected to the fluctuations of the weather, to the variety of temperaments, to the ideas personal to the artist, to his feelings and his intimate dreams. Whence the necessity, expressed in *Racine et Shakespeare,* of modernity in the arts: the theater of the nineteenth century had to respond to the contemporary conditions of habits and beliefs; writers had to serve up to the French people of 1824 or 1825 the "dish" capable of giving them the greatest possible pleasure.

Baudelaire followed Stendhal in affirming the relativity of an idea which Platonists presented as an absolute concept. Thus one thinks of the former's report on the Exposition Universelle of 1855: the Beautiful in itself is unknowable, each civilization has developed its own idea of the Beautiful and thinks that that idea is the right one; one cannot reach a clear-cut decision regarding these divergent views, since the hierarchy of civilization has never been established; moreover, any individual exiled for a few years in a distant country will certainly change his *credo* in matters of morals and aesthetics. *Le Peintre de la vie moderne* (1863) attacks again "the theory of the unique and absolute Beautiful," by proposing the twofold makeup of the Beautiful, formed certainly of "an eternal, unvarying element," but with which there is associated "a relative, circumstantial element which will be, if you wish, all in all or altogether, the epoch, fashion, morals, passion" (*OC* 2:685).

The Beautiful, the True, and the Good—as pure ideas—are unrecognizable, and the pursuit of these ideals leads the artist into an aesthetic dead end: in subjecting all aesthetic pursuit to the triad of pure ideas, the Platonic system revealed itself as arid and impracticable. At any rate, such is the conclusion drawn by Baudelaire in his correspondence: "Every seeker after pure ideality in matters of art is a heretic in the eyes of the Muse and of art" (Letter to Alphonse de Calonne, 8 January 1859, *COR* 1:537),[3] as well as at the end of "Le *Confiteor* de l'artiste," in *Petits Poèmes en prose:* "The study of the beautiful is a duel where the artist cries out before being vanquished" (*OC* 1:179). The same theme appears in at least two poems from *Les Fleurs du Mal,* "Les Plaintes d'un Icare" (edition of 1868)—the love of the beautiful, in the strict meaning of the term, consumes the poet—and above all "La Mort des artistes": only death will perhaps be able to put the artist in contact with the "grande Créature," or the "Idole," "dont l'infernal désir les remplit de sanglots" [the Idol . . . whose infernal enticement fills them with sobs] (*OC* 1:127).[4] The ideal work of art, the desire for which consumes the Platonists, is destined to remain forever an absent work of art.

The Platonist aesthetic is based on the indissolubility of the triad of the Beautiful, the True, the Good. It will be the author of *Les Fleurs du Mal* who will oppose that theory with the most devastating refutation: *"The time is*

*mad and raves in everything, but more especially in the field of art, because of
the HERETICAL confusion of the Good with the Beautiful*" (letter of 8
January 1859, *COR* 1:537); "What is beautiful is not more honest than dis-
honest" (*OC* 2:142); "the famous doctrine of the indissolubility of the
Beautiful, the True, and the Good is but the invention of modern would-be
philosophers" (*OC* 2:111).[5] The Baudelairean aesthetic, on the contrary, is
founded on the denial of the equivalence of the Beautiful—the Good: so
even the title of the 1857 collection affirms the link which exists between
Beauty—the flowers—and Evil.

In art Baudelaire became the opponent of Platonism and, in our view,
some critics have been wrong in exploiting the lines in which the poet presents the work of Edgar Allan Poe.[6] One cannot, in the absence of a clear-cut
argument, attribute to the author of *Les Fleurs du Mal* the Platonist ideas of
the American writer which Baudelaire describes and indeed expounds but
does not endorse. The independence manifested with regard to Platonism is
also demonstrated in the famous sonnet "Correspondances": the title is indeed Swedenborgian, but the content of the poem quashes such a rapprochement. As Claude Pichois emphasizes:

> The title, seemingly Swedenborgian, threatens to confuse the
> reader, to lead him to believe that the first stanza has devolved
> from the symbolic communication of the material world and
> the spiritual world. The puzzle remains (has Baudelaire intend-
> ed this?), but it begins to be clarified if one considers that
> Baudelaire gave to the word *correspondances* a personal meaning
> in harmony with line 8 ["Scents, colors and sounds respond to
> one another"]. (*OC* 1:843)[7]

In fact, several interpreters, among whom, in spite of everything, is included Jean Pommier, have remarked that Baudelaire refrained from building bridges between the visible universe and the invisible. The spectacle
of nature finds equivalents in a supernatural world, but *surnaturel* for
Baudelaire is not synonymous with *céleste* or *divin*. In this respect, it is of interest to set the "Correspondances" of *Les Fleurs du Mal* against a poem of
the same title unearthed by Jacques Crépet.[8] "Les Correspondances" of the
Abbé Constant (Eliphas Lévi) appeared in 1845 in the collection *Les Trois
Harmonies. Chansons et poésies:*

Formé de visibles paroles,
Ce monde est le songe de Dieu;
Son verbe en choisit les symboles,
L'esprit les remplit de son feu [. . .]
C'est là que lisent les prophètes;
Et ceux dont les yeux sont ouverts
Sont eux-mêmes les interprètes
De l'énigme de l'univers . . . (Cited in *OC* 1:840)

[Formed of visible words, / This world is God's dream; / His word chooses the symbols for it, / The spirit fills them with its fire. / It is there that the prophets read; / And those whose eyes are open / Are themselves the interpreters / Of the enigma of the universe. . . .]

In the case of Abbé Constant, and in the tradition of "official" romantic thought, it is very much a question of recalling the Swedenborgian doctrine of correspondences. On the other hand, it is clear that the poem of *Les Fleurs du Mal,* which deliberately ignores terrestrial/divine equivalents, has no point of reference with such a doctrine.

After the first edition of *Les Fleurs du Mal,* Baudelaire's anti-Platonism will not vary again, as is evidenced particularly in the sonnet "Les Aveugles" in the edition of 1861 and in the article devoted the same year to Victor Hugo. The latter text has been analyzed in detail by Pierre Laforgue, who has demonstrated that, in passages with double or triple meanings, Baudelaire made fun of the poet's literary priesthood or royalty, central themes of Hugolian thought. Baudelaire's article of 1861, under the guise of a eulogy, would describe Hugo as a poet of an obsolete aesthetic, a writer of times past, repeating tirelessly a few ideas in vogue around 1830.

As for the sonnet "Les Aveugles," it evokes directly the Platonic symbol of blindness, but to poke fun at it; *L'Homme qui rit,* in 1869, would again reveal that blindness, according to Hugo, had always remained the symbol of sight and the perception of pure ideas and the truth (Milner 1994, 1996). Now Baudelaire's poem makes fun of the blind: they are "affreux," "vaguement ridicules," and their eyes "d'où la divine étincelle est partie" [which the divine spark has left], are looking no one knows where, lost in the endless dark (*OC* 1:92). The blindness is transformed in *Les Fleurs du Mal* into a negative symbol, which—far from evoking the capacity, reserved for a few chosen ones, of grasping the forms—accuses those who are affected by them of rejecting the reality of the world. The characters in Baudelaire's sonnet do not ally themselves with the *voyants:* blind advocates of a system, they are like strangers on earth. Moreover, this blindness of the Platonists also was denounced in Baudelaire's report of the Exposition Universelle, *Beaux-Arts:* the "mad doctrinaire of the Beautiful," "locked up in the blinding fortress of his system," makes a blasphemy of life and nature; he has "forgotten the colour of the sky, the shape of vegetation, the movement and smell of the animals," and his "tensed fingers, paralyzed by the pen, can no longer run along the huge keyboard of *correspondences!*" (*OC* 2:577).[9] This was clearly an affirmation that the Baudelairean correspondences are not vertical earth /Heaven connections.

But if Baudelaire is not a Platonist, what then is he? He belongs to a line of creative artists who, faced with Hugolian romanticism, developed an original aesthetic, born out of opposition to the Platonist or idealist system. The *Salon de 1846* was to affirm, in a famous but somewhat sibylline passage, that romanticism did not consist of a choice of subject nor of exact truth, but "in the manner of feeling" (*OC* 2:420). Through this formula, Baudelaire extended his hand to the first users in France of the word "romantisme"— namely Rousseau, the marquis of Girardin, and Pierre Le Tourneur, the translator of Shakespeare—well before that aesthetic was spoiled—*dixit* Stendhal—"by the mystical Schlegel." According to Le Tourneur, who is keen to find the precise meaning of the word *romanticism,* it goes much further than *pittoresque* or *romanesque;* applied to a landscape, it joins "together the physical and moral effects of perspective"; it designates also a sensation which "arouses in the affected soul tender feelings and melancholy ideas." When a valley is "romantic," Le Tourneur continues,

> [t]he eye is pleased to look at it and soon the melted imagination
> fills it with interesting scenes; it forgets the valley to enjoy the
> ideas, the images that it has inspired. (See also Pichois 1959;
> Peyre 1971, 71; and Milner and Pichois 1985, 11–12.)[10]

The "manner of feeling" which Baudelaire evokes in 1846 seems scarcely removed from the "sensations" of Le Tourneur, which conjure up a physical thing to which is given a moral meaning. The use of the term *romantic*

appears to enter in from the moment the subject gives life to the world, or in
any case when there is established between the two poles of the self and of the
world a certain relationship, founded on analogy: the impressions originating
in the contemplation of nature awaken, through a game of correspondences,
feelings—but not of absolute feelings—in the consciousness of the spectator.

> Cieux déchirés comme des grèves,
> En vous se mire mon orgueil;
> Vos vastes nuages en deuil

> Sont les corbillards de mes rêves,
> Et vos lueurs sont le reflet
> De l'Enfer où mon cœur se plaît. (*OC* 1:78)

[Skies torn like shores, / In you my pride admires itself; / Your
vast mourning clouds // Are the hearses of my dreams, / And
your glows are the reflection / Of Hell where my heart is happy.]

These are the tercets of "Horreur sympathique," a poem belonging to
the second edition of *Les Fleurs du Mal*. The word *sympathique* is to be understood here in its primary meaning, that of its Greek origin, evoking participation in the suffering of another and in the sharing of feelings. The first
stanza of the same text speaks also of a "ciel bizarre et livide, /Tourmenté" [a
strange and livid, tormented sky], like the fate of a libertine. In nature the
poet finds, not exact similitudes (fate or pride cannot be confused with sky
any more than clouds can carry the grief of dreams), but resemblances,
analogies, correspondences. Nature is offered as the reflection or as a kind
of translation, a word to which we will have to return, of the individual's
states of soul.

"Horreur sympathique" does not illustrate an isolated theme in *Les
Fleurs du Mal*. We could have quoted, among other texts, the sonnet
"Brumes et pluies": "Rien n'est plus doux au cœur plein de choses funèbres,
/ Et sur qui dès longtemps descendent les frimas, / ' blafardes saisons, reines
de nos climats, / Que l'aspect permanent de vos pâles ténèbres" (*OC* 1:101)
[Nothing is sweeter to the heart full of mournful things, / On whom the
wintry weather has for long been falling, / O pale seasons, queen of our
climes, / Than the permanent look of your pale worlds of darkness"]. Or we

could have cited the last of the four pieces, called "Spleen," in which the sky weighs down on the narrator's mind, the day is sad, the earth is a prison cell, and the rods of rain are like prison bars. Here, without doubt, we are touching on a major and particular character of human perception: the spontaneous association in sense experiences of physical elements and moral impressions. The sight of the world awakens moral ideas in human consciousness: a moonlight is melancholic, a flower evinces joy, an isolated tree, sadness, a dark sky, remorse. The list can go on and on. From the outset, it suggests the fruitfulness of an aesthetic based entirely on sense experience.

This special attention to the world allows the artist to "invest all of nature with a supernatural interest, which gives each object a deeper meaning, more voluntary, more despotic" (*OC* 2:596). One can see quite well that, in such a context, the word *surnaturel* is not to be approximated to *céleste* or *mystique* and does not have even any religious connotation. The inspiration of things, the supernatural dimension which the writer attaches to them, are the moral ideas they harbor and which the medium of art reveals. The world of moral impressions constitutes also a "sur-nature." For all that, it is not pointless to note that Baudelaire has borrowed the word *surnaturalisme* from Heinrich Heine, who transferred this term from the theological to the aesthetic domain.[11] Above nature, there is not only the divinity, or the pure ideas, there is also the moral world. Supernaturalism—what Baudelaire discovers at work in, for example, Delacroix—consists of changing the material world by uncovering not its religious meaning, but its moral treasury (*OC* 2:546). Half a century after Baudelaire, Proust, to indicate the degree to which, like the author of *Les Fleurs du Mal*, he was to plumb the sense of material things, uses the term *métaphore*, clearly devoid at that time of all religious meaning.[12] But, for all that, it does not follow that the search for such metaphors entails ipso facto the denial of the existence of God: supernaturalism has nothing to do with religion, but it does not deny it. On the contrary, one would even be tempted to say, if one followed Baudelaire's formula: it is because "God has offered the world as a complex and indivisible whole" that it is in order to look again, in the moral world, for the equivalents of material things (*OC* 2:784).

The question of the Beautiful, which is at the origin of this essay, exemplifies the split which ran through French literature in the nineteenth century. We have examined the conception of the Beautiful created by the writers faithful to Platonist inspiration. We must here quote the lines dedicated to the Spanish painter Ribera in 1850. His paintings gather together what can be called, by way of caricature, "l'arsenal réaliste": the lowly classes, beggars, gypsies, bandits, lackeys, all afflicted with physical deformities more or less pronounced. Gautier admires the painter's approach and writes:

> if, through a very modern and very Spanish attitude, he [Ribera] prefers character to beauty and rehabilitates those three monsters, terrors of ancient art: poverty, ugliness and old age, it is not only that graces repel him: . . . but, in the name of realism, he is protesting against the abstractions of Greek idealism, and brings into the domain of art all these evils formerly rejected, and, through the powerful seal of approval he gives them, raises them in style and gives them letters of nobility. (Gautier, *La Presse*, 27 August 1850)[13]

Ribera "prefers character to beauty." The sequel to the passage shows clearly to what "beauty" Gautier is alluding: linked with Greek idealism, it is found at the heart of the Platonist system and represents the external image of the ideal on earth. To such a quest for Beauty is opposed, in the words of Gautier, a poetic of "character"—that is to say of the moral meaning of things: a thing is beautiful, not because it possesses one or other of the marks generally attributed to the idea of Beauty (unity, universality, harmony), but because it has a sense which the artist is seeking to transmit. These are precisely the convictions Baudelaire expresses in the manuscript of *Fusées*.

> I have found the definition of the Beautiful,—of my Beautiful. It is something fervent and sad. . . . An attractive and beautiful face, a woman's face, shall I say, it is a face which, at the same time . . . makes one dream of desire and sadness,—or a contrary idea, that is to say a zeal, a thirst for living, associated with a resurgent sense of bitterness. . . . [A beautiful male face] will contain also something passionate and sad,—spiritual needs, ambitions secretly rejected,—the idea of a rumbling force, unused,—sometimes the idea of a vengeful insensitivity. (*OC* 1:657)

We see that beauty according to Baudelaire is not Platonist; the beautiful forms are not those arousing the intuition of eternal realities, but really those bearing moral significance—sadness, melancholy, bitter disappointment, joy, passion for living, etc.

All in all, the Baudelairean definition of beauty refers to a kind of secular Platonism, in which reality retains its symbolic value but no longer reflects back to any form or ideal no matter what. So, one witnesses during the nineteenth century the development of a double conception of the symbol. One is inspired directly by Platonism (these are the vertical correspondences) and seeks to reattach earth to heaven. The other flows from the Baudelairean conception of horizontal correspondences (or synaesthesia) and affirms—strictly in human terms and without reference to the divinity —the unity of the moral world and the material world; it does not tie the Beautiful to the qualities of the proportion, harmony, or symmetry of things, but with the inner self of the observer. "If such a composition of trees, mountains, water and houses, which we call a landscape is beautiful, it is not so by itself, but through me, through my own favor, by the idea or the feeling which I attach to it" (*Salon de 1859, OC* 2:660). The Baudelairean "essences" are revealed as even more volatile or, at any rate, more transitory, than things themselves, and they can vary infinitely; by contrast, in all the doctrines emerging from Platonist inspiration, the forms are reputed to be fixed and eternal.

The artist's task is to restore these moral impressions—in other words, and to recall the words which Baudelaire applies to Gautier, "to define the mysterious attitude which the objects of creation hold in the face of human observation" (*OC* 2:117). With normal perception leading from things to ideas, the artist, for his or her part, must make the same transition, but in reverse: going from the moral impressions to things, seeking, and here again Baudelaire serves as our guide, "in external and visible nature examples and metaphors which [serve] to characterize pleasures and impressions of a spiritual order." (*OC* 2:148).[14] The notion of translation finds its whole meaning in such a context. Baudelaire uses this word on many occasions to signify that the major value of a work of art resides in the original impression the author is struggling to reconstitute. "A beautiful picture is faithful to the dream which brought it into being" (*OC* 2:626). In other words, a picture representing a landscape is beautiful in so far as it succeeds in awakening in the viewer the very feeling which made the painter find it beautiful. Thus, it is not the subject matter which counts in painting ("the beauty of a painting does not depend on the things represented there"),[15] but the moral fruitfulness, the power of suggestion of the picture, its capacity to translate the feelings experienced by the artist in regard to that which he is painting. Before the drawings of Constantin Guys, the viewer's imagination reconstructs vividly the impression produced by the concrete things on the mind of the author (*OC* 2:698). Concerning a cartoon of Carle Vernet depicting a gaming club, Baudelaire praises the composition for displaying "much seriousness, a pleasing severity, a hardness in approach which suits the subject quite well as the game is a passion, violent and controlled at the same time" (*Quelques caricaturistes français, OC* 2:545). It is the treatment of the subject—and not the subject itself—which constitutes the sense, or the moral significance, accorded to the game by the painter.

How is this transfer done? The major role played by memory in the creative process comes in here. Baudelaire explains in the *Salon de 1859*:

> Allow me . . . to return again to my mania, I mean to the regrets I have at seeing the part played by imagination in landscapes becoming more and more reduced. . . . Yes, the imagination makes the landscape. I understand that a mind being applied to take notes cannot surrender itself to the fantastic imagery contained in the spectacle of nature which is present; but why does imagination flee from the studio of the landscape artist? Perhaps the artists who cultivate this genre mistrust their memory far too much and adopt a method of immediate copying, which matches perfectly the laziness of their minds. (OC 2:664–65).

This method of "immediate copy" outside any mediation of memory distances painters not only from true art, but also just as much from their first ambition, the faithful reproduction of a landscape. Baudelaire writes yet further on: "the majority of our landscape artists are liars, precisely because they have neglected to lie" (*OC* 2:668). Clearly, the truth in the picture does not belong to those who copy, but to those who use the prism of their memory or their imagination (in so much , of course, as one can distinguish between these two faculties). It is from such a perspective that we have to grasp Baudelaire's views on photography, which, in his eyes, represents the negation of art.[16] Baudelaire admires Constantin Guys because he draws from memory, from the image inscribed in his brain, and not from a model or from nature. Whereas realistic description subjects the artist to details and finally drowns him in them, the "involvement of re-enlivening, suggestive memory" (*OC* 2:699), as proved by Constantin Guys, allows him, on the other hand, to create effects, impressions through his drawings. It is for memory to "digest" the reality—that is to say, to accord a place and a value relative to the signs which fill the visible universe.[17] The artist or the writer has to be able, like Constantin Guys, to turn away from his model at the moment of creation and place his trust in the work of synthesis, combination, and transformation realized through memory. The process of creating a literary work is therefore identified with an operation of re-creation or recomposition of reality by memory, alone capable of reconstituting the effect, which art is seeking to transmit.

One of the chapters in *Le Peintre de la vie moderne* has as its heading "La Modernité." Without doubt, in today's literary criticism, there is no word more hackneyed than this one. Baudelaire has obviously something to do with this. But an examination of the principles which underlie his aesthetic allows us, perhaps, to approach this specious concept and to uncover the slow and progressive development in France, in the nineteenth century, of literary modernity, with Baudelaire, but also with Stendhal, Chateaubriand, Balzac, Gautier, Nerval, Flaubert, and finally Proust. Modernism is art freed from Platonist guardianship and, consequently, from any religious intention or background. Art to the measure of the human.

The Linguistic Turning of the Symbol

Baudelaire and His French Symbolist Heirs

William Franke

THE process of symbolization begins when one thing is used to stand for something else. A stone thrown into a pit for the purpose of counting whatever sort of objects may be considered a primitive symbol. A link is thereby forged between items that have nothing to do with each other in the nature of things, simply by virtue of the one's being made to take the place of the other. Some such model as this generally informs the notion of the symbol current in linguistics and semiotics and in a broad spectrum of empirical disciplines where phenomena of signification are studied scientifically. The aspect of the symbol that is stressed in these fields is its arbitrariness or conventionality and the fact that it is *not* the object it symbolizes, but just some substitute for it in the object's absence.[1]

For poets, and generally in aesthetic theory, the symbolic has quite a different meaning. The symbol distinguishes itself from other types of signs (or as against the sign altogether) by virtue of its making concretely present the thing it signifies. This function of presencing has consistently been described in the language of "participation," with the implication that the symbol is actually a part of the larger whole it represents—*pars pro toto*. In Coleridge's famous formulation, the symbol "always partakes of the reality which it renders intelligible; and while it enunciates the whole, abides itself as a living part in that unity of which it is the representative."[2] Consequently, in aesthetics the idea of the symbol has tended to imply an intrinsic affinity with what is symbolized (to the point of *being* it, at least in part) and often the fundamental unity of all things—all things

15

being reflected in the symbol as in a microcosm or monad.[3] In addition to the monadology of Leibniz, Hegel's doctrine of the concrete universal and Kant's notion of an a priori intuition which is not "schematic" but rather "analogical" (*Kritik der Urteilskraft*, sec. 59) supply some of the German idealistic underpinnings for this originally romantic conception of the symbol.[4] Another important source can be found in magic and totemism, as is signaled by the interest of symbolist poets from Baudelaire to Yeats and beyond, for example, to James Merrill, in the occult. In occult tradition and lore, the symbol participates in reality to the extent of being able effectively to transform it, typically through the manipulation of tokens, rather than remaining just an external representation devoid of any real efficacy and power over what it represents (Lévi-Strauss, "L'efficacité").

That the symbol is a part of the whole it represents (and by universal analogy this expands to include the whole universe), that it thereby makes present what it signifies, presenting it, precisely, *in part,* means also that the symbol may be said to signify not merely by virtue of convention but by its "nature." What it actually is in itself and not just what it may be arbitrarily used to stand for determines what the symbol signifies. To say a "sail" was seen on the horizon in order to mean that a ship was seen (Coleridge's own example) is in some sense a natural mode of expression. There is something not entirely arbitrary about using a sail to represent a ship. A ship is indeed in a certain manner present in a sail; it is present in part. And a sail *is,* approximately, a ship: that is, it is a piece of a ship.

The goal of giving access to nature beneath the level of social conventions of signification has been fairly constantly in view throughout the history of symbolic expression in poetry: it is epitomized by the myth of Orpheus as the singer-poet whose music tames beasts and even moves the inanimate elements. His mastery over the natural world indicates that his poetry is the very language of nature (Bays). The endeavor to return to a state in which language would signify by virtue of its being and intrinsic nature rather than by conventions socially imposed was a program already of the romantics. Hölderlin's "Nun, nun, müssen die Worte dafür, wie Blumen, entstehen" [Now, now, must words therefore like flowers originate] in "Brot und Wein" can be taken as emblematic of the need for rediscovering language as a natural thing. This is the ideal of a poetic language that would be literally things, in which the breach between sign and referent that characterizes (and curses) postlapsarian language would be repaired.[5]

The symbolist tradition from Hölderlin to Rilke activates this Orphic claim for poetry in a particularly intense and self-conscious, even at times self-ironic, way. The notion often holds a powerful attraction still for contemporary poets—as witness the undiminished fascination with Orpheus—however far they may be from considering it possible to realize.

The art of the symbol, accordingly, at least from the romantic period on, was supposed to make beings speak, or to provide by the symbol a channel that would make their natural speech audible. Baudelaire crystallized the idea that language should ideally be the natural speaking of things in some essential verses in "L'Invitation au voyage":

> Tout y parlerait
> À l'âme en secret
> Sa douce langue natale. (*OC* 1:53)

> [There everything would speak / To the soul in secret / Its sweet native language.]

These lapidary lines seem to envisage a language unmediated by arbitrary conventions and by meanings imposed by practical functions of communication, deaf to the things' own native voices. Things speaking to the soul in their own native language, attuned to its own inner being, communicate in virtue of what they are. What speaks in the symbol or in the space to which Baudelaire voyages in the poem is everything, *tout*, since by universal analogy any particular thing speaking its sweet native language—that is, the language of things—speaks for all beings and perhaps for being itself. Of course, Baudelaire is also, in decisive ways, fiercely negative on nature, loathing it as ugly and evil, yet his "*flowers* of evil" are nevertheless themselves produced by descent to precisely this soil in order to transform it into art. It is all the more necessary, therefore, to begin from these romantic doctrines in order to account for his transmutation, in effect a denaturalization, of the symbol.

In the symbolic universe, all things are interconnected, and all are immanent in each individual thing. This is to say that the world is composed of correspondences: its qualities "answer to one another," as Baudelaire puts it in "Correspondances" ("Les parfums, les couleurs et les sons se répondent"), just like the mutually defining elements of a language. Indeed, as the linguistic metaphor of "answering" suggests, the things that make up the world, at least as it is reflected in poetry, *are* the elements of a language. Baudelaire was fond of describing all nature as a vocabulary for the artist's use ("La nature n'est qu'un dictionnaire").[6] However, although he evokes the romantic topos of the language of things—as again in "Elévation": "le langage des fleurs et des choses muettes" [the language of flowers and of mute things]—Baudelaire turns out ultimately to be more interested in re-creating the whole order of things as a language and therefore as *not* natural. The implication is less that language should return to a state of nature and more nearly the reverse—that even nature might be subsumed into language.

Baudelaire's closed, symmetrical stanzaic forms and the interiorization of the world in the supposedly authentic dimension of "cœur" contribute to construing reality as a language where everything is differentially defined, so that all elements are ordered by internal relations into a self-enclosed system.[7] In "L'Invitation au voyage," "things" such as "les soleils mouillés" and "ces ciels brouillés" are not just kindred natural phenomena. They actually create each other in relation to one another—for example, by the reciprocity of their rhyming and the differential play of assonances and consonants—in the splendor in which they poetically exist, each as distilled out of the other and as fused together into one whole. The experience of reading a Baudelaire poem is (or at least can be) one of being carried away to a sphere where all things and sensations are transubstantiated by appearing within the structural wholes of the poem. The world is presented as essentially translated into a poetic idiom and as articulated in a harmony of purely formal, mutually defining values. Things sublated thus into a system of correspondences or relative differences have been turned essentially into language.

Romantics, and long before them writers of the Middle Ages, had conceived nature as language—that is, as a system of signs, or, metaphorically, a book. However, the creed that the experience of everything as one is a possibility engendered specifically by poetic language became operational first for the symbolists, and they recognized Baudelaire as having opened up this possibility. The sensuously symbolic power of his verse made it a superior, all-encompassing kind of "seeing" to which a veritable universe accrued. Hence Baudelaire could be hailed as *voyant* and a "vrai dieu" by Rimbaud. Baudelaire's essential achievement and legacy to symbolism is to have convincingly created the experience of how everything (at least as sensed and felt by an individual) can be known in and as language. Feelings and perceptions themselves become an alphabet to be used according to the grammar of poetic art. Even when it is strongly evocative of a specific historical epoch and milieu, Baudelaire's poetry refers to these external phenomena only as essentially transfigured by their representation in and as poetic language: "Tout devient allégorie" [All becomes allegory]—"Le Cygne." Baudelaire tended to use *allégorie* interchangeably with the term *symbole* (for example, at the end of "Un voyage à Cythère"), since both serve equally well to indicate the linguistic transfiguration of the real.[8] In this perspective, which is the soul of symbolism, language is not just a reality but all reality, and perhaps suprareality as well.

Language tends to become identical with all it represents in Baudelaire's poetry: it is the part which concretely embodies and becomes symbolically identical with the whole. This is not to be confused with a metaphysical thesis that there is nothing but language.[9] It is rather a poetic experience of everything becoming accessible to be known symbolically—that is, as identical, on the model of part and whole, with the concrete, sensuous instance of the poem itself. A symbol is the presence of a unity that is not completely given as such to the senses but is present in language through the partial, or rather participatory, identity of symbol and symbolized. The poem as symbol is, at least in part, what it represents. This results directly from the drive toward identity at work in language as symbol. The symbol annexes to itself everything with which it comes into contact. It makes everything it touches over into itself. By virtue of its intense sensuality and almost hallucinatory inebriation, Baudelaire's language becomes the palpable presentation or incarnation of a whole (symbolic) universe.

The symbol proposes to participate in a larger reality, but for the symbolist this means, by a logic of supplementarity, that it ends up producing virtually, in the element of language, the reality it was supposed to symbolize. Its synthetic energy becomes the creative force that constitutes the world it symbolizes. For the symbol is invested with a force for becoming symbolically the whole that it is not literally, either by throwing things together into unity *(symballein)* or as the part of a token *(symbolon)* that represents, in the absence of the missing half, the whole of which it was originally part. The drive to identity at work in language as symbol is concentrated and heightened by the harmonious language of lyric based on symmetries and correspondences—that is, on various forms of repetition of the same; for example, rhythm and rhyme. All such devices of the lyric imagination serve in the production of varieties of identity.

Identity that is forged by the very symbolic nature of language, brought out and enhanced by the form as well as the intent and meaning of Baudelaire's verse, surfaces as a totally obsessive trope in a poem like "L'Invitation au voyage." The *incipit*—"Mon enfant, ma sœur" [My child, my sister]—creates identity immediately by its grammar of apposition. This already suggests some collapse of natural boundaries of difference, a promiscuous mix of distinct kinds of kinship. All intimate relations seem to be embraced together in one, an incestuous intimacy disregarding essential differences between progeny and sibling and, implicitly, lover. The country to which the voyage is directed is itself at least partially or approximately identical with the beloved ("pays qui te ressemble"). The skyscapes and weather are for the poet-speaker but the reflection of the beloved's eyes and their stormy emotions. Even love and death collapse together in identity by conjunction: "Aimer à loisir, / Aimer et mourir" [To love at leisure, / To love and die], as loving here becomes at the same time a suspension of activity and a dying. This world of complete identity is expressed finally in the last stanza of the poem in that the ships traveling from the furthest limits of the earth nevertheless move wholly within the sphere of the beloved's desire: "C'est pour assouvir / Ton moindre désir / Qu'ils viennent du bout du monde" [It is to satisfy / Your least desire / That they come from the end of the world]. The external world here is totally at the service of, and has no determination or identity independently of, the innerness of desire. By thematizing the principle of identity in this way, the poem gives a lyric image of how language in fact operates in symbolist poetry—namely, by identifying itself concretely with what it represents and erasing the difference between representation and reality, the inner world and the outer.

The intrinsic relation of language and world in symbolism is grounded not only in the Neoplatonic trope of participation, but also, particularly for romantic theorists of the symbol like Coleridge, Goethe, and Hamann, in the language of revelation, *Offenbarung,* which intimates a prophetic precedent for symbolist poetics. In the biblical tradition of *Logos,* the Word of God creates all things and, consequently, all creatures are symbols bespeaking their Creator. Hence this paradigm, too, induces to construing language and world as communicating with, and indeed as intrinsic to one another, at the most originary level. Baudelaire explicitly alludes to the Creator Word's becoming flesh ("Et verbum caro factum est") in his preface to *Les Fleurs du Mal.*

Whether Neoplatonically or biblically backgrounded, whether conceived in terms of participation or of creation as revelation, symbolist poetics are predicated on a peculiarly privileged relation of language and world. Indeed the absorption of all reality into language as *poiesis* may be taken to be the key premise of the entire symbolist vision. The consequences of this fundamental premise, however, turn out to be diverse and even contradictory. On the one hand, reality puts up no more resistance: all is simply fused into unity in an exquisite and unrestricted universal harmony forged in and by language. On the other hand, the collapse of all extralinguistic reality into language leaves language empty of real substance and consequently disoriented. Without being anchored to anything real beyond itself, language has trouble maintaining even its own unity and integrity.

The essential tension between these opposite sorts of consequences of its pan-linguisticism can, in fact, be detected in every aspect and dimension of symbolist art. Ineluctably, together with the presence of the object in and to the symbol, its immanence to language, comes also an emptying of all objective content. The symbol contains everything immediately within itself, but only at the price of becoming a pure ideality devoid of relation to anything beyond the purely linguistic sphere. Every supposedly external object of language collapses into just a linguistic artifact. This makes it possible ultimately to dissolve the presumed external sources of language, including subjectivity and all its attendant postulates, into material forces and drives conceived of as working and manifest immanently in language. And it is this direction in which symbolist poetry subsequent to Baudelaire and down to our own times decisively moves.

Baudelaire used his art of the symbol in order to discover the mysterious and profound unity ("une ténébreuse et profonde unité") of all things based on revelation by the word or on correspondences in a Neoplatonic order of being. But that this is peculiarly the poet's prerogative, a secret reserved for disclosure by the master of words, suggests that it is a unity that exists essentially in the order of language. As the purely linguistic status of the vision proclaimed in symbolist poetry becomes more overt, the synthesis Baudelaire's poetry celebrates shows itself to be not just a synthesis of what is supposed to be higher reality but equally, and paradoxically, an exclusion from and avoidance of the real. Hence the "double aspect" of symbolism individuated by Paul de Man in his homologous essay "The Double Aspect of Symbolism."[10] It is because the poet in the solitude of his individual consciousness finds himself alienated from the world that he attempts, in vain according to de Man, to recover lost unity by means of his symbolic language.

Given this double aspect of symbolism, together with the aspiration toward an ideal life of unity goes a discomfiting and even shocking avowal of the ultimate truth of dissolution and death. It is only too clear that the ecstatic experiences so exuberantly enjoyed are dependent upon and even transpire within, wholly within, language. Language is the element in which the symbol lives and dies. It is a synthetic, unifying medium, but it is also in itself purely formal, empty of substance, a kind of dead artifact destined to be identified with the dead letter of writing. Consequently, its use to synthesize unity is inevitably artificial. The pure religion of art, practiced self-consciously as a calculated linguistic craft or alchemy, is constrained to exploit the very sorts of mechanical and material means that the symbolist artist otherwise affects to despise. Thus, to the extent that it is an act of faith, symbolism is almost inevitably in bad faith, for it is acutely aware of its own artifices and, in effect, of the contradiction of striving to *synthesize* unmediated experience of the whole harmonious unity of things.

This precarious posture of symbolist poetry is held intact by Baudelaire, buoyed up on the exuberance of his discovery of an almost all-powerful verbal magic. As the historical distance from this burst of creative inspiration lengthens, it becomes more difficult for the sheer passion of poetry to either make good or render irrelevant the self-deceptions that go into the making of the symbol. It is language that permits the total, unified knowledge sought by symbolists, yet language is also at the same time a false, or at least a fictive, element of such knowledge. What is "merely" linguistic is also in a sense nothing. The nothingness and death with which symbolist voices are so seductively obsessed has its remote motivations in this predicament. Irrepressibly, this sense of an encroaching emptying out and annihilation of reality by language asserts itself as a dominant mood throughout French symbolist poetry starting from Baudelaire's own poetry precipitated into the abyss *(le gouffre)* opened up by its own infinite expanse unlimited by any reality it cannot absorb. Indeed death comes to be figured as the very perfection sought, and the goal of knowledge by poetry's symbolic *gnosis* is represented as being reached precisely in death.

As Walter Benjamin perceived, Baudelaire's poetry presents a challenge to conceive language in its purity. In introducing his translation of *Tableaux parisiens,* he describes his attempt to translate the pure essence of language itself. Translation allows pure language "to shine upon the original more fully. It is the task of the translator to release in his own language that pure language which is under the spell of another" (Benjamin 1969, 227). However, while insisting on the absoluteness of language, taking inspiration from Baudelaire's poetry, the last work of lyric poetry with European-wide significance ("Die 'Fleurs du mal' sind das letzte lyrische Werk gewesen, das eine europäische Wirkung getan hat"), Benjamin also encompasses the other, inseparable aspect of symbolism in analyzing Baudelaire's lyric art as a way of coping with shock, the most distinctive modern experience, as registered first in Baudelaire's poetry. Originally shocking experience can be confronted and digested by being assimilated into a total structure of meaning—that is, essentially as language, but a language scarred with the traces of trauma. Baudelaire's lyric production represents a highly conscious reworking in and as lyric language of lived stimuli that have left the psychic mechanism traumatized, and Benjamin deciphers beneath the smooth surface of the mellifluous verses the ruptures and impasses of Baudelaire's quintessential experience as inaugural of the modern. The apparent wholeness of language into which experience was lifted by symbolic lyric in fact shows through to another aspect of language, especially of prophetic or messianic language, as consisting essentially in ruptures and abrasions. Still on the basis of its sublation of reality into language, symbolism's language thus reveals quite a different, unsuspected face marked by materiality and fragmentation. Baudelaire's language read profoundly translates the breakdown that the modern age was witnessing, whereby the aura of things that connects them with their context and past by involuntary memory disintegrates ("Über einige Motive bei Baudelaire").

Benjamin's reflections confirm the two aspects of symbolism and adduce a sort of historical, material account of their derivation. But it is also possible to interpret how the drive toward unity and presence inherent in the symbol converts into disunity and rupture with the real by its own internal logic, by the very fulfillment of its own impulse to total unity and the consequent cutting asunder of the tension between reality and symbol, language and world. The grand symbolic vision of the identity of All leads not only to a total structure or monism of the universe: it entails equally a shattering into autonomous fragments, since each individual element is wholly self-contained, indeed is in itself all-containing. The totally relational identity characteristic of language and therefore also of a linguistic universe turns into an equally total self-sufficiency of every particle, since each is endowed with an absolute identity already in itself, unconditioned by any external relations—all relations having become internal to it. In symbolism, everything has become language, but as a result language no longer mediates anything extra-linguistic. Without any real content, language becomes purely image or, as is suggested by other forms of symbolist art, purely musical incantation: it is unbounded, but is lacking in any rule or concept such as only an external limit could provide, and this leads eventually to language's being threatened even in its own internal cohesion.

The breakup of language and of everything in language was to be overtly pursued by Baudelaire's poetic successors, and it has been discovered retrospectively as subtext in Baudelaire himself by recent critics, especially in Benjamin's wake.[11] It can be understood as resulting ineluctably from the logic and dynamic of the symbol itself, with its absolute exigencies of identity, presence and immediacy, achieved no longer just by means of, but actually in and as, language. For once language has totally penetrated nature, leaving no remainder, nature is turned wholly into artifice. Nature can no longer supply the paradigm of organic unity after which language models itself in romanticism. Rather, everything becomes subject to the nature of language as an artificial synthesis with no substance in itself and therefore in a constant state of dissolution. When the universal identity forged by the symbol turns into an identity of all with language itself, the symbolic order of things is poised to collapse in upon itself, to implode in an uncontrolled proliferation of pure form. Baudelaire's transmission of the romantic doctrine of the symbol radicalizes and in effect reverses it, resulting in its no longer effecting union with all that is, but rather causing an alienation from nature and the real. Although he at times embraces the idea of a harmoniously ordered universe of natural correspondences, he lays the groundwork for its undoing in and by the symbol, which becomes the dynamite that explodes the universe eventually into Mallarmé's constellations of unmasterable chance. Precisely these disintegrative implications of the unrestricted identification of all with language have manifested themselves persistently in the course and direction of symbolist poetry in

its development ever since Baudelaire. (For sometimes contrasting views
on this descent, see Charles Altieri.)

Baudelaire was a believer in the identificatory power of the symbol, and
he remained the undisputed master of this creative faculty for the symbolist
poets that followed him. Yet he did not believe in the all-embracing, benevo-
lent Nature in which symbols were supposed to be embedded, and into
which they beckoned invitingly, binding all things, including whoever
could interpret them, together into one whole. For Baudelaire, this romantic
dream had become a nightmare and, consequently, the symbol, in significant
ways, sinister. Indeed, he was haunted by the symbol and its solicitations to
communion with a Nature that he loathed. In "Obsession," Baudelaire re-
coils from nature, from its great forests which frighten him, as do cathedrals
with their windy organs ("Grands bois, vous m'effrayez comme des cathé-
drales; / Vous hurlez comme l'orgue"). He would like the night to be without
stars, for their light speaks to him, and it is a known language, whereas he is
in search rather of the empty, the black and naked, what is divested of signs
and therefore devoid of significance:

> Comme tu me plairais, ô nuit! sans ces étoiles
> Dont la lumière parle un langage connu!
> Car je cherche le vide, et le noir, et le nu! (*OC* 1:75)

> [How you would please me, O night, without these stars /
> whose light speaks a known language! / For I seek the empty, the black
> and the naked!]

This constitutes an anguished palinode that effectively retracts the soul's en-
chantment with the sweet native language of things in "L'Invitation au voyage." Here Baudelaire is horrified of nature and its language, indeed of
nature as language, and not because it is strange but because it is all too familiar. The "regards familiers" of "Correspondances" reappear in order to
become terrifying. The forest is experienced as a cathedral whose significance is frightfully overdetermined, rather than as the mysteriously alluring
temple of "Correspondances." Nature now is already fully codified: the cries
of the woods that reply to one another out of their depths ("Répondent les
échos de vos *De profundis*") are already articulated as a church liturgy. They
are natural rites in a manner reminiscent of "Correspondances," but now

precisely their symbolic force makes them a negative, indeed a nightmare experience.

Baudelaire is repelled not so directly by nature as by the significance of nature, which is a form of human culture, indeed a language. The ocean's waves, with their heaving and tumult, are execrable because they are already found by the mind within itself ("Je te hais, Océan! tes bonds et tes tumultes, / Mon esprit les retrouve en lui"), just as the defeated man's bitter laugh full of sobs and insults is found in the enormous laugh of the sea. Even night fails to be other, and darkness—"les ténèbres"—consists in canvasses ("des toiles") painted on, or to be painted on, by human signs. Nature offers no escape from the human, and the human has become just as abhorrent as the natural. The symbolic-linguistic mechanism that reduces everything to language is at the bottom of this viciously circular mirroring, since everything that can be reached through language is reduced to identity. All that is known is known through the identity of signs circulating in the linguistic system: it is all too familiar and too wretched, in effect a prison house of language from which there is no exit.

Of course, what Baudelaire loathes at bottom is himself, because that is what he sees at the bottom of Nature. He begins the desperate struggle to escape himself by crying out after the name of "the other" that is still the watchword of so much of French, left-bank culture today. What he is trying to escape is the viciously narcissistic self-reflexivity of the symbolist quest that is palpable in a poem like "La Chevelure," in which the poet imagines plunging his amorous head into the black ocean in which "the other" is enclosed:

> Je plongerai ma tête amoureuse d'ivresse
> Dans ce noir océan où l'autre est enfermé . . . (OC 1:26)

The "other" is sought in desperation in order to escape the self, but it is indeed already an other that is "enclosed" (enfermé). It risks being confounded with the blackness of the self's own spleen. In the universe of total identity there is really no escaping the self. The seeker necessarily voyages endlessly in quest of le nouveau and l'inconnu. The absolute identity of everything is the truth of the symbol that Baudelaire found himself imprisoned by and from which he chafes to escape. All this he bequeathed to his poetic posterity.

Baudelaire adopts the symbol as a basic strategy but denaturalizes and also denatures it in the process. The universal identification of each with all that is characteristic of symbolic vision and the basis for the correspondences of things takes a peculiar turn when the identification of all things in the symbol is taken to be an identity of all with language. This is, in effect, what the symbolists explicitly do, rendering manifest the revolution in poetic language brought about *in nuce* by Baudelaire. It means that the identities of the symbolist vision, rather than being natural, indeed the deep structure or essence of nature, turn out to be purely artificial, indeed nothing but language. There is still an all-pervading logic of identity, but it takes on a very different significance, in important ways just the opposite of the significance it had in romanticism. The natural order of things is no longer reassuring and restorative, healing human breaches and diseases. The order of things is only linguistic and therefore only a reflection of the human world of cultural artifacts and in fact already infected with the sickness of the self.

Baudelaire pursues to its furthest limits the logic of identity inhering in the symbol. He identifies everything with everything else. But the result he obtains is not oneness with the mystery of nature and the universe (even though he leaves some traces of a suffering longing for an encounter with the Other or the Unknown), but rather an expansion of language so as to actually encompass everything, beyond simply serving as the instrument of establishing the symbolic identity of all being. It remains only for this linguistic mechanism to expose itself as such, and to collapse for lack of external support, in order to produce the brilliant artificial paradises and chance constellations of subsequent symbolism. Thus is set the program that symbolist poets, eminently Rimbaud and Mallarmé, were to follow. It is the linguistic turning and totalizing of the symbol achieved substantially by Baudelaire that constitutes the premise for the shattering even of language itself, no longer held intact by anything beyond it, that was to be pursued to its furthest extremes by later symbolist poets.

The identification of everything with language has remained an absolutely central preoccupation of French poetry and poetics in the twentieth century. It is at issue, for example, in the way Francis Ponge's *Le Parti pris des choses* hovers between treating words as natural things and then again ruthlessly unmasking this fiction and fighting against language in the name of "la chose même," which escapes it. Yet, given the double aspect of the symbolism inaugurated by Baudelaire's poetry, whereby the breaking down of language, which collapses from within, belongs together with the absorption by language of the world of things and its becoming itself a thing (acquiring thereby also the thing's vulnerability to amorcelation, dismemberment, and dissolution), even this sort of resistance to the idealizations inherent in language suggests in indirect ways how subsequent poets continue to remain Baudelaire's heirs. For although Baudelaire stands as the great poet of mysterious and profound unity in the symbol, in which domain "Tout n'est qu'ordre et beauté / Luxe, calme et volupté" [All is but order and beauty / Luxury, calm and voluptuousness], it is nevertheless possible to see how this complete freedom from discord and all external constraint contains the seeds of its own destruction—of the shattering of language as total system into infinite disunity and limitless dis-semination. This is the decisive creative innovation that makes Baudelaire's poetry so seminal for symbolist poetry in its widest ramifications.

Gautier as "Seer" of the Origins of Modernity in Baudelaire

Lois Cassandra Hamrick

> Modernity.—Does the noun exist? The feeling it expresses is so recent that the word might well not be in the dictionaries.
>
> —*Le Moniteur universel,* 25 May 1855

The year is 1855 and Théophile Gautier is reviewing the English paintings he has recently seen on display at the Exposition Universelle. Among the numerous British entries are seven pictures having little in common with each other by William Mulready (1786–1863). "Each of these canvases is treated in a different, often conflicting manner," observes our critic in wonderment (Gautier 1855c, 19). Indeed, one of the first things that had struck Gautier on opening day of the exposition was precisely this peculiar "difference" which seemed to define the "originality," or what some were calling the "eccentricity" of the English art and which set the British apart from their European counterparts:

> The distinctive traits of England are a frank originality, a strong local flavor; England owes nothing to the other schools. . . . An English painting, whatever its merit, is immediately recognizable to even the least practiced eye.—Its inventiveness, taste, line, color, touch, feeling, everything is different.—One feels transported into another world very far away and very unfamiliar. (Gautier 1855a, 1:7)

For Gautier, this "other world" is marked by a "distinctive kind of art, re-
fined to the point of being affected, bizarre like a Chinese curio" (7).[1] Yet it
is this same "bizarre" character which gives British painting its "modern"
aspect. For, concludes our critic:

> [a]ntiquity has no place in English art. An English picture is
> modern in the same way that a Balzac novel is modern; the most
> advanced civilization on Earth can be read in minute detail, in
> the sheen of the varnish, in the preparation of the panel and the
> colors.—Everything is perfect. (7)

Interestingly enough, in his attempt to come to grips with the word *modernity*
as it relates to English painting, Gautier is actually pinpointing characteristics
which will surface again several years later in his writings devoted to the life
and work of his disciple, Charles Baudelaire. In all, Gautier produced four
studies on Baudelaire: a *notice,* which appeared in an anthology of French
poets, published by Eugène Crépet in 1862; an obituary article in 1867; a
study based on parts of the aforementioned texts which would be incorporat-
ed into the *Rapport sur le progrès de la poésie* (1868), commissioned by the
Ministry of Instruction; and, finally, the most substantial study—the one of
which Gautier was most proud—that would appear as a preface to *Les Fleurs
du Mal,* volume 1 of Michel Lévy's 1868 edition of Baudelaire's *Œuvres complètes.* It is the 1868 preface, along with the 1862 *notice,* which focus most
closely on the modern nature of Baudelaire's production.[2]

For the inexperienced eye, the relationship between these studies and
the reviews of the English paintings shown at the exposition may not be
readily apparent. Yet a close look will reveal two types of parallels. First,
from a thematic perspective, these texts reveal similarities in the various aspects of that recent "feeling," hesitatingly referred to in 1855 as "modernity." These include a predominance of such unusual features as originality,
eccentricity, and an oddness referred to as *bizarrerie.* Even more interesting
is the process by which these aspects are first identified, and then highlighted and analyzed. Indeed, the reader with a keen eye will not fail to notice
that it is precisely the faculty of *seeing* that becomes the vehicle by which one
can begin to reach an understanding of what it means to be modern. "Never
was an eye more avid than ours," confessed Gautier as he assumed the edi-
torship of *L'Artiste* in 1856 (Gautier 1856b, 4). It is this extraordinary eye of

a person whose passion is fastened on the visual which provides the means of entry into an "other world," a world where "everything is different," in short, a world distinctly *modern*. It is this same eye which is able to situate modernity within a broad literary time frame, thereby *fore*-seeing the legitimate place of modernity in the future canon of French poetics and fiction.

The "avid eye" of Gautier is therefore no ordinary eye. On the one hand, this is the eye of a critic who has been charged with assessing the value of a literary or artistic work. On the other hand, it is also the eye of the "poet-artist" who has undergone practical training in art at the studio of the painter Rioult. Later, our poet-artist will "throw away the paint brush for the pen," opting to paint with words, rather than pigments (Gautier 1978, 3). The artistic instruction will leave its mark, however, and the result will be a practiced eye, casting its sight both *outward*, toward the material world, and *inward*, toward the individual world of the poet-artist.[3] Finally, let us not forget that it is this same gift of sight that accounts for the process known as *transposition d'art*, for which Gautier remains today so famous.[4] In short, what we find is an eye capable of setting in motion a kind of "transfer" mechanism by which elements found in one context are transposed to another. So it is that we find in the world of Baudelaire as "seen" by Gautier a certain number of features identified as "modern," which have already been "seen" in other contexts,[5] and in particular in the realm of the English painters.

The Word Modernity

But just what is the status of the word *modernity* at this time? A review of the dictionaries reflecting language usage of the period reveals that the word did not become a part of the vernacular until the Second Empire. Hence Gautier's hesitation in 1855, when he wonders whether the noun exists. The uncertainty surrounding the term appears to linger in Baudelaire's own mind, even as he is composing his now famous study, *Le Peintre de la vie moderne,* published in 1863. Referring to Constantin Guys, Baudelaire writes: "He is looking for that quality which you must allow me to call 'modernity'; for I know of no better word to express the idea I have in mind" (*OC* 2:694).[6]

Yet if the status of the noun remains shaky, the adjective *modern,* derived from the Latin *modo* (ablative of *modus*), has long been a part of standard usage. Moreover, the ablative *modo,* denoting way *(manière)* of doing,

is closely allied with *mode*—that is, "fashion" or "custom" *(moeurs).*[7] *Mode,*
in turn, is a key element in the emerging notion of "modernity": that is, the
idea of belonging to "a new period, the present time, our own era" ("aux
temps nouveaux, à l'âge actuel, à notre époque"; *Grand Dictionnaire universel,* 11:362). It is this sense of temporality and its close rapport with the
notion of "types" of beauty tied to such variables as those implied by the
idea of *mode* that will first strike Gautier while traveling in England in
1843[8]—that is, two years before Baudelaire in his *Salon of 1845* defends
the "heroism of modern life" as having legitimate aesthetic value (*OC*
2:407).

Is it only a coincidence that during this trip Gautier will make his discovery about the variability of the artistic ideal and its relationship to *la
mode* as he is standing before a series of English fashion plates in the studio
of portraitist Alfred Edward Chalon (1780–1860)? In any case, this first
English experience marked for Gautier the beginning of a long period of reflection on the problem of the relativity of beauty. These reflections, which
resonate with echoes from the thought of Diderot and Stendhal, will lead in
1858 not to an outright defense of the modern costume per se (as is the case
with Baudelaire), but rather of the contemporary portrait as a document capable of seizing the moment, thereby according to the present a historical
value.[9] It is, moreover, while tackling the problem of the contemporary portrait and its lack of prestige as a genre in 1852 that Gautier is prompted to
use the word *modernity* for the first time:

> It is wrong, in our mind, to affect a certain repugnance or at least
> a certain disdain for the types which are purely contemporary.
> We believe, for our part, that there are brand-new effects, unex-
> pected aspects in the intelligent and faithful representation of
> what we will call *modernity.* (Gautier 1852)[10]

For Gautier, however, *la mode* and *les types modernes* (modern types of
beauty) are concerns more nearly suited to the area of literature or to art
whose aim is to recount or narrate, rather than to the plastic arts. In Gautier's
view—and this is also true for Baudelaire (*OC* 2:496, 687)—it is therefore the
creator of the *La Comédie humaine* who best expresses the themes of modernity in France. For Balzac has an unusual quality: he is a man "of his time."
"He owes nothing to antiquity, accepts . . . nothing from the mythologies or

traditions from the past."[11] Balzac sets himself apart by the "absolute modernity of his genius" (Gautier 1874, 107). In so doing, however, Balzac remains almost insensitive to plastic beauty (108). If Gautier (unlike Baudelaire), due to an "early (artistic) education and a particular instinct," prefers as a model Venus de Milo to that of the elegantly attired *Parisienne,* our critic nonetheless acknowledges that a notion of (modern) beauty in which artifice and costume *(la toilette)* are integral components is a defensible, albeit radical, position. Thus observes Gautier apropos of Baudelaire's preference for the woman who combines her "profound charm" with "the eloquence of her *toilette*": "Such an original way of comprehending modern beauty reverses the question, for such an understanding considers ancient (classical) beauty as primitive, gross and barbarous, which is undoubtedly a paradoxical opinion, but which can be very well supported" (Gautier 1986, 153). Moreover, Gautier considers the invention of the prose poem as "one of Baudelaire's glories, if not his greatest glory," precisely because this literary form fills a gap in traditional French poetry, whose structure lends itself with difficulty to expressing the "fugitive nuances" of modern life (165).

Finally, it is probably more than just a curious coincidence that on more than one occasion it is a visual experience prompted by an encounter with English art which will move Gautier (and he will be followed in this by Baudelaire)[12] to reflect on the importance of different elements underlying the notion of modernity in art. In 1843, as we have seen, it is the English fashion engravings which Gautier sees during his London stay that trigger a reflection on the relativity of the artistic ideal throughout the ages. "In every era, artists have an ideal which they pursue and render as best they can," Gautier (1856a, 204) reports in *La Presse* after visiting Chalon's studio. Later, in 1855, the English paintings on display at the Exposition Universelle incite our critic to comment on their peculiar "local flavor," which "owes nothing to the other schools." It is this focus on "local flavor"—that is, on what is particular and relative, as opposed to general and universal—that allows the spectator "to enter deeply into the private life of the country" (Gautier 1855–56, 1:20). In short, for Gautier, the modern aspect *(le moderne)* of contemporary English painting is revealed in much the same way as the contemporary mores of the characters would be made manifest in a novel: through the act of (pictoral) reading. To the careful eye of our artist-critic, the English painting becomes, then, like a Balzac text, reflecting both *le mode* (the manner) and *la mode* (the customs) of a people at a given moment in the history of civilization.

Needless to say, it is another English artist, Constantin Guys, who inspires Baudelaire to write his much celebrated study, *Le Peintre de la vie moderne,* a study which, in turn, will inspire numerous "modern" and "postmodern" critics intent on seeking the meaning of modernity. Gautier, who knew Guys, acknowledges having owned around sixty drawings, sketches, and watercolors by "this pencil humorist" and having given some to Baudelaire. "[Guys] had a very keen sense of modern corruption . . . and in his sketches, he too, gathered a bouquet of flowers of evil," notes Gautier in the 1868 preface (Gautier 1986, 151–52). Is it any surprise that this self-same master of drawing who was capable of creating his own "flowers of evil" would have a special appeal for the author whose volume of poetry is devoted to the same subject? Once again, the voice of Gautier proves informative:

> [Baudelaire] was struck by this spirit, this perceptiveness, this power of observation, all literary qualities which were translated through drawing. He liked the complete absence of antiquity, that is, the absence of classical tradition, in these drawings, and the profound feeling of what we will call *decadence,* short of another word which could express our idea better. (152–53)

A Way of Seeing

"Decadence"—for Gautier (as will also be true for Baudelaire), the idea of decadence is linked to a certain way of seeing. For this reason, when Gautier attempts to define the problem of decadence in the case of Baudelaire, it will be to the mechanics of vision that our critic will turn in order to explain the extreme originality of the poet:

> [Baudelaire] saw things from a special point of view, with the result that the lines were changed, like the lines of objects seen from a bird's eye or looking down from the ceiling, and he grasped rapports which were imperceptible for others and whose logical oddness (*bizarrerie*) was striking. (116)

Understanding the modern character of Baudelaire is, then, in the end a question of sight (or more precisely perhaps, *insight*). We should not forget that for Gautier, "seeing is the same as having" (Gautier 1856b, 4). Seeing implies "possession" or "appropriation" of the object. But in this instance, the "object" of the act of seeing is the "subject" of the artistic act: that is, the poet or artist whose work is being scrutinized. Thus "seeing" implies possession of the "soul" of the poet-artist, to borrow the language of Gautier.[13] This means momentarily adopting the particular ideal ("l'idéal particulier") of the artist or author. "Seeing" supposes a displacement toward the "other" in order to "grasp"[14] precisely those "rapports" which remain "imperceptible" for those persons whose eyes cannot "see." "*Oculas habent et non vident, aures habent et non audiunt.* The Gospel was doubtlessly alluding to the newspaper reviewers *(les feuilletonistes)* of painting and music," observes a sly young Gautier in 1836. "It takes lengthy study in order to learn to see. Half of genius is in the ability to see," he adds.[15] In Gautier's case, this ability allows him to "*Britainize* his genius" ("britanniser son génie"; *OC* 2:123)— to cite Baudelaire—in order to penetrate the "other world, very far away and very unfamiliar," the world of the English painters. Likewise, Gautier undertakes to direct his glance through what he calls elsewhere in his writings the "prism" of the artist[16] so as to be able to examine the artist's own "individuality" (Gautier 1986, 123), the artist's own personal "world." Finally, it is by appropriating the Baudelairean mindset that Gautier is able to demonstrate the superiority of a special genius who, to those whose eyes have not been opened, appears to be simply a producer of "concerted *bizarrerie*" or gratuitous "mannerism" (123). In the 1868 preface, Gautier notes in this regard:

> Baudelaire is often accused of concerted *bizarrerie,* deliberate originality obtained at any price, and especially *mannerism.* Before going any further, this is a point that needs clarification. There are people who are naturally affected. . . . They see things from an uncommon angle which modifies the aspect or perspective they have of these things. . . . Baudelaire had such a mind. So when the critics insisted on seeing work, effort, extravagance, and biased paroxysm in Baudelaire, there was actually only the free and easy blossoming of an individuality. (123)

However, the same critic who "displaces" himself in order to adopt the point of view of the *other* is himself a poet-painter having his own interior "world" and his own "mannerisms." Consequently, as a painter, Gautier sees the modern aspect of his discipline from a particular angle. In so doing, Gautier draws on a set of images which Baudelaire himself had used in the early 1860s when wrestling with the same problem of decadence in the work of Edgar Allan Poe.[17] The Poe text thus provides a metaphorical prototype which will be artistically "transposed" by our critic-painter into the Baudelairean framework.

In both the text on Poe and in Gautier's pieces on Baudelaire, the imagery adopted—that of the sun setting at the end of a long literary "day"—accords a positive value to the notion of decadence. For the sunset here is freed of any negative connotations the image might otherwise convey in a system of metaphorical values in which the descent of the sun is equated with decline, deterioration, or a falling away from an irretrievable ideal. Gautier develops his vision as follows:

> Literature is like a long day: there is a morning, there is mid-day, there is an evening and a nighttime. Without going into any needless discourse about whether the period of dawn should be preferred to twilight time, it is imperative to "paint" things at the moment at which one finds oneself and with a palette having the colors needed in order to render the effects "of the hour." Does not the setting of the sun have its beauty, just as the morning had a (different) beauty? (Gautier 1986, 124)

If the setting of the sun here is to be understood as a part of a cyclical phenomenon in which literary expression manifests itself in various phases that can be likened to different moments of a day (dawn, midday, twilight, night), it is important to note that none of these moments is designated as an ideal phase or point of perfection against which the other phases can be measured. There is no "scale of literatures," explains Baudelaire (OC 2:320). In a similar argument, Gautier points out that it would be fruitless to debate whether dawn must be given preference over twilight (Gautier 1986, 124). Consequently, the night can be just as glorious as midday, when the sun is at its zenith. Similarly, the decadent style is just as viable aesthetically as the finest classic expression. In the absence of a model to emulate, one must take as parameters those of the moment in which one finds oneself. In other words, in a world having no absolute Ideal serving as the aesthetic standard, it is the particularities of modernity which have led to the development of the decadent style. In transposing a set of images of temporality borrowed from the writer whose work he is defending, Gautier succeeds in creating a new vision of Baudelaire's decadence and in so doing situates the poet's particular aesthetic within the larger context of modern French poetics.

"Painting" Baudelaire's Modernity

As was the case in English art, the new perspective brought by Baudelaire, coupled with his break with the traditional stylistic mould, were met with shock and dismay by a public "blind" to the intrinsic value of such innovation. Yet the "shock" factor is not the only point of convergence to be found between English painting and what we might call the Baudelairean *tableaux*. For if the British canvases stand out from the academic norm because of the particular "local flavor" they reflect of the world's "most advanced civilization," the Baudelairean *tableaux* are no less peculiar in their rendering of the spirit of a new era radically different from that of former times. For this is an era in which life has become "more complex, weighed down by more notions and more ideas" than was the case in the classic period, when the "great masters of the past" were producing in an environment where "all forms, all images, all feelings had a charm of virgin novelty" (Gautier 1986, 123–24). It is precisely this new complexity of life, maintains Gautier, that requires another type of expression, another "palette" of colors, for traditional language is no longer adequate:[18] "The great quality of the nineteenth century is not exactly its naiveté, and in order to render its thought, its dreams and its postulations, it needs an idiom which is a little more heterogeneous than the so-called classical language" (124).

Borrowing once more from the work of the writer he seeks to defend, Gautier proposes to justify the idea of decadence by positioning the phenomenon as the natural outcome of art which has reached the state of "extreme maturity" (124). As a critic who is also a painter, however, Gautier will enhance the visual dimension of his argument by heightening the color and augmenting the relief of the original imagery as first sketched out in the text on Poe. Whereas Baudelaire's setting sun symbolizing the approach of the decadent period "will soon inundate the western horizon with varied colors" (*OC* 2:320), Gautier's setting becomes a veritable blaze of variegated colors of apocalyptic proportions. For the sun's rays over the decadent period have become oblique, producing "the great final blaze," a mass of brilliant colors all afire and in the process of decomposing: "copper reds, . . . green golds, turquoise tones melting with sapphire" (124). Moreover, the "dazzling columns" alluded to by Baudelaire in the Poe text (*OC* 2:320) become for Gautier "strange and monstrous clouds penetrated by streams of light" in which the critic sees "the gigantic collapse of an aerial Babel" (Gautier 1986, 124). Gautier may be recalling here the work of yet another English artist, John Martin (1789–1854), "le grand peintre des énormités disparues," whose fantastic vision and monstrous proportions can be found "transposed" in certain pages of Gautier's 1838 short story "Une nuit de Cléopâtre."[19] In the 1868 preface, however, the diversity of these different exotic colors and forms carries a special metaphorical weight not found in the *nouvelle.* For the "1400 words of the Racine dialect are not sufficient if an author has the difficult task of rendering modern ideas and things in all their infinite complexity and multiple coloring" (125). Indeed, translating "the last hour of civilizations" requires a complete "range of infuriating colors pushed to the most intense degree" (133). The style of decadence is "the last word of the Word which has been charged to express everything and which has been pushed to the extreme" (124–25).

However, as in the case of the English painters whose "range of strange tones" astonish at first more than they please the eye (Gautier 1855–56, 1:7), the poetic work of Baudelaire gives an initial impression of being "difficult and obscure" (Gautier 1986, 133). Moreover, as Gautier notes with reference to a picture by British painter Maclise (1806–1870) entitled "Epreuve du toucher" (Ordeal by touch):

> It is only with great difficulty that French eyes will decipher this painting which is so brilliantly English. . . . Our eyes are not made for these combinations of impossible colors, these lighting effects from weird reflections, this transparent light from alabaster lamps. . . . From a material stand-point, the artistic process has no rapport with ours. These colors which are so bizarre are applied in a manner which is even stranger still. (Gautier 1855–56, 1:13)

It is clear in both cases that the contemporaries of Baudelaire and Gautier lack the proper criterion for judging works which, in their eyes, appear "so eccentric, so strange" (33–34). For in both instances, it is a new artistic idiom which is at work, an idiom at odds with traditionally recognized norms.

Although there is similarity in the reaction of the French public to the eccentricity perceived in these two examples, it is important to note that there is dissimilarity in the *causes* of this eccentricity. In the case of the English, antiquity has nothing to do with the fact that their art is modern. Thus there is no official *break* with the ancient model, but rather *absence* of a model. Indeed, the English painters, whose inspiration came largely from the northern countries (Dutch and Flemish art in particular), never experienced the constraints of a strong academic tradition such as that known in France. Unlike the French, the English had no centralized system in which the *Prix de Rome* furnished the dominant criterion for the instruction of art. As a result, British artists did not develop the skills in drawing human anatomy which were necessary to ensure success in more traditional areas such as the painting of mythological subjects (Gautier 1855–56, 1:51). It is this lack of a uniform model which leads to an emphasis on "individuality" and an artistic production in which "everything is different," in which "capriciousness" reigns—in short, in which the "bizarre" becomes the identifying "stamp" of its modernity (7–9).

For Baudelaire, on the other hand, the classic example is a reality. In fact, strictly speaking, with Baudelaire, there is no clean "break" with the classical model. Rather, there is *transgression*. There is *decadence*. There is *fusion*, as has been shown by Claude Pichois, who sees in Baudelaire the "Janus" of French poetry, capable of looking at the same time toward the past and toward the future.[20] Finally, there is *evolution* toward "that late splendor, when nuances decompose, flare up, revive, and triple in intensity" (81). For Baudelaire, the "bizarre" becomes a veritable aesthetic: "the beautiful is always bizarre," declares the poet in his own review of the Exposition Universelle in 1855 (*OC* 2:578). Himself an admirer of "those charming [English] artists," of "those favored by the bizarre muse" (*OC* 2:609), Baudelaire recognizes that it is his "maître" Gautier who had spoken "the first and the best about this English School" (*OC* 2:123). The parallels in their views of these partisans of the "bizarre" are, in fact, quite striking.

The "Other" Is Multiform

Yet what for Baudelaire constitutes an indispensable ingredient in an aesthetic concept emphasizing *le beau individuel* (individual beauty), remains for Gautier just one artistic element among many other possibilities. For Gautier, an artistic approach in which the "bizarre" is a salient feature is a particular kind of art belonging to an "other world." This world has its own rules, its own mechanism. To access this world implies a displacement on the visual plane, but this displacement is temporary: "Why deprive oneself the delicious pleasure of being for a time another . . . ?" asks Gautier in 1856 (Gautier 1856b, 4). The mind of Gautier is, to cite Baudelaire, "a cosmopolitan mirror of beauty." In other words, this is a mind capable of appropriating the viewpoint of countless artists of different nationalities and character. "As a critic," Baudelaire reminds us, "Théophile Gautier knew, loved, explained . . . Asiatic beauty, Greek beauty, Roman beauty, Spanish beauty, Flemish beauty, Dutch beauty, and English beauty" (*OC* 2:123).

If one were to apply Rimbaud's formula, "*JE est un autre*" (I is an other)[21] to Gautier, it would have to be an "other" having multiple forms *(un autre multiforme)*. For the "I" can, depending on the context, become several "others." In the case of the English painters, the process of appropriation begins with "astonishment" *(l'étonnement),* for the oddness *(la bizarrerie)* and the strangeness *(l'étrangeté)* of their paintings transgress the French Academic norm. But for the person who possesses the gift of *seeing,* this momentary *astonishment* leads to the seduction of the spectator by the objet d'art. Thus observes Gautier concerning his experience standing in front of the English paintings in 1855: "At first, one is more astonished than charmed; but soon the eye gets used to these ranges of strange and charming tones, these satiny lights, these transparent shadows" (1855–56, 1:7). Further on, Gautier observes upon seeing Maclise's painting "Ordeal by Touch":

> when one looks a long time at this color, which at first is so disquieting, one ends up finding unbelievable subtleties, an extreme harmony. . . . Its charm overtakes you, as might happen in a foreign land with respect to fruits which are rejected at first and over which you go wild later. (14)

Finally, as a poet-painter, Gautier is well versed in the technique of transposition by which an art work is "transported" into the realm of literary art.[22] In order to effect this operation, there is necessarily displacement. In reacting to the highly original character of Baudelaire's work, Gautier seems to be engaging in a similar operation. But here what is being "transported" is not a work of art, but rather the mechanism of displacement itself. Indeed, consciously or not, when faced with the patently "modern" aspect of Baudelaire's expression, Gautier appears to be following the same process of transfer that came into play when he "Britainized" his mind at the 1855 exposition. For the Baudelaire whom Gautier chooses to depict is, first of all, the Baudelaire who astonishes by his "deliberate *bizarrerie*," the Baudelaire who is disturbing because of his affected originality and his mannerism. It is the Baudelaire who could not prevent the reader from being surprised by such very different verse as that found in *Les Fleurs du Mal* (Gautier 1986, 133). But this initial stage, in which the shock effect is a dominant component, leads to a second stage in which the "bizarre" is reexamined through the writer's inner prism which enables this quality to be seen in the metaphorical context of the unfolding of the long literary "day." It is at this point that the initial astonishment gives way to a sweeping reevaluation of the notion of decadence as a logical stage in the progression of art and civilization toward "extreme maturity" (124). Yet if for many of Baudelaire's contemporaries, decadence signaled the setting of the sun after a glorious literary day, for future generations of Baudelaire readers, the sunset would be perceived to be in reality a sunrise. For this is the dawn of a new era in poetics, an era in which the word *modernity* becomes firmly entrenched in the literary lexicon.

Gautier as "Seer" of Baudelairean Modernity

Of all of Gautier's boisterous declarations, the best known is probably one recorded by the Goncourt brothers in their *Mémoires,* where he is reported to have said: "I am a man for whom the visible world exists" (Goncourt 1956, 343). Ironically, it takes a "sharp eye" to decipher the full import of this statement. The reason is that, in the case of Gautier, taking into account the "visible" is not a simple procedure by which visual data from the exterior world are recorded in the mind of the observer. What we are "seeing" in Gautier is something more complex. For the "avid eye" of our critic, who is at the same time poet and artist, seems to possess a certain "transfer" mechanism which allows the reconstruction, or rather, the *re-creation* of the *world* of the *other* from elements often already *seen* in other *worlds,* whether literary or artistic. As a result, for Gautier, the modernity of Baudelaire is a modernity defined through the faculty of sight: it is a modernity as *seen* by his master. Finally, it is a modernity that can be perceived only through the *œil visionnaire*[23] of a critic-poet-artist who had experienced *la bizarrerie* and *l'étonnement* himself as the young author of *Albertus* (1832) and *La Comédie de la Mort* (1838).[24]

PART II

Poetry and Painting

Strangers in the Park

Manet, Baudelaire, and *La Musique aux Tuileries*

Sima Godfrey

I N late 1867 or early 1868, Edouard Manet wrote to Charles Asselineau, friend and biographer of Baudelaire, to offer him two portraits for a posthumous edition of the poet's work.

> My dear Asselineau, I believe you are working at this time on an edition of the works of Baudelaire? If you put a portrait at the beginning of "Spleen de Paris," I have one of Baudelaire with a hat, in other words, as a *flâneur*, which might not look bad at the start of this book. I also have another, bareheaded, more impressive, which would go well in a book of poetry. I would very much like to be given the task, and, of course, in proposing myself, I *would give* you my plates. (Cited in Cachin 1983, 158)

Reprinted with five etchings of Baudelaire in the catalog for the 1983 Manet retrospective (157–58), this brief letter has had a critical history all its own. Scholars of Manet have repeatedly turned to it for the purpose of dating the various portraits of the poet that Manet may have begun as early as 1862 and completed as late as 1868. Manet had known Baudelaire since 1859, and he had already painted his portrait once in the plein air composition *La Musique aux Tuileries*. Indeed, the "Baudelaire en chapeau" that Manet mentions in the letter (Cachin 1983, nos. 54, 55) clearly derives from that portrait, painted in 1861–62. Antonin Proust, Manet's biographer and friend, recalls the close friendship that bound the two men at that time.

Eduard Manet, *La Musique aux Tuileries*, 1861–62.
Photograph reproduced by permission of National Gallery Publications, Ltd.

> For Manet, the eye played such an important role that Paris has
> never known a flaneur like him, nor one who wandered about so
> effectively (Paris n'a jamais connu de flâneur semblable à lui et
> de flâneur flânant plus utilement). . . . He went to the Tuileries
> gardens almost everyday from two to four o'clock to draw plein-
> air studies under the trees [. . .] Baudelaire regularly accompa-
> nied him. (A. Proust 1913, 29, 39)

Manet's epithet for the etching of Baudelaire with a hat—"en promeneur"—thus recalls both an earlier painted image of the poet and the history of a friendship between two flaneurs and artists who together turned the
Tuileries gardens into a vast open-air studio. The second portrait of
Baudelaire that he alludes to—"tête nue, plus important"—derives just as
evidently from a photograph of Baudelaire taken by Nadar in 1862 (Cachin
1983, 159, fig. b). Manet's letter, although undated, was clearly written
sometime in or after the autumn of 1867—that is, after the painter and his
family had moved to the Rue Saint-Pétersbourg and after the poet's death
(31 August 1867). It thus allows for the rough dating of the series of portrait etchings to a six-year period between 1862 and 1868. Neither close in-
vestigation of Manet's emerging graphic style nor the confusing and
possibly incorrect dates attached to these portraits in Asselineau's book
(*Charles Baudelaire: Sa vie et son œuvre*) have served to fix their respective
dates with any more precision.[1] The brief letter to Asselineau has, as a result, provided art historians with the major piece of evidence they have for
situating these works in Manet's career; hence its importance (Cachin
1983, 159–60).

The information art historians have traditionally extracted from this
letter may be categorized as follows:

1. Chronological—the occasion for and the address on the letter
   identify a more or less verifiable time span from late 1867 to
   1868.

2. Commemorative—evidence of the friendship and intellectual
   sympathy between Baudelaire and Manet, the poet and the
   painter of modern life, is confirmed by Manet's eagerness to
   participate in a posthumous edition of the poet's work.

Such information, however, is limited both within the context of this letter and within the larger documented context of Baudelaire and Manet's years of association. So limited, indeed, that it calls equal, if indirect, attention to the more obvious references in the letter that have been selectively elided: namely, Manet's specific identification of the image of Baudelaire in a top hat with the volume of prose poems *Le Spleen de Paris* and his secondary association of the portrait of the bareheaded poet with a book of verse—that is, *Les Fleurs du Mal*. The partial reading (or misreading) of this one brief letter—for all its familiarity and repetition—may serve as an example of the peculiar sort of art-historical blindness that might be called "the use and abuse of poetry."[2] Or—to echo a polemical statement by Leo Steinberg— "why poetry is a closed book to the art historian."[3]

Steinberg has argued that the literary scholar's quotation of painterly images, extracted from their formal context and from the conventions and history of painting that inform them, often skews the reading of their overall significance. So, too, a biased critical focus can affect the inverse quotation, or misquotation, of literary texts by art historians. Even in a historical example of such high profile as the artistic solidarity of Baudelaire and Manet, there are startling instances of pertinent information in the poetry of Baudelaire that has been systematically skimmed over by art historians.

Such is the example of the Manet letter—often cited but rarely read. For the most part, art historians have been so pleased and so distracted by the exceptional quality and exceptional insights of Baudelaire's art criticism as to imply that this is where the historical truths of art must lie. In particular, they have paid worthy attention to Baudelaire's famous essay *Le Peintre de la vie moderne* (published in 1863, but composed in 1859–60) for the aesthetic program it maps out, a program that admirably expresses, it is true, the peculiar energy and apparent purpose of Manet's paintings of modern life done around this time. The characterization of the "painter of modern life" as a dandy, a flaneur, and a man of the crowd functions as an illuminating gloss on the artistic activity of Manet in the early 1860s—the time, we are told, when he strolled the streets of Paris in the company of Baudelaire.

The election of this essay as the pertinent Baudelairean intertext for Manet's work in the early 1860s thus seems not only tempting but inevitable. But is it exclusive? Manet, after all, volunteered his portrait of Baudelaire in a top hat not as an accompaniment for *Le Peintre de la vie moderne,* nor any other edition of the essays on art, but specifically as the

frontispiece for the volume of prose poems, published after the poet's death
as *Le Spleen de Paris*. For during the years when Baudelaire was frequenting
the Tuileries with Manet and writing his essay on the painter of modern life,
he was also vigorously at work on that set of poems that would dramatize
the modern aesthetic expounded in the essay in a new and self-consciously
modern literary form.[4]

One prose poem in particular, "Les Veuves," draws our attention with
specific reference to the historic and aesthetic conjunction of Baudelaire
and Manet. Written around the time of *Le Peintre de la vie moderne,* it was
published first in the *Revue Fantaisiste* on 1 November 1861 and later in
Arsène Houssaye's journal, *La Presse,* on 27 August 1862.

Like Manet's famous crowd painting of 1862, *La Musique aux Tuileries,*
Baudelaire's poem takes as its setting the "jardins publics"—artificial
refuges of natural beauty and calm that punctuate the changing urban landscape of Paris in the Second Empire. The poem opens with a reflection on
the many tales of private loneliness that haunt these spaces of leisure.

> And toward these places poets and philosophers love to direct
> their avid speculations. [. . .] they feel themselves irresistibly
> drawn toward everything that is feeble, destitute, orphaned, and
> forlorn. (Baudelaire 1970, 22)

The quintessentially Baudelairean theme of loneliness in the crowd
finds its symbolic articulation in the image of widows who circulate among
the throng.

> Which is sadder, and more saddening, the widow holding by the
> hand a little child with whom she cannot share her thought, or
> the one who is completely alone? I do not know. . . . I once fol-
> lowed for many hours one of those solitary widows; [. . .]
> Finally, in the afternoon under a lovely autumn sky, [. . .] she
> sat on a bench some distance from the crowd to listen to one of
> those concerts offered the Parisian public by military bands.
> (22–23)

The final image of this first "tableau" ends at the site of an open-air
concert in a public park, and this setting triggers the visual memory of yet

another widow observed, not solitary like the first, but accompanied by a young boy. Like the old clown of the subsequent poem ("Le Vieux Saltimbanque"), she materializes visually out of the festive color and activity of the crowd.

> I can never help casting a glance, which if not universally sympathetic is at least curious, at the mob of pariahs that crowd around the enclosure of an outdoor concert. The orchestra pours its festive, martial, or voluptuous airs into the night; glittering gowns trail on the ground; glances cross; the idle, having nothing to do, attitudinize and pretend to be indolently relishing the music. Here nothing that is not rich and happy [. . .] except that rabble over there leaning on the outside enclosure [. . .].
>
> But on this particular day, in that crowd of work blouses and calico dresses, my attention was caught by a figure of such nobility that it stood in shocking contrast to the environing vulgarity. ("J'aperçus *un être dont la noblesse faisait un éclatant contraste avec toute la trivialité environnante.*")
>
> This was a tall, majestic woman whose whole bearing expressed a nobility such as I cannot remember ever having seen before, not even in the collections of aristocratic beauties of the past. [. . .] Her sad, emaciated face was in harmony with the heavy mourning ("le grand deuil") she was wearing. [. . .] Why then does she choose to stay in a milieu where she offers so conspicuous a contrast? ("Pourquoi donc reste-t-elle volontairement dans un milieu *où elle fait une tache si éclatante?*")
>
> But drawing near to her out of curiosity, I seemed to understand the reason. The tall widow was holding a little boy by the hand who, like her, was dressed in mourning. (Baudelaire 1970, 23–24, emphasis added)

What is first striking in this long passage is the glittering portrayal of the elegant crowd at an outdoor concert that recalls the title and imagery of Manet's painting *La Musique aux Tuileries*. No concert, however, is literally represented in that painting; the music functions figuratively as the stated occasion for a fashionable gathering. "At this time," Théodore Duret recalls, "the palace at the Tuileries where the Emperor held his court was the center of living luxury which extended into the gardens. The music that was played there twice a week attracted a worldly and elegant crowd" (30–31). But where Manet seems preoccupied primarily with that worldly and elegant crowd, in which he and the poet may play a role, Baudelaire, in his poem, seeks to penetrate beyond it; to observe "cette tourbe qui s'appuie là-bas sur la barrière extérieure," the lowly crowd that is excluded by the cost of admission from the indulgences of the rich and idle. Literary critic Christopher Prendergast, in his pairing of "Les Veuves" with *La Musique aux Tuileries* makes this very point, criticizing along the way art historians who have smoothed over the evident thematic difference between this prose poem and the painting. "Yet on the face of it, there is little affinity between text and image. Manet's version seems the natural choice for the committed boulevardier he was, and, while it could be read as being close to the spirit of *Le Peintre de la vie moderne* and the worldly sketches of Guys, there is *certainly nothing in it of Baudelaire's emphasis in the prose poem on figures of estrangement and dispossession*" (emphasis added).[5] It is "the feeble, the destitute, orphaned and forlorn," Baudelaire says, who irresistibly draw his eye away from the scene, desolate characters, more like Manet's *Buveur d'absinthe* (1859), which Baudelaire had seen in the artist's studio, and which has often been qualified as "Baudelairean" for its fascination with urban squalor.[6]

The fact remains that, viewed against Manet's celebration of the inclusive multitude in *La Musique aux Tuileries,* Baudelaire's "Veuves," by contrast, is very much a reflection on exclusion and solitude. The widows he spots in the park are notable precisely for their isolation from the crowd, a specific crowd that is itself excluded from the self-enclosed world of music and gaiety in the afternoon. Baudelaire's poet-philosopher looks on that crowd from the outside, too, much as we, the spectators of Manet's painting are separated from its society by the modern wire-backed chairs that form a decorative enclosure for the assembled gathering.

Looking at Manet's painting, it is clear even from a superficial glance at this crowd that this is no accidental encounter of afternoon strollers; the participants in the foreground are for the most part well-defined individuals who have been packed into this tight space not by chance, nor by any physical constraints, but by the memory of the artist, in whose imagination they all occupy relative roles. Indeed, much of the documentary interest generated by this painting has been directed to singling out from the crowd those identifiable figures who simultaneously inhabit the space of Manet's private world of association. No one has been so bold or so naive as to assume that at any one moment they all shared the same public space in a Parisian park, although T. J. Clark has come close to reading the painting that way.[7] They represent in sum a personal allegory of Manet's social world, not as it ever appeared precisely in reality, but rather as it might have appeared telescoped by the mind's eye of the artist.[8] A multitude of subjective associations are combined into this dense world to offer us no objective picture, but instead—as Baudelaire would have it—a picture of nature, or society, as it might have seemed, filtered through the idiosyncratic desires of the artist's imagination and memory.

From his recollections Manet recomposes a new world in this painting, a world that aptly contains his own portrait. Standing at the edge of the painting, he dictates, as it were, our reading of the "table of contents" from left to right. Many are the other faces in the crowd that have been picked out from the mass—Albert de Balleroy, Champfleury, Zacharie Astruc, Aurélien Scholl, Fantin-Latour, and Baudelaire himself, who speaks with Théophile Gautier and Baron Taylor (he stands at the compositional center of the left half of the painting). In the right half of the painting one recognizes Madame Lejosne, Madame Offenbach, Eugène Manet, Jacques Offenbach, and Charles Monginot. Beatrice Farwell stresses the specific identifiability of the figures as the constitutive feature distinguishing the fashionable world of this painting from the more desolate society of *Le Vieux Musicien* (painted the same year): "the people in Manet's *Concert* are all individuals, while the old musician and his friends are all types" (91). But there are anonymous "types" in the Tuileries crowd as well; some, like Baudelaire, are faceless, too, and lend themselves to the "avid speculations" of the detached observer.

To be sure, the composition contains its own invitation to the viewer to enter it right at the center, where the distinct features of the foreground figures on the left give way to looser, vaguer brushstrokes; some of these materialize into people with the active engagement of the spectator's eye. And what does that eye see?

In the middle of the picture, set between the tall tree trunk that arches to the left and the standing figure of Eugène Manet (in ivory trousers, black frock coat, and top hat) there is a gray area that is oddly blurred by comparison with the well-defined features of the dapper Eugène. The legible access

to that area is provided by Eugène Manet's top hat, which inclines slightly to
the left to point to a faceless woman directly behind him, a woman who
suddenly emerges visually from the broad strokes of gray. This veiled image
in black with a young child in her arms is a peculiarly mysterious figure in
the lively crowd. She is grouped with no one and addresses no one, and her
very aloofness bespeaks an unusual state of isolation in the midst of sociable
activity. Indeed, I maintain that she is herself "une image voilée" of that very
widow with a young child whom Baudelaire spots in the crowd in the prose
poem of 1861.[9]

Like the lonely widows of Baudelaire's poetic world, Manet's widow is
invisible to the crowd, and it is only the avid eye of the artist, man of the
crowd, which singles her out from the mass. Faceless, like the poet himself,
she demands an enormous act of imaginative sympathy to be acknowledged
at all—such are the distracting effects of bright colors and heedless pleasure.
Much like the explicit information in Manet's letter, she is at the very center
of the picture and, yet, how rarely has she been seen. Art historians and
sympathetic literary critics alike have missed her, referring to the "central
area" of the painting as "indistinct, almost impenetrable" (Adler 1986, 44).
Prendergast himself, in his otherwise compelling reading of this painting
and its ironic "pantomime of etiquette," comments: "The painting of the
woman in the left foreground replicates the signs of 'decorum,' but elsewhere the signs are far less clear. Indeed, in the centre, they are virtually unreadable" (182). "There is certainly nothing," he asserts about this painting,
"of Baudelaire's emphasis . . . on figures of estrangement and dispossess-
sion." Interpreters have again been blinded by the verifiable facts of the
painting—the well-defined portraits of well-known faces—and in the head-
long pursuit of historical fact, the poetic reference has been lost.[10]

What is one to make of poetic hypotheses such as those I have just advanced? It would be presumptuous to claim that they disqualify earlier interpretations of *La Musique aux Tuileries* on the grounds of iconographical
oversight. In truth, my script for the putative dialogue between Manet's
painting and Baudelaire's prose poem hinges on intuitions that I can no
more demonstrate than can the critics who would see this picture as a plainly bourgeois transcription of Second Empire leisure. What can be deduced,
nonetheless, from these "avid speculations" are the different sets of presup-
positions and ignorances that an art-historian and a literary historian may
bring to a well-known—if not so evident—artistic "collaboration" such as

that of Baudelaire and Manet.[11] Perhaps, in the end, it is the art historian who will best alert the literary scholar to potential blind spots in his reading of and speaking to painting. In surveying the art historical reception and interpretation of one Manet painting in conjunction with Baudelaire's writings, I have, in turn, been impressed by two instances of blindness or blurring that repeatedly qualify the commentary on *La Musique aux Tuileries*. One of these pertains to the selective reading of visual evidence in the painting; the other relates to the selective reading of textual evidence in the poet's work.

It is well known that when *La Musique aux Tuileries* was first exhibited along with thirteen other paintings by Manet at the Galerie Martinet in February 1863, it elicited the harshest reaction from critics and public alike. Emile Zola recalls the intensity of the outrage:

> It was two other pictures, "Le Ballet Espagnol" and "La Musique aux Tuileries" which put flame to powder. An exasperated picture lover went so far as to threaten that if "La Musique aux Tuileries" was left any longer in the exhibition hall, he would resort to violence. (Zola 1991, 157)

One is hard pressed today to imagine what, in this rather polite picture, might have provoked such a violent response—a response repeated throughout the press coverage of the exhibition. Unlike the scandal initiated by the Olympia painting two years later, there is no evidence of moral outrage in the attacks on the picture. The criticism was primarily leveled at the formal execution of the painting, in particular at the areas of strident brushwork and painterly indeterminacy that offended the eye of the viewer and confounded his reading. Paul de Saint-Victor, writing in *La Presse,* 27 April 1863, describes Manet's paintings at the Martinet exhibition as "des charivaris de palette." "Never have we seen lines grimace more horribly, nor tones of color screech so. . . . His Concert in the Tuileries Gardens burns (*écorche*) the eyes, much as the music at a fair makes ears bleed." Hippolyte Babou, writing four years later in *La Revue libérale,* attacks the painting more specifically for the blotchiness of its portraits:

> A canvas entitled *La Musique aux Tuileries* presents me with the Baudelaire blotch (*la tache-Baudelaire*), the Gautier blotch, and

even the Manet blotch; I didn't see a Zola blotch. It has been further noted, and rightly so, that this mania for seeing things in
blotches (par taches) invariably leads to a kind of uniformity of
impression that reduces, effaces, and degrades the human face;
which explains why, in all these paintings, the heads are almost
always marbled and streaky (jaspées ou écaillées), sketchy and
confused. (289; see also Cachin 1983, 126.)

Even Zola, in his passionate defense of the painting, recognized that a
startling technique of representation had disrupted the harmony of the
painting's surface and ostensible subject matter.

I can understand why this lover of the arts was angry. Imagine a
crowd, maybe a hundred persons, milling around in the sun-
shine under the trees in the Tuileries. Each face is just a single
blob of paint, barely defined, where details are reduced to lines
or black points. Had I been there, I would have asked this lover
of the arts to stand at a respectable distance from the picture; he
would have then seen that these blobs are alive, that the crowd is
talking and that this is one of the artist's characteristic canvases,
one in which he has obeyed to the utmost what his eyes and tem-
perament have dictated. (Zola 1991, 157–58)

How odd descriptive accounts such as these must seem to the twentieth-century eye, inured as it is to the boldness of Manet's technique.
Whereas contemporary critics of Manet could not read the portraits for the
taches, our own contemporaries have, just as exclusively, avoided the *taches*
for the portraits. And yet, surely, the most remarkable visual feature of this
painting is the jarring coincidence of different manners of brushwork; that
is, different modes of representation—conventional portraits and streaky
blobs—on one surface. For there is no doubt about it: on close observation
this is a very strange picture. And if nineteenth-century viewers were
too startled visually by the unfinished sketch of a face—like the face of
Baudelaire or the face of the widow, who, in the poet's words, "fait une
tache si éclatante"—to comment on the more legible areas of the painting,
twentieth-century readers of this painting have minimized the formal prob-
lematics that issue from the visual oddness of, for instance, the central scene

in this picture or, for that matter, the relation between the extreme left and right sides.

Whereas the one edge of the canvas proposes a familiar nineteenth-century iconic representation of Manet, the other asserts, to borrow Richard Shiff's use of the term, an indexical reference to the Manet. The one represents the person of the artist; the other represents the artist's style and touch. In his article "Performing an Appearance: On the Surface of Abstract Expressionism," Shiff, taking the example of Manet as a modernist prototype, retraces the theoretical relations of indexicality to iconicity . . .

In an age of mechanization and mass industrial production, painting, always labor-intensive, assumes the symbolic meaning of individual effort and creative originality (or at least singularity). The marks on the painted surface each function as a kind of individualized signature, especially if they have formal consistency. So to the extent that a painter's marks look like each other more than they resemble the external world they "represent," they can function . . . indexically, signifying the presence of an artist who is a creative individual. Style, indexically, is more a matter of making marks on a surface than of arranging the parts of a represented subject matter. One's style of marking identifies one's character, one's manner of performance. Strong character would entail strong style, and that would entail a very visible mark of the hand (the appearance of strong performance).

All this is more of modernist mythology, and it was once controversial. Ingres, in his academic moments during the nineteenth century, did not approve: "Touch should not be apparent . . . Instead of the object represented, it makes one see the painter's technique; in place of thought, it proclaims the hand." (Shiff 1987, 100)

Ingres, like the baffled viewers at Manet's exhibition, is here advocating "an art of iconicity" (to visualize "the object") and resisting the rise of modernist indexicality (assertion of "the hand"). Ironically, in resisting or ignoring Manet's various stylistic assertions on the surface of his canvas, modern readers of *La Musique aux Tuileries* have done the same. For if we accept Shiff's definition of the aim of modernism as "the attempt . . . to fuse iconic

appearance to indexical performance" (103), does it not follow that in
Manet's painting, the willful juxtaposition of manifestly different tech-
niques of representation itself constitutes the significant reflection on "the
painting of modern life" that twentieth-century critics would extrapolate
from the subject matter alone? In selectively reducing the information in
this painting to a tableau of Second Empire sociability—the example of T. J.
Clark might again be cited—it would seem that art historians have, like
their single-minded precursors of the 1860s, smoothed over the painting's
internal conflicts and thereby produced a painting that is more unidimen-
sional than even Manet's lack of modeling might have made it appear.

Such reductions are, furthermore, most often performed in the name of
Baudelaire, whose treatise on "the painting of modernity" this painting
would illustrate perfectly. To be sure, for this painting to illustrate that ad-
mirable essay, it would have to acknowledge formally, and not just icono-
graphically, the special energy of modern art that is, for Baudelaire, born
out of tension, like an electrical charge: the collision of the eternal and the
ephemeral, of the fantastic and the everyday, of the poetic and the historic.

Traditionally, art historians and literary historians alike have tended to
read *Le Peintre de la vie moderne* as an essay on "The Painting of Modern
Life," stressing the art object (painting) and its modern subject matter. It is
this misplaced emphasis that has led so many readers to regret the choice of
Constantin Guys as the hero of that piece, since his artistic production
hardly seems to merit the weight of this thoughtful and passionate statement. But the essay is about the persona of the Painter himself, about his
idiosyncratic manner of relating the phantasmagoria of his private imagination to the public displays of modern life about him; and, above all, it celebrates his uncanny knack for capturing that tense and fleeting relation on
paper, by hand.[12] For Baudelaire, the specific figurations which dramatize
that fragile representation of private phantasm and public world, reside,
however, not in the art criticism, where he can only describe their aesthetic
potential, but in his poetry, where they enact their "magical" effect. It is this
distinction, or the failure to recognize it, that has entailed the selective misreading of textual evidence to which I alluded.

The example of the shadowy widow is a case in point. There are more
general instances of the art historian's disregard for poetic intertexts that reflect Baudelaire's thinking on art—poems that do not necessarily refer explicitly to painting. Even Michael Fried, one of the more careful readers of

Baudelaire, in his essay "Painting Memories: On the Containment of the Past in Baudelaire and Manet"—an essay reworked in his more recent book, *Manet's Modernism*—is careful mainly in his reading of the art criticism, minimizing the literary texts that coincide—intellectually and chronologically—with the essays on art.[13]

In that essay, Fried insists upon the importance of Baudelaire's aesthetics of memory for Manet, with reference to the following quotation:

> The critic should arm himself from the start with a sure criterion, a criterion drawn from nature, and should then carry on his duty with a passion; for a critic does not cease to be a man, and passion draws similar temperaments together. (In Baudelaire 1965, 45)

Accepting Fried's argument that Baudelaire's "sure criterion" of art is memory—and I believe this to be the case—we may wish to reconsider the entire sentence that authorized this intuition. It would appear that, like many of the scholars he takes to task, Fried has stopped short of the second half of the statement. Whereas Baudelaire qualifies his initial proposition with the following caveat: "for the critic does not cease to be a man," Fried goes on to describe the "pictorial thought" of a critic who does not cease to be a critic. And memory for him, and for his interpretation of Baudelaire's understanding of the creative process of art, signifies primarily—if not exclusively—the memory of *paintings*. This is an odd conclusion indeed to draw from a poet whose poems are so thoroughly obsessed with the workings of memory, and with the externalization of inner phantoms into eloquent images. When, in his essay, Fried does introduce the inevitable topic of the role of private memories (as opposed to the memory of paintings) in Baudelaire's early criticism, he announces: "two further lines of inquiry all but propose themselves." One line leads to "Freud's writings," and the other to an essay by Walter Benjamin on Baudelaire's poetry. No pertinent lines, it would appear, lead to Baudelaire's poetry itself.

What are the implications of this selective use of Baudelaire's writings? It would seem that, as in the readings of *La Musique aux Tuileries*, a large textual forest is being misrepresented for a few well-defined trees. The complex theory of memory, repression and desire that is enacted in Baudelaire's poems—itself a prototype of Freudian discourse—is flattened into a pat intertextual system: paintings contain the memory of other paintings, poems remember other poems, etc. Fried's effective reduction of the "stock of memories" that Baudelaire invokes in his art criticism to a storehouse of paintings thus not only deprives the poet's writings of the competing structures that inform and energize them, but also deprives Manet's pictures of whatever poetic reference might be playing alongside the visually commemorative details.

In conclusion, whereas over time literary critics have had to be convinced of the poetic value of Baudelaire's art criticism, art historians may still need to be convinced of the art-critical insight of the poetry. In the case of Manet, whose painting so explicitly acknowledges "the poet of modern life," to refuse the poetic resonance of *La Musique aux Tuileries* is to remain blind to the "tache éclatante," and the stoic widow standing still at its center.

The Subject of *Le Peintre de la vie moderne*

Timothy Raser

WHILE critics of Baudelaire's *Le Peintre de la vie moderne* disagree about almost everything else, they do agree that its subject is not what it appears to be. This is strange, for, unlike a poem or a novel, an art-critical essay would seem to possess a nominal subject, a subject that can be determined with some precision: the real works of a real artist. One might think or hope that such referentiality would guarantee at least some common ground for criticism. The contrary, however, seems to be the case. Pierre-Georges Castex, for example, resists the notion that Baudelaire, the great poet, and, he hopes, the prophetic critic, could have chosen a minor illustrator as the subject of his most influential essay: "The complete painter of modern life cannot be identified with a fashion-artist, even an inspired one." However suggestive the works of Constantin Guys might be, or however stimulating he might have been to Baudelaire's thought, it is unfortunate that the essay wasn't about a greater artist: "Certainly Baudelaire could have found richer material, if not for an analysis of modernity in the meaning he understood by this notion, at least for an analysis of the modern genius of painting, in the works of Edouard Manet" (Castex 1979, 74). But it is hard to imagine what a "richer material" would have contributed to an essay which, by all accounts, is a seminal formulation of modernist aesthetics, and, by all accounts, an essay worthy of careful study and close reading, whatever its subject might be. For Castex, Baudelaire's value as critic depends on his ability to single out great artists before wider recognition, and his value as theoretician depends on his ability to formulate a notion—modernity—that will capture the preoccupations of the greatest artists of his day. This contention—from 1969—has had a significant following,[1] its most notable instances being in the field of art history, where both Anne Coffin Hanson and Timothy J. Clark have used the essay as the starting point of analysis of more recognized painters—Manet in the case of Hanson; Manet and Monet in the case of Clark.

Nor is the resistance to the subject of the essay limited to art history or to Constantin Guys: as early as 1971, Anita Brookner took issue with the subject of modernity, which was to dominate Hanson's and Clark's uses of the text, enabling application to Manet and Monet. By contrast, Brookner places the emphasis not on modernity, but on life when she considers "The Painter of Modern Life": "The essay is about life—and only incidentally about modern life—by someone who is already sick and has always regarded himself as disabled" (Brookner 1971, 83). The thesis is plausible, above all because it takes into account biographical information—Baudelaire's illness—of great importance for the year of the essay's publication. However, such a thesis stands or falls with the dating of the essay: if the essay was composed in a time of good health, its value is less, and this dating of the essay is far from certain.[2] Claude Pichois, for example, in the magisterial presentation of the essay in his edition of the *Œuvres complètes,* places the greater part of its composition in the years 1859 and 1860, years of relative health.

Beyond its titular subject, the essay contains theoretical considerations of the nature of beauty, and these reflections have also been taken, given the unfamiliarity of Guys and his work, as the "real" subject of the essay. These considerations, furthermore, have often been applied to Baudelaire's poetry, and the stakes of designating them as subject of the essay have correspondingly increased. Essential to any account of this kind is the distinction, found in the first pages of the essay, of a fluctuating and a stable element in beauty, and Baudelaire's assertion that both elements are present in any beautiful object.[3] This distinction has given rise to many interpretations of his poetry, especially of his prose poems—for example, "Le Thyrse." However, this definition of beauty is even more problematic than the canonical definitions it hopes to replace (where beauty consists entirely of certain predictable and stable elements), for the transitory element of "dual" beauty proves impossible to define. David Carrier has shown that this transitory element is, in the final analysis, everything, and if everything from the present is of interest, simply because it is present, the definition becomes unusable: "Both the past and the present can be interesting: the one because it is past, the other because it is present. This suggests, perhaps incorrectly, that everything is interesting; it sounds like a deep point, but is Baudelaire saying anything more than that someday our images of contemporary scenes too will show scenes of the past?" (Carrier 1985, 57–58).

There can be no doubt that it was a dissatisfaction such as this that led Paul de Man to read the essay against its "theoretical" thrust. Like those authors who have underlined the notion of modernity and the desire, among modern artists, to capture the "present," de Man also points out the themes of speed, energy, and action that guide the description of Guys and his works. At the same time, however, de Man insists on the paradox of any discussion of modernity. The artistic representation of the nonartistic, the *representation of the present*, involve the cancellation of the nominal subject by its opposite: "The paradox of the problem is potentially contained in the formula 'représentation du présent,' which combines a repetitive with an instantaneous pattern without apparent awareness of the incompatibility" (de Man 1983, 156). Such an aporia could be allowed to stand by labeling it something like "the paradox of modern art." Instead, de Man pushes further and discovers, in the moments where Baudelaire formulates it, the emergence of a theme of writing: "The more realistic and pictorial they (descriptions) become, the more abstract they are, the slighter the residue of meaning that would exist outside their specificity as mere language and mere *signifiant*" (160). The appearance of the theme of writing is caused by the awareness the writer experiences as he tries to represent action, movement, or modernity, that the only tools he has are those of their opposite: duration and repetition, essential features of language. Thus, the more Baudelaire strives to "represent the present" or to "extract modernity" from "life," the more he in fact succeeds in allegorizing language.

Writing, however, is not a privileged subject in the essay; it is not one which tends to be the irrevocable allegory of all others. At one point, for example, Baudelaire expresses the regret that Guys's album of drawings was never presented to the emperor, but are instead "now scattered in several different places" (Baudelaire 1964, 21). He thus associates the figure of the emperor with that of an authoritative presence: his viewing of the drawings would somehow have validated them. And when the emperor returns in the following chapter, he is indeed assimilated to writing: "The emperor of the French, whose face he has learnt to curtail to an unerring sketch which he executes with the assurance of a personal signature" (24). Here at last we recognize a meaning rather than appreciate a form; a signature replaces an image, and the insistence on a figure of writing is all the more promising as it is invested with the possibility of deciding, once and for all, the value of Guys's drawings: The emperor, who can be recognized, will authorize us in turn to recognize the beauty of Guys's drawings. But here again the subject is evasive: no sooner is the emperor evoked as a recognizable figure than his authority recedes behind the glitter of his surroundings:

> At the front of a box . . . the Emperor is leaning forward slightly, so as to get a better view of the stage: below him, two personal bodyguards are standing at attention in a military, almost hieratic state of immobility, while their brilliant uniforms receive the splash and sputter of the footlights. On the far side of the barrier of flame . . . the actors are singing, declaiming, and gesticulating . . . on the near side there yawns an abyss of dim light, a circular space crowded with tier upon tier of human figures; it is the great chandelier, and the audience. (24)

As the emperor disappears in favor of the chandelier, the theme of writing, and with it, recognition, recede in favor of the theme of superficial beauty evoked on the first pages of the essay.

Not about Guys, not about modernity, not about the present, action, or, finally, about writing, is the essay about nothing? What is plain from this review of criticism of the essay is that the essay says one thing and means something else. This feature has been labeled "semiosis" by Michael Riffaterre, and is, he claims, the defining feature of poetry (1978, 1). Indeed, the essay has always been qualified as "poetic": "This is not a work of simple criticism . . . Felix Leakey likened it to the *Cygne* . . . and Georges Blin found it to be 'the greatest of Baudelaire's prose poems'" (*OC* 2:1418).[4] If anything, however, *Le Peintre de la vie moderne* applies the principle of semiosis more systematically than does Riffaterre: not simply does it mean something other than what it says, but *whatever* it seems to say, its meaning lies elsewhere. One could think of the essay as an extreme illustration of Baudelaire's complaint from the contemporary poem "Le Cygne": "Everything is becoming an allegory for me" (*OC* 1:86).

I would like to examine the essay's descriptions and its narrative to determine whether the displacement of the subject that has so often been pointed out also characterizes other, major features of the essay and whether, correlatively, this displacement doesn't characterize the essay as a whole.

In the first paragraph, Baudelaire presents Guys indirectly while attacking the notion of canonical art: consecrated examples of classical beauty displayed in authoritative settings where they need only to be recognized:

> The world—and even the world of artists—is full of people who can go to the Louvre, walk rapidly, without so much as a glance, past rows of very interesting, though secondary, pictures, to come to a rapturous halt in front of a Titian or a Raphael—one of those that has been most popularised by the engraver's art; then they will go home happily, not a few say to themselves, "I know my Museum." (Baudelaire 1964, 1)

Such an attitude eliminates appreciation, replacing it with recognition, and reduces aesthetics from a sensory experience to a moment of cognition. This attitude relies on authority: the "aesthetic" experience takes place in a museum, the Louvre in particular, and results in celebrating canonical artists: Titian or Raphael. Significantly, the museum-goer considers only paintings already made famous by engraving—that is, he rereads already familiar images. If the experience of Guys is to be different from this manifestly degraded result of classical aesthetics, it should be because his works are new and unknown, appreciated via the senses rather than validated by cognition. Criticizing the museum-goer, Baudelaire thus promises to appreciate Guys for his novelty rather than for conformity to rules of beauty, and if his works are beautiful, it is because they are *aesthetic* (that is, sensory) rather than regular. The later themes of childhood, youth, novelty, energy, etc., thus support the thesis advanced in the first paragraph. Baudelaire's use of "M.G." to designate Guys[5] also supports the thesis: the artist cannot be recognized—and, hence, must be appreciated—if his name is not revealed.

And yet, the essay unfolds like a murder mystery, an exercise in detection, where the object is cognitive, to learn and know something unknown at the outset. "Who is this white-moustached cavalry-officer, with so vividly-drawn an expression," Baudelaire asks (Baudelaire 1964, 19–20). "*Myself at Inkermann,"* Guys replies. Elsewhere, M.G.'s pictures of society resemble the reports of a journalist dispatched to lay bare the truth behind everyday appearances: behind the laziness of soldiers in their barracks are "strange adventures"; behind the materialism of the dandy is a modern stoicism; behind the wives of "good" families are the prostitutes their husbands visit. If the thesis is that beauty should be enjoyed and appreciated, another current of the essay states that the modern city should be known. Here, too, it seems, the "subject" of the essay is displaced in its initial statement by something quite different.

This displacement is visible in the descriptions as well, especially apparent in the long chapter "Des Femmes et des filles." Initial considerations of the women of the capital are aesthetic: well-to-do wives display themselves at the theater, in a spectacle of jewels, eyes, skin, and teeth. No question of who these women are disturbs the resolutely superficial presentation. But elsewhere, in cafés and small theaters, other women appear, no longer defined solely in terms of their appearances: these are "mistresses," "wanton beauties," and "courtesans" (35–36). And not simply does identification replace the enjoyment of pure appearance accorded to "respectable" women, but it is doubled with increasingly explicit moral judgments: the light bathing them is "infernal," movement toward them is labeled a "descent," the world they inhabit is called "the last degree of the spiral," and their attraction is not beauty, but Evil: "She has her own sort of beauty, which comes to her from Evil" (36).

To sum up, not simply does the essay mean something other than what it says, it does so systematically, or pathologically. It's not a question of determining a "real" subject behind an apparent subject, but accepting that whatever subject is attached to the essay is in turn displaced by another subject. This is true of immediate subjects such as "Guys," "life," and "modernity," but also metasubjects such as "the present" and "allegory." Even the claim to appreciate appearances is displaced by an impulse to know, and aesthetics is replaced by writing. This displacement could even be called Baudelaire's aesthetics: his works include a purely superficial sensorial enjoyment, which is doubled by moral judgments. The outstanding example, of course, is the title of his *Fleurs du Mal.* But even such a hackneyed identification has its use: if the evasiveness of the "subject" of *Le Peintre de la vie moderne* springs from Baudelairean aesthetics, it would follow that the other examples of that aesthetic are equally evasive.

It seems to me manifest that the source of these displacements is not an error of judgment that would have accorded Constantin Guys the stature reserved for Edouard Manet; nor is it the illness that dominated the last years of Baudelaire's life. De Man's contention that the impulse to capture the nonlinguistic generates a thematization of its opposite—writing—seems closer to the mark, but needs some elaboration, for de Man looks at the essay as a theory of modernity, a theory that, as David Carrier has shown, also has many difficulties.

In order to determine the source of the displacements, I would return to the essay: even if Manet is a more appropriate subject for Baudelaire than Guys, and even if writing is a persistent theme, one must entertain, at least provisionally, the notion that Guys's drawings are its subject. But when one does so, features of art-critical discourse come to the fore. On the one hand, as Castex assumes, art-criticism contains judgments, discriminations enabling the author to direct his /her reader to some works and away from others. But on the other, it contains descriptions, situating and elaborating the judgments. These descriptions depend absolutely on deictics, pointers in the text that designate which painting, statue, or engraving to consider. This feature is characteristic of the art-critical salons Baudelaire wrote in 1845, 1846, 1855, and 1859, "these useful handbooks" (Baudelaire 1965, 1), as he put it, which provide judgments and comments for paintings displayed at the yearly exposition. These deictics, pointing away from the writer to something else punctuate the essay: from the "J'ai sous les yeux" of the fourth paragraph to the recurrent "ce" and "ces" used to designate images in pictures before him, to the "ici," "voici," "tantôt," "maintenant" Baudelaire insistently uses to postulate a place, time, and subject different from the "here" and "now" of the essay itself. "And now we are at Schumla, enjoying the hospitality of Omer-Pacha . . . And here are the *Kurds at Scutari* . . . the bachi-bazoucks . . . we find that historic cavalry charge celebrated by the heroic trumpet-blasts of Alfred Tennyson . . . (Baudelaire 1964, 19–20). But the "here" and "now" of the essay are part of this system: there can be no "then" without the determination of a "now," no "there" without a "here," and the "here" and "now" of an essay written in Paris (or was it Honfleur?) in 1860 (or was it two years earlier?) but read in Nashville in 1998 are, to say the least, uncertain. It is hardly necessary to invoke Hegel to point out that using markers of the "here" and "now" does not simplify but complicates the references of any text.[6] For every deictic, one can ask "Which here? Which now?" Every time

Baudelaire refers to Guys's drawings with a "voici," an "ici," a "maintenant," or a "ce," the drawings seem to evaporate like the present itself: is this the right drawing? Is he talking about the drawing or the engraving? Is Baudelaire talking about the experience of the city, or its inscription as a drawing/engraving? Every effort to come closer to "la vie moderne" elicits a swarm of questions that take one away from it, just as St. Augustine found that any attempt to circumscribe the moment led one further from it, not closer to it (Ricœur 1983, 27–29). And yet, such deictics are necessary in any referential text, and absolutely necessary in art criticism, where the basic gesture of pointing and designating is inscribed in the very discourse. If one can't point, one can hardly talk about the visual arts.

These tools are of course prevalent in art-critical discourse, and necessarily so. But it also seems that their use is insistent in *Le Peintre de la vie moderne,*[7] and, moreover, that Baudelaire thematized them: the very questions that have made the essay so engaging, the questions that have set critics apart on their assessment of the essay's subject, are precisely questions that arise from the use of deictics.

One of the functions of deictics is to specify: words being general in their application, the use of a deictic (in the present case, the verbal substitute *voici*) is necessary in order to specify which place, person, group, or artist is meant. This is exactly the problem raised by Baudelaire's use of "M.G." instead of the proper noun that would have specified the essay's subject: Is it about Constantin Guys or painters more generally? If it's not about Guys, perhaps it's really about Manet, etc. Likewise, Baudelaire's invocation of *modernité* as the artist's prey calls for, but does not receive, specification: is the essay about 1860 or about the "modern" more generally, whenever that might occur? And, if so, is it possible, as David Carrier has suggested,[8] for the essay ever to be out of date? Is it about life (and the eternal questions of age, illness, and death), or is it about modern life, whatever that might be? Is it about the City, or about the City of Paris in 1863 as recorded by Constantin Guys? Both answers have their supporters. Finally, and most generally, is the essay about experience, whether strictly visual or, more generally, sensual, or is it about sign systems (whether linguistic or pictorial), which can never do justice to the details of a particular experience? By constructing the essay around such problems, Baudelaire highlights the nature of art-critical discourse, whose ambition is forever to specify further.

This claim can be easily tested, and no text of Baudelaire's, or anyone else's for that matter, lends itself so readily to inspection as the poet's "Les Phares," found both in the 1857 and 1861 editions of *Les Fleurs du Mal* and considered by many as a primer for Baudelaire's aesthetics and art criticism. An enumeration of the names of eight great artists, the poem adds to these names, in a stanza dedicated to each artist, a short evocation of his works, and then, having evoked the eight, analogizes them to a series of signal towers along a coast, relaying a message over time and distance. The subject or subjects of the poem would thus be great art or great artists, arranged in a sequence that has attracted as much attention as the names of the artists themselves. The image of the lighthouse has seized the imagination of several critics, who see in it an alternative model of artistic evolution to that of genius,[9] and such artistic "progress" could be construed as another subject of the poem.

With a single exception, each of the eight stanzas dedicated to a single artist starts with that artist's name; the rest of the stanza, descriptive of his works, is placed in apposition to the name as if the name and the works were the same thing. But whether the proper noun designates the artist or his works, in both cases it points, specifying a man among men, a work (or group of works) among works. The specified artists follow each other in sequence,[10] but the meaning of that sequence is not in question now: what is in question is how these designations relate to art criticism.

The poem ends with three stanzas more general in nature and of greater import for the understanding of the poem as a whole than analysis of those images used to depict individual artists. In these three stanzas, the preceding eight are summed up as "Ces malédictions, ces blasphèmes, ces plaintes, / Ces extases, ces cris, ces pleurs, ces *Te Deum*": the works of the artists are equated to forms of verbal expression, ranging from inarticulate cries to formed prayers, from blasphemy and curses to expressions of ecstasy. What is immediately apparent, however, is that the verbal equivalents of plastic works of art are reductive and interchangeable. The density and particularity of the imagery attached to each artist are lost when the cries, prayers, etc. are reduced to a single cry repeated by a thousand sentinels: "C'est un cri répété par mille sentinelles." And not simply are the works reduced, but they are repeated, in a sequence as dull and regular as the artists themselves were varied and original. Finally, what the artists' works are reduced to is the least articulate of utterances: not a message, certainly not a prayer or a legacy, but a cry to a posterity that fails even to take cognizance of those who cry. The apparent subject of the first eight stanzas changes radically: if art is an inheritance, the bequeathing of a legacy to successive heirs, it doesn't make it through probate. Certainly, this is an unusual outcome for a poem universally understood to praise the arts and to illustrate Baudelaire's dependence on them.

While it would be implausible to evoke any direct acquaintance with German philosophy with respect to Baudelaire, the preface to Hegel's *Phenomenology* comes again to mind here, if only because he and the poet approach the same problem: the failure of consciousness to base itself in the senses. Whether Baudelaire speaks successively of Eugène Delacroix, of works known as Delacroix, of a constellation of images and finally of a string of verbal utterances, his evocations of the painter become successively more general, more abstract, and less attached to the painter or his works, just as for Hegel the effort to determine a substance through the senses by enumerating its properties leads not to greater specificity, but to greater abstraction.[11] Hegel of course was to use this failure as a stepping stone toward an analysis of a more certain consciousness. But for an art critic, the failure of words to capture the specificity of sensation can only be deeply disturbing: if one can't describe or particularize a work, how can one possibly speak of it, much less judge it?

It might be for this reason, or in answer to this question, that as Baudelaire's qualifications of the works become most abstract, his designation of them becomes most insistent: his "cries," "blasphemies," and "prayers" are preceded by the frenzy of the demonstrative "ces," seven plurals followed by four singulars in the repeated expression "c'est," expressions which attempt to make up for vagueness of their qualification by the precision of their pointing. Even though he doesn't know what to call the works, and even though he seems to get further away with each effort to describe them, the poet claims to refer to them, if only by pointing.

I would note two things here: the first concerns the date of "Les Phares," a poem first published in *Les Fleurs du Mal* in 1857, but one of the stanzas of which was used in the reprint of Baudelaire's *Exposition universelle,* thus suggesting composition as early as 1855. Antoine Adam notes "stylistic resemblances" (280) with the poet's *Salon de 1846* and claims they indicate an early composition of the poem; Claude Pichois discounts this early dating. But even if "Les Phares" dates only from 1857, it shares a linguistic concern with *Le Peintre de la vie moderne* well in advance of that essay. Likewise, even if it celebrates canonical artists such as Rubens, Rembrandt, and Michelangelo, artists, precisely, about whom the essay avoids speaking, it shares the gesture of judgment with *Le Peintre*. And, of course, the poem is in verse, while the essay is prose. So even if *Le Peintre de la vie moderne* is apparently about the modern (just as "Les Phares" is apparently about the canon), both, because they are art-critical, must deal with the problem of pointing, whether they designate the present moment or an individual work, and whether they point in prose or do so in verse.

Secondly, the problem of designation remains regardless of the interpretation given to the descriptive stanzas of the poem: whether "evocations" or descriptions, whether their order is significant or not, whether the artists are great or of no consequence, analysis of the poem must deal with the fact that in the space of three stanzas the poet spends eleven demonstratives on descriptions that should stand on their own. That the problem returns regardless of interpretation of the eight descriptive stanzas indicates Baudelaire's sensitivity as art critic and his awareness of the genre's founding paradox. Art criticism must judge works of art, apply a general concept to an individual instance, singling it out from others, and evoking its particularity. As it does so, however, the language used makes judgment more, rather than less, general. And worse, the more criticism describes and designates, the further it strays from the work, and back into language. The subject of "Les Phares" can no more be determined than can that of *Le Peintre de la vie moderne,* for both texts have located their subject outside of themselves and are created by pointing at it, in a movement that forever draws the reader away from criticism as text, toward its ostensible object, only to fall back on itself as language fails to become plastic.

Off the Charts

Walter Benjamin's Depiction
of Baudelaire

Kevin Newmark

"**B**EHIND the masks which he used up, the poet in Baudelaire preserved his incognito." Such a description, which Walter Benjamin makes in passing during the course of the chapter on modernism in his essay "The Paris of the Second Empire in Baudelaire" is not just typical of the images Benjamin uses to characterize the texts by Baudelaire he is interpreting; it is also an apt emblem for Benjamin's own very curious and enigmatic writing: behind the masks, the incognito. Behind the masks, it would be much more logical to expect, and satisfying to find, there should rather be the grounding identity that is served by the masks. Just as, behind all the pseudonyms, presumably, stands the unique proper name. Is the incognito here not itself just another figure for the kind of hidden knowledge that can always be disclosed beyond the ultimate removal of all masks? Should the metaphoric expression that is used here to characterize the nature of Baudelaire's poetry, behind x is preserved y, not put both mask and incognito on the same side of the poetic equation, reserving for the other side of the interpretative act the secret meaning that has been concealed behind the masks? What exactly is represented by such an image of poetry's modernity? How can we understand the image of a mask placed upon the incognito, and how could such a bizarre metaphor ever be put to work for a future understanding of either the modernity of Baudelaire's poetry or Benjamin's reading of it?

In other words, faced with a theory of lyric poetry that promises to bring to light only the incognito, or unknowability, that has been preserved there, how can we do anything but finally ignore or forget it?

Un vieux sphinx ignoré du monde insoucieux,
Oublié sur la carte, et dont l'humeur farouche
Ne chante qu'aux rayons du soleil qui se couche . (*OC* 1:73)

[An ancient sphinx, unknown to a careless world, / forgotten
from the map, and whose incomprehensible strains / sing only
in the glow of a setting sun.]

These final lines taken from "Spleen II" seem to announce ahead of time the
fate of such an enigmatic theory of poetry as Benjamin's. But before joining
those insouciant individuals who leave Benjamin off the map of contemporary receptions of Baudelaire, perhaps we should return for just a moment,
the time in which it takes for the sun to set or turn dark, to read what else he
says about Baudelaire's incognito. "The incognito was the law of his poetry," Benjamin writes. "His prosody is comparable to the map of a big city in
which it is possible to move about inconspicuously, shielded by blocks of
houses, gateways, courtyards. On this map the places for the words are
clearly indicated, as the places are indicated for conspirators before the outbreak of a revolt. Baudelaire conspires with language itself" (Benjamin 1983,
98). The incognito Benjamin characterizes as the law of Baudelaire's poetry
is also described here in the figure of a *map*: Baudelaire's prosody is like a
map on which the places for the words, rather than merely forgotten, are
clearly indicated.

However, there is also something strange about this image of a map on
which the places for the conspirators are clearly indicated. The places for the
conspirators are marked out distinctly enough, and yet they themselves are
not actually there, as though the figures on the map were also masks behind
which Baudelaire's incognito waited to reveal itself as precisely that which
cannot be fully known, indeed, as a potential outbreak of violence and revolt against the known. "Oublié sur la carte," it should be remembered, can
also mean forgotten *on* the map rather than simply left off it.[1] For Benjamin,
the map is a mask, then, a certain kind of chart whose images indicate the
places where nothing of a future revolt can yet be seen. What is thus clearly
represented in its very invisibility to the naked eye, what is shielded and
therefore concealed behind all the houses, gateways, and courtyards that can
always be represented on such a map of modernity, is a potential conspiracy
against these same images. And even more strangely still, Benjamin's text

also clearly indicates who these conspirators are: "On this map the places for the *words* are clearly indicated. . . . Baudelaire conspires with *language* itself" (98).

"Oublié sur la carte": if Benjamin always resists inclusion within any simple mapping of Baudelaire studies, would this not also be because his theory of Baudelaire's poetry hinges in this way on an incognito that is not just that of Baudelaire, but more radically still, an incognito of the poetic *word,* of what he calls "language itself"? The suggestion that Baudelaire's poetry constitutes a kind of map that indicates not what it represents, but rather what cannot be represented there, is clearly an interesting one.[2] But to go on to suggest that the ultimate incognito preserved in this way behind all the masks on the map is that of a language in revolt against the current mapping of knowledge is truly baffling. For what could it possibly mean that Baudelaire's poetry, which is after all nothing but a chart composed of words, represents only the places for other words that are not yet in place, but whose job, when they do come, would be to break out and revolt against what is known, and therefore representable on all such maps?

There is, of course, one very important text by Baudelaire himself where the question of the incognito surfaces in direct connection to the theoretical issue of representation, though at first glance it seems more like a theory modeled on pictorial than poetic representation. The work in question, *Le Peintre de la vie moderne,* describes its ostensible subject, the painter Constantin Guys, as a "great lover of crowds and incognito" (*OC* 2:688). Nonetheless, it should be clear to any reader of the text that the figure of the anonymous painter is itself a convenient mask that Baudelaire uses there only in order to represent his own theory of poetic activity. The poet, like the painter, is therefore represented in the mask of one whose most obvious task is precisely that of representation. Just as Benjamin suggests in his essay, behind this particular mask of Baudelaire, the poet as painter, is preserved the incognito, the painter who loves the anonymity of crowds as well as his own incognito. But since the incognito to which Baudelaire refers in his essay on modernity seems itself merely to mask a theory of poetry that would ultimately be based on painting, or representation, it could hardly turn out to be as enigmatic as Benjamin's mapping of poetic incognito as the unknowability of language itself. Or could it?

Written, Baudelaire says, as an attempt to elaborate an aesthetic theory that would be truly historical rather than purely abstract, *Le Peintre de la vie moderne* seems at first to rely entirely upon a straightforward principle of representation as mimesis. "But [those painters from the last century] *represent* the past," Baudelaire says, "and it is the painting of present customs that I would like to examine today. . . . The pleasure to be derived from the *representation* of the present has to do not only with the beauty with which it may be adorned, but also with its essential quality of being present" (684). At this point, though, Baudelaire's conception of the historical dimension of the artwork appears rather traditional as well as potentially misleading. Baudelaire seems to be arguing here that each historical moment has its own mode of being present to itself, and any given historical moment achieves adequation through *representing* this presence to itself. "Man ends up resembling what he wants to be," is one of the formulations Baudelaire uses in this section, and it also catches the sense in which the concept of history being articulated here understands the past as that which once was but is no longer present to itself.

Baudelaire's model of modernity can be read at this point as a rather thinly disguised form of historical positivism, a model in which the artwork would simply mirror, or represent, whatever conventions, ideals, and beliefs are operative and present to themselves at any given moment. Baudelaire uses the word *phantom* in the opening pages of his essay to refer to the modern element inherent to every historical period, but the phantom here can only be understood to mean that the past present moment necessarily becomes a phantom for every current present, which itself can occur only through its emergence and therefore separation from the past. For this reason, Baudelaire can go on to claim that nothing could prevent such a phantom of the past from always becoming present once again, in a new representation, as it were, since its essence resides in a former adequation among all its elements.

The pseudo-historical model elaborated here is a simple one of sequential and fully ordered synchronic states that follow without interruption one upon the other, and it thus avoids all the hermeneutic negativity that would have to be confronted in a truly historical conception of art. "The transitions are handled as smoothly here," Baudelaire writes, "as in the animal kingdom, without the slightest lacuna or surprise" (685). The work of art, like human nature itself, may involve a duality, but it would be a duality that is patterned on a correspondence of internal and external elements. This model makes the work of art into the outward manifestation, or representation, of an internal essence, just as, and Baudelaire does not fail to include the reference, the human and variable body can be said to incarnate the divine and eternal soul. To gaze through the documented history of past aesthetic representations is therefore to be brought face to face with the individual moments of a universal system. "One need only add to the vignette *representing* each period," Baudelaire finally declares, "the philosophical thought with which it was so preoccupied, a thought whose memory is inevitably suggested by the vignette, to see what profound harmony rules all the elements of history" (685). The French word *régir*, which means to rule or govern, and which points directly to the judicial register of law and law enforcement, serves as well to remind us precisely at the point of its most desirable harmony that the concept of representation alluded to here is grounded in political as well as aesthetic considerations. The rule of *régir*, unlike the more absolute rule of *régner*, would thus be a form of governance in which the achievement of harmony results from the adequate representation and visibility of all of the elements within the whole rather than by simple decree. In an essay devoted to the painter of modern life, Baudelaire the liberal democrat himself paints a rather rosy picture of the power of representation to achieve harmonious social as well as artistic ends. The map in question is not just a picture, it is as well a political organization of space.

Of course, it is not simply the case that all reference to violence and potential revolt has disappeared. But the specific way the violence is related to representation in this model, which is itself fundamentally representational, will turn out to be a contingent rather than truly disruptive feature within the system. When it comes to Baudelaire's description of how the painter Constantin Guys produces his representations of modern life, one notes a process marked more by a form of disturbance and agitation than by its ultimate goal of harmony. The passage in question is all the more interesting to the extent that it represents representation as a struggle rather than a simple state of equilibrium:

> Now, at an hour when others are asleep, [the painter] is hunched over his table, darting onto a sheet of paper the same glance that earlier in the day he had fixed upon things in the world, fencing with his pencil, his pen, his brush, squirting water from his glass up to the ceiling, testing his pen on his shirt, in a rush, violently active, as though he were afraid the images might

escape him, quarrelsome, even when alone, and he is banging into himself. (693)

There is a certain kind of violence in this representation, and it is represented as in some way belonging to representation. The strokes of representation must themselves possess violence, but this is in the end a violence consciously applied for the sake of representation, and not a conspiracy or revolt against it. It occurs in this passage in the mode of mere hurry or precipitation, lest the fleeting moment of the present that is to be adequately represented slip away from representation.

The painter, our most reliable representative of representation as a political and aesthetic model, does battle, but he is doing battle first of all with the empirical limitations of painting. What the painter therefore battles against is the constraints of frame and clock, or space and time, and for the sake of faithfully representing whatever might otherwise fail to achieve full representation. Thus, the violence involved could be called strategic, since it is calculated within an economy of gain and loss. In this model, the cost of violence inscribed within the painter's brushstrokes can always appear to be well worth their relative price. Parrying the violence that otherwise would threaten the unrepresented and therefore incognito objects of representation, the violence of the painter seizes the images of things before they disappear entirely, so that nothing will be ultimately left off the map. The disarray, such as that of the painter who remains awake while the rest of the world sleeps, is predicated on a momentary interruption of order rather than a full-scale revolt, and it is carried out in view of an ensuing state of reestablished order and superior harmony: "And everything is reborn upon the paper," Baudelaire goes on to say of this nocturnal labor, "natural and even more than natural, beautiful and even more than beautiful. . . . All the materials that were heaped upon the memory now undergo classification and arrange themselves into a harmony" (694–95).

Lest we forget, however, that, following Benjamin, our initial question concerned the adequacy of representing poetic activity by means of painting, we should notice a new element that intervenes in the process. Baudelaire makes the final harmony of representation depend upon an act of recollection, an act which, unlike every other empirical object of painting, always remains incognito to the extent that it is not itself susceptible to adequate representation. What should therefore be noted is that the pseudo-historical scheme that earlier represented poetry as painting, and that represented painting as the faithful and enduring representation of a fleeting present, ends here in a mere fiction. As Baudelaire well knows, the temporality of memory is by no means simply synchronic with respect to its power to recall or reproduce images. Unlike the kind of painting that is represented in the first pages of the essay, this kind of painting must be understood to contain elements that are historical in a very different sense. Like the imagination, memory, for Baudelaire, is always historical in that it does not simply represent a past that has already been present to itself; its power to alter and transform the materials it works into something wholly different also opens onto a future that remains strictly unknowable. As such, it is capable of producing "images" that have no prior equivalent on any map, and thus do not simply represent by means of any known correspondence.

In any case, Baudelaire begins to make clear in this passage that it is only thanks to their having first passed through the faculty of *memory* that all materials eventually available even to the painter can then be reordered in a harmonious classification and arrangement. By this point it is far from certain that memory can still work in the same way for the painter and the poet and thus it calls into question the very harmony that is represented here. It could well be that the ultimate limits of representing the work of poetry by the work of painting first become legible in this turn by Baudelaire to memory rather than perception for his theoretical model of representation.

Indeed, a little further on in the essay, Baudelaire includes a chapter called "Mnemonic Art," and it is there that he describes the artwork in a way that is no longer simply compatible with representational models, like that of painting. Furthermore, it could not be said that painting just so happens no longer to function here as an adequate model for poetry, and that poetry and painting simply part company peacefully, each in accord with its own principles. Much more radically, Baudelaire begins to displace the terms of his argument in such a way that it becomes clear that painting itself must now be considered as one possible type of poetic effect, or mask, among others. Painting becomes a poetic mask of representation so noiselessly effective in its own self-fulfilling operation that it is most easily confused with and subsequently taken for poetry's incognito. But such a mask placed upon the incognito of poetry cannot entirely ignore or efface the operations of memory that make it, too, possible.

The actual disruption of the representational model as painting occurs when the artist is confronted by nothing other than the so-called model. For "the true artist," Baudelaire has to admit, "whatever model precedes the finished work becomes much more of an *encumbrance (embarras)* than an aid" (698). This is because, Baudelaire goes on to say, "confronted with the model and the multiplicity of details that it comprises, [artists] experience a disturbance, akin to paralysis, of their principal faculty" This faculty, of course, is that of memory itself, which, according to Baudelaire, is stocked with "written images" *(images écrites)* that are not simple reproductions "taken from nature." Following the logic of the passage, these written images, or words, are produced through a form of activity that is characterized by Baudelaire as both an "abbreviation" and "exaggeration" on the part of memory.

And this work of abbreviation and exaggeration is anything but representational in the sense of offering faithful representation to all its constituents. In one of the most curious formulations of the entire essay, Baudelaire insists that, within this type of representation, both the origin and the end of the process remain subservient to a power of memory that can only be called "despotic." Capable of violating at any moment every given order, abbreviating and exaggerating whatever and whenever it records, the power of this memory necessarily fails to respect what it eventually serves to represent only in an aberrant synthesis, or arabesque. This model of representation as the failure of poetry's language to represent, as the radical revolt against a model of representation as painting, is as far from the earlier model we saw in Baudelaire as can be imagined. But that does not mean that things are allowed to come to rest there. The very interruption of the model of representation by the nonrepresenting memory is represented in Baudelaire's text as a new combat, a kind of struggle for power that no longer pits the artist against the merely empirical limits of faithfully representing the fleeting object of his self-conscious activity.

This time, the struggle is a duel that produces the work of art as an impossible encounter between the pole of representation as pure *sight* and the pole of nonrepresentation as mnemonic *synthesis*. "There ensues," Baudelaire writes, "a duel between the desire to see everything, to forget nothing, and the faculty of memory that has acquired the habit of an energetic *absorption* of the general tone, the silhouette, and the arabesque of contours. An artist who has a perfect feel for form, but who has become accustomed especially to exercising the memory and imagination, will be assaulted at that point by a riot of details, all of which demand justice with the fury of a crowd enamored of absolute equality. All justice will be necessarily violated, all harmony destroyed and sacrificed" (698–99). This is a very different picture of the work of art from that of the harmonious totality Baudelaire referred to earlier in the essay, and one that is much closer to his actual poetic practice, especially in the prose poems of *Le Spleen de Paris*. It pits a theory of art as description, or representation based on perception as sequence, against a theory of art as arabesque, or the sudden absorption and elimination of all perceivable details in the stroke of a single, simultaneous, instant. Of course, it is no accident that this is the very moment Baudelaire's text most resembles the description Benjamin gives of the crowded city waiting to explode with conspirators, since this is the moment in Baudelaire's poetic theory when what is being described is the production of poetry as language itself.

In Baudelaire's text, *arabesque* names a mode of writing as abbreviation and exaggeration, like that of allegory, moreover, that ultimately represents in a synthesis, or mask of words, that which has no observable equivalent.[3] The arabesque, then, is first of all a force—memory as the imposition of contours without detail—that does not preserve anything prior to its own notations in words. Or, rather, the power of this memory, as it abbreviates and exaggerates all that it touches, cannot be said to preserve anything except by way of simultaneously effacing, or forgetting, it as well. That is why, when Baudelaire returns on the next page to this force of synthesis as non-adequation, he will refer to what is actually seized in the arabesque as a *fantôme* (699). This time, though, the phantom cannot be seen as a past presence awaiting resurrection in a present representation, since it never was there as such in the first place. Rather, the effacement of all particularity is coextensive with memory's production of the *image écrite,* a phantom representation that slightly but decisively displaces the representational model carried along by it.

Unlike the duality Baudelaire described earlier between the two aspects of the artwork, and which he compared to the correlation of body and soul, the tension between representational and allegorical modes that is inscribed in this duel is not itself representational. There is no correspondence or inner harmony to be found here, and the text ends up fragmenting itself in an allegory of riot, anarchy, and explosive injustice. The revolt that is inscribed in this allegory is no longer strategic, it cannot possibly calculate all the effects it will have had on representation, since it is a mode of assault and counterassault that underlies the very attempt to institute itself as a system of representation. The anonymous crowd's demand for absolute equality in this text is also the point that comes closest to a fictitious state of absolute indifference, the "chimera" that would spell the end of representation and that is described in the dreariest of terms in the prose poem "Chacun sa chimère." The violence that interests us in this text is therefore not solely that of the anarchical crowd, which as such and on its own remains powerless to bring anything into being but the simple demand for justice. Rather, it is the necessarily explosive confrontation between this crowd of irreducible details and the invisible force of synthesis that alone is capable of subordinating such aimlessness to order.

Nonetheless, the fact that the synthetic force cannot help but do violence to the individual elements of the crowd that it by turns abbreviates and exaggerates does not, at least in this passage, attenuate their continuing *demand* for better, fuller, ever more complete forms of justice. To the extent that in them justice is actually violated, they demand it all the louder, since the synthetic force at work here is always applied within earshot of the crowd's demand. The mnemonic duel that breaks out in Baudelaire's exposition at this point thus places the text in a state of permanent suspension; with no possible resolution *present* to the passage, it necessarily points toward a *future* in which both synthetic force and the crowd of details demand their due at once. In other words, Baudelaire's text becomes truly historical at the moment it inscribes this explosive material in an image—that of the phantom—that demands immediate and full representation for what in fact will always defy adequate representation, its own incognito.

As Baudelaire's essay suggests by way of the allegorical representation of the riot, there can be no system of representation, no map, that is, of relative equivalencies between different orders, that does not issue from some inaugural breach of representational models. The moment that Baudelaire calls *synthetic* is this necessary imposition of an order on what otherwise would disappear in an endless enumeration of colorless details, or what Baudelaire also calls in "Spleen" II "un Sahara brumeux," a desert covered in fog. In the thematic imagery crossing painting with fencing, which Baudelaire uses consistently to illustrate this inaugural interruption of representation, the moment of the sudden drawing of the contour or arabesque, can also be described as a kind of stroke waiting to happen: that of a conspiratorial sword or pen that can always become a more or less corrupt means in the hands of the one who wields it. And in this very passage, Baudelaire does indeed have recourse to such an image, describing it by way of periphrasis as "the fiery rapture of the pencil or brush that almost resembles a frenzy in its attempt to seize the phantom before it escapes." The word *fureur* in this context, like the title of Char's collection, *Fureur et mystère*, reminds us that the mnemonic work in question, whether represented as painting or fencing the phantom, is at bottom the work of poetry, since it points to the rapture of inspiration, the momentary folly or violence that by convention announces the poetic act of inscription.

As such, the stroke of poetry reveals yet another series of consequences for the representation of poetic language and the type of incognito inhering to it. A few pages before the chapter on mnemonic art, Baudelaire mentions the way inspiration itself strikes: violently. That is, he represents with a most striking image the way that inspiration both revolts against and inaugurates the possibility of thought as representation. "I would even dare to go further," he says, "and claim that inspiration has some relation to a *stroke*, that every sublime thought is accompanied by a nervous shock that is more or less powerful and reverberates all the way to the cerebellum" (690). *This* stroke of violence is exceedingly difficult to talk about. First of all, Baudelaire himself does not use the word *stroke*, but rather the French word *congestion*, even though it is clear he means what we call a *stroke*, or apoplexy; that is, a ruptured blood vessel in the brain.

The true difficulty resides in the fact that Baudelaire's text continues to offer an image or mask, the stroke, for the one act of inexplicable violence that conspires against the functioning of the human subject's brain, effectively blocking access to its own representations, memories, images, and thoughts. And further, he suggests by way of this mask, which strips the subject of its own knowledge, of itself or anything else for that matter, that it is just such a revolt against the brain's ordinary functioning that lies at the source of all poetic activity. Indeed, the text itself has to interrupt its own sequential depiction of poetic language at this point in order, poetically, to produce this one *image écrite* for it, no matter how inspired or uninspired any one of us might find this particular equivalent for the work of poetry. The image of the stroke as it is written in Baudelaire's text does not therefore leave intact our understanding of the phantomatic duel as a self-conscious act of a self-present subject. The rupture occurring between crowds of details and synthetic forces also produces a rupture within the subject capable of thinking or writing about them, dislocating in a stroke its own capacity to be present to itself. In this way, Baudelaire's depiction of the struggle with the phantom must also be read as a struggle where the true incognito is not just that of the objects of representation, but belongs as well to its agent or subject. Never fully present to itself as such, the phantom thus names the incognito of a poetic subject that can only write in the words of poetry by forgetting itself as a subject.

Baudelaire's use of the stroke here allows us to return to the production of poetic language as well as to the kinds of representation that can be assigned to it. What Benjamin alerts us to when he speaks of Baudelaire's incognito is the potential for words to break out in a revolt against all images, or masks, that serve to construct our usual map of poetic understanding, including the mask of the thinking, self-recollecting subject. Our reading of *Le Peintre de la vie moderne* discloses the way that such an incognito can be read in Baudelaire's own text as a kind of intellectual short circuit, or *stroke*, suffered by the subject who forgets itself in the very act of writing poetry. So, too, does Baudelaire associate the stroke that separates the subject from its own knowledge, not with the end of poetic language past, but rather with its future modernity, and thus with the incognito of all riots to come.

In the case of both writers, the theoretical reflection on the work of poetry discloses the ways that systems of representation are not only interrupted but also inaugurated by conspiring with poetry. In Benjamin's text, the inscription of a poetic unknowability that disrupts dominant systems of representation as total visibility is itself described in the mask of invisibility he uses in his own text. And we have just seen how Baudelaire's deflection of the representational strokes of the painter through the nonrepresentational strokes of the arabesque can finally be marked out only behind the mask of a phantomatic stroke of poetic apoplexy. Accordingly, there can be no map of representations, and that includes any modification of an existing system of representation as well, without the imposition of a poetic act that radically suspends and redirects all representative coherence. And we should make no mistake about it, such acts contain their own kind of violence.

It is a violence, though, only in the sense that, always as an *image écrite*, it can strike all that it touches with a force of displacement powerful enough, as in the cases of Baudelaire and Benjamin, to make other forces legible, and thus to enable anything whatsoever to happen, even nothing at all. It is therefore a real revolt and not a real revolt, and both at the same time; in other words, it is the incognito of genuine revolt. The places marked out for such a revolt always demand the most scrupulous attention, even as they also contain the possibility of disappearing before our very eyes. What happens right now in such places, or what will happen next, does not belong to this particular force of displacement to foresee and certainly not to enforce all on its own. The strokes of violence that can enable and always interrupt any given system of representation, any given map, are not simply to be mistaken for the strokes of violence that can then issue from them. For this reason as well, it is all too easy to ignore or forget the poetic conspirators whose place is marked out in the masks of Baudelaire's and Benjamin's modernity. But to the extent that they are written, however invisibly for us to see or know, they are always only forgotten *on* the map, enigmatic phantoms there, always again waiting to be read.

"La Belle Dorothée," or Poetry and Painting

Yves Bonnefoy

Translated by *Jan Plug*

I

Baudelaire paid close attention to the most immediately sensorial perceptions, and he was also altogether sensitive to the relations of simple beauty
that can be established between colors. There he could find the happiness of
a moment and even what he sometimes did not hesitate to call a kind of intoxication. That is what appears, for example, in his reflections on Boudin.
"In the end," he writes in the *Salon de 1859,* "all these clouds in fantastic and
luminous forms, these chaotic darknesses, these green and pink immensi-
ties, suspended and added to one another, these gaping blazes, these black
or purple, wrinkled, rolled, or torn satin firmaments, these horizons in
mourning or streaming melted metal, all these depths, all these splendors
rose to my brain like an intoxicating drink or the eloquence of opium" (*OC*
2:666).

Something intensely experienced, this reception to color and to its immense possibility. For one rare moment, in the poet of *Les Fleurs du Mal,* we
even see sketched out by way of perception—in this case guided, to be sure,
by the work of an artist, intensified by its refraction in the prism of a painted
work—a participation in elementary forces, in the "depths" of natural or, to
put it better, cosmic occurrence: but let us not forget that such moments of
enjoying simple matter do not reveal what is truly Baudelaire, and he, moreover, knows it and immediately lets it be known. There is tragic potential in

85

these spectacles of the skies, in these "darknesses," this "mourning"; he could have perceived there reflections of the soul's restlessness, could have had a foreboding there of those forms, unimaginable on earth and yet human, that so easily rekindle thoughts of the Ideal: yet, on this occasion, immediate impression wins out over his concern, which surprises him. "The strange thing," he adds, "is that, in front of this liquid or aerial magic, I did not once complain about the absence of man" (*OC* 2:666). The human drama to which his oeuvre is so constantly attached has been forgotten, for this moment of what one would today call pure painting, and if I have cited this passage at such length, it is to show how and how much Baudelaire himself knew how to be a painter in words—and such a painter, already more Turner than Boudin—despite his most instinctive tendencies.

Concerning those Boudin canvases that for us are entirely exceptional works, it is true that Baudelaire immediately emphasizes that he sees, and wants to see, in them nothing other than "studies." He esteems their author greatly; he takes pleasure in saying so; but he also hastens to assure us that this excellent painter knew before everyone, in these moments of joy in color, "that all that must become a painting by means of poetic impression recalled at will." Boudin "does not pretend to pass his notes off as paintings," Baudelaire assures us. As for Baudelaire, it is clear that he will not be able to stick for long to only these events of perception, which he deems too little impregnated with meaning. That he knows how to recognize beauty in color, that he even senses there all the energy and light it can give the spirit that seeks, let us have no doubt; nonetheless, this beauty for him must, "by means of poetic impression," give a sign by which the disquieted spirit signifies itself to itself.

It is certain that this sign that Baudelaire privileges will have appeared to his eyes only when the intensity, the vividness, sometimes the strangeness, of perception have allowed his desire to imagine—if not catch a glimpse of—higher reality: that world of the Ideal toward which his thought turns this time with the exultant sensation of a mystery, that of our divided condition between heaven and earth, but with also, simultaneously, pain. Pain, for this intensification of color—and one could say as much about form, sometimes susceptible to exalting elegance—will be but a threshold that will remain uncrossed, the poet having to live, forever, in what he experiences as an exile. For an instant the suggestion of the world of the senses will have been welcomed, questioned, interpreted in a great surge of hope, but quickly will but recapture the lucidity that makes of the painter a completely different artist from that Boudin of the Normandy beaches. To paint will be, first, to give oneself over to the imagination—that "queen of the true," "married positively with infinity"—that seeks to deliver life from its straitjacket of finitude and to substitute for it a world in which the Ideal is outlined. "A good painting, faithful and equal to the dream that gave birth to it, must be produced like a world," says the *Salon de 1859* (*OC* 2:626). But immediately afterward, if not even already, the work of truth will take place, which will be to recognize that the imagined world is precisely only that: a dream.

Colors, the harmonies of two or several tones, their iridescences, their play: as intoxicating as all that might be, can only be notations, only beginnings. And the painting, the work of art that fully merits to be named thus, will be the vision that will soon be blackened by the storm of disappointed hope—that storm, that fury, our true "dignity," nevertheless. What, in fact, can the attention to sense perception be worth if, through satisfaction in the beautiful effects on a bit of canvas or the simple curiosity of the abysses of matter, it resigns itself to demanding nothing for the human condition? Betraying that "dignity," which is, in frustration, to sacrifice nothing of the highest desires, it will have been but the renunciation that, through ignorance or forgetfulness of the Ideal, makes the bed of artistic decadence, and equally so in painting: as so often is the case, according to Baudelaire, at this turning point of the 1860s when Manet will have no difficulty, he remarks sadly, being worth more than others.

Let's put it differently: true painters, for Baudelaire, are only those invoked by "Les Phares," in which, from stanza to stanza, the same scheme is repeated: a first plane of sensible reality, sometimes still seductive, sometimes already discredited by the artist's melancholy; and beyond, always, the glimpse and then the absence of higher reality. To be sure, Rubens, the first named because he is not really among those who count for Baudelaire, Rubens is "un oreiller de chair fraîche" (a pillow of fresh flesh); life flows in his work like light in the sky. But immediately afterward, there is Leonardo da Vinci, "un miroir sombre" (a sombre mirror) in which only glaciers shine, then Rembrandt, he a whole world of moans and filth that only a ray of winter sun "abruptly" crosses. As for Watteau, he is a flame in which figures are caught like nocturnal insects; night is the basis of his work; and Delacroix, finally, the painter par excellence, so informed by spiritual nostalgia, is the tearing to pieces of red and green with the livid gap of a "despondent sky" in the distance. Painting, says "Les Phares," is "ecstasy"; it is "tears"; it is "a cry," "a call": in no way pleasure at perception.

That is an idea of painting, a notion of art, to which I will content myself with adding that, for Baudelaire, it remains the essential thing; it takes the lead over simple pleasures; it decides everything. He is never satisfied with sensation alone, not because he does not find it very attractive, but because the obsession with the human as spiritual reality is too strong in him. Thus he becomes attached—for example, in "La Chevelure"—exclusively to aspects of the female body or its finery, its fragrances, that allow his imagination, "wedded to infinity," to take flight anew toward higher reality: but to experience, the moment after, a disappointment that can even vilify the woman who is supposedly too "natural." Baudelaire will accuse; he will insult. However, he can understand that the partner, still more than he, is a victim—hence the surge of an almost brotherly love. What a paradox. It is, then, for having passed by way of Art, this solitude, that he finds himself again with another being in a relationship of affective solidarity. I thus evoke "Le Balcon."

II

There is nothing very original about these comments, but I did not refrain from making them because they are going to allow me to take up a particular poem, "La Belle Dorothée," piece XXV of Le Spleen de Paris (OC 1:316–17). As inclined as Baudelaire might be to a painting that transcends sensation, that aims at the Ideal, that dedicates itself to the image and to the cult of images, it so happens—or appears to have happened—that he let himself be caught up in certain texts by what is immediate, what is simply itself, in sensorial perception without for once seeking further. In such cases a question is sketched out: under the apparent immanentism of these notations, is there not a mental reservation, a disquiet, that is not reducible to perception as such? I thus come to "La Belle Dorothée," a poem that is perhaps more revealing of certain intimate movements of Baudelaire's dialectics than its modest intention would have us believe.

There is certainly a level on which "La Belle Dorothée" is conceived as what Baudelaire, in the case of Boudin, would have called a "study." We think, on first glance, that the relations of colors in this poem are for the simple delight of the eyes. There is no subject here in the sense Delacroix would have wanted it: in a street one imagines as white as the nearby beach, put differently, on a background that sharpens and accentuates the tones, dulling thought, the beautiful young woman, Dorothy, "advances, alone," and everything we will know about her is going to come over a long time through visual notations and, more precisely, colors. The "immense azure," the white ochre of the sand, the pink of the dress, the red of the umbrella, and in this latter the prismatic decompositions of the Impressionists or of yet more modern painters, the blue—of the hair—in at once intimate and violent relation with the black of the skin, and the very strong though fleeting sparkle of the teeth between the very purple lips: these are colors that surely impose themselves upon the attention of the reader, colors this time that are only color, the immediate datum of ocular perception, not those forebodings of spirit by the ambiguous grace of which they become signs or symbols for the imagination that dreams of correspondences between the sensorial and the spiritual. There is nothing here of the emotion that rises in Delacroix from the conflicting harmony of dark green and red. Nothing that carries into a dimension perpendicular to sensation by means of analogies that create depth; everything is played out in the complementarities of surface on a canvas that itself remains visible, under the brush. Baudelaire, moreover, knew how to impart to his writing a circularity in the phrases, in the paragraphs, that tightens perfectly around visual impressions in a verbal present tense that can be called showing, speech, to be sure, but speech that dissipates in the obvious.

"La Belle Dorothée," a "study" then, if by this word we mean a painting that sticks to what the eyes see, without ever undertaking the deciphering of the figures that would make them significant, to the benefit of the desire to change life. "La Belle Dorothée," a study, and even in a fairly restrictive sense, for we have seen that Boudin, interested in strollers on the beaches but also and especially in the beauty of the clouds, saw in these latter ruptures and abysses right into the depths of matter, questioning the world of appearances and thus awakening metaphysical anxiety—while "La Belle Dorothée" seems to keep the mind on things and beings as they are, in a horizon of simple nature, in order simply to utter the words of the vocabulary of which a Delacroix would make a sentence. This "painting" is the most literal possible. And it is literal to the point that it is legitimate to imagine, at least for a moment, that this Dorothy who only is and only wants to be her superb appearance is understood by Baudelaire as the allegory of a

painting that would itself only want to be the life of the senses. A less exalted
painting than the ones celebrated in "Les Phares," but one that would not
have held the poet's sympathy any less, before the opportunity presented by
certain works of his era.

I think of Fromentin, for example. Fromentin, whose light is much
more that of "Dorothée" than Boudin's skies and beaches, and of whom
Baudelaire said in that same *Salon de 1859* that he esteemed him and even
felt close to his "gentle and calm contemplation" of the world. In fact he—
the poet of a "fury" Fromentin knows nothing about—would like to feel
and on occasion to exist like those Orientals that this painter understood so
intimately: "One can presume," writes Baudelaire in front of these exhibited
paintings, "that I am myself affected somewhat by a nostalgia that is carry-
ing me toward the sun; for from these luminous canvases an intoxicating
vapor rises for me, which soon condenses into desires and regrets. I find
myself surprised in envying the lot of those men stretched out under these
blue shadows, whose eyes, neither awake nor asleep, express, if indeed they
express anything, only the love of rest and the feeling of happiness that an
immense light inspires" (*OC* 2:650). "Blue shadows," a spirit that is no
longer anything but its adherence to these blue shadows, or to the vividness
of the "red umbrella": "La Belle Dorothée" would be not only pure visuality,
but would speak on behalf of the painters who lay claim to it.

Why, moreover, would Baudelaire not have wanted, for once, to paint
in this way, to write and bear witness in this way: he who was capable, aesthetically, of seeing as a Fromentin can see, who in his own life had the opportunity, never forgotten, to perceive what uncomplaining destinies can be
born of light? "Desires" and "regrets": it is also from his past that the "intoxicating vapor" rises; in front of Fromentin's "luminous canvases" he re-
members the islands he visited in the Indian Ocean, Mauritius, the Ile
Bourbon, where, moreover, he knew a Dorothy, if not two. There, "in the
midst of the azure," how "calm" the voluptuous pleasures are, how heavy
the fruits in the basket, among flowers. Actually, it is like the legend of Saint
Dorothy, the young Cappadocian who was martyred under Diocletian. She
was advancing, to her death; she, too, "strong and proud as the sun," when
Theophilus the scribe asked her, ironically, to send him "fruit and flowers"
from Paradise. "It shall be so," the young woman replied, when at the final
moment an angel appeared before her, with a basket of apples and red roses
from Paradise, "Take them to Theophilus," said Dorothy; and Theophilus

the scribe converted. It was the miracle of the roses (Réau 1958, 403–4). Didn't Baudelaire himself convert on Ile Bourbon, at least for a few beautiful days, in the face of the facts of being? Can he not understand, today, in front of Fromentin's simple and clear paintings, that painting can be the young faith that can give anxious humanity the basket of what is? The allegory of painting, this is the Dorothy of the poem, this body that "advances" into color, dissipating the imaginary as she does so, the allegory of an art that would be done with original sin, which was to dream what is not.

My hypothesis will be daring. But I will nonetheless note that Baudelaire takes care to tell us that Dorothy has a "little sister"; that the young woman's only worry is to have to buy back this sister, who is the slave of a miserly master; and that she therefore amasses "piastre upon piastre" to do so, which means that if she advances thus into the light, as beautiful as can be for the senses, full of joy at being herself, nothing but herself, it is also for a meeting from which she will benefit. Who is Dorothy's "little sister"? In an allegory of painting, can one resign oneself to not seeking the "sister art"? I think "La Belle Dorothée" is almost on the point of announcing that a painting that would only be painting would tear poetry from its modern slavery, that of a mercantile society that dooms it to the chains of a chimera; and that if it is at the price of selling itself, this painting would do so, like Dorothy, happily because freely, in the manner of the original "naked eras" that were "free of lies and anxiety." A painting that would cool the forehead with palm leaves. That would deliver the spirit from its "painful secret."

III

Do not hesitate to reproach me for this reading of "La Belle Dorothée," which I agree is without rigor, for it is this whole level of a poem-painting, of a painting simply of perception and its joys, that I believe it is appropriate, certainly not to reject, but to recognize as troubled by another reflection by the poet. Troubled in its depth, for, indeed, there is a depth.

To make myself clearer, I recall, first, that this pleasure at perception, which makes an attractive figure of Dorothy and her memory a regret, was not without reservation on the part of Baudelaire, from the very time he spent on the Ile Bourbon or, first of all, in Mauritius. Proof of his ambivalence, at the very least, at that time, [is] the poem "Déjà!," piece number XXXIV of the *Petits poèmes en prose,* which is late, to be sure (it only appeared in December 1863), but is thus contemporary with "La Belle

Dorothée," a fact which is not without importance; which, moreover, precisely evokes those days when Baudelaire arrived at one or the other of the
islands. The boat, in fact, on which we are invited indeed was drawing near a
shore. This would soon be "a magnificent, dazzling land"; "it seemed that
the music of life freed itself into a vague murmur, and that from these
coasts, rich in all sorts of verdure, rose up, to a height of several leagues, a
delicious odor of flowers and fruit"—"a mysterious perfume of rose and
musk," Baudelaire will say also. A true basket of feast days. And the passen-
gers are also joyful; they forget the suffering and desperation of the previous
countless hours, but one among them, who is the poet, on the contrary feels
"sad, inconceivably sad."

Baudelaire explains precisely the reason for this sadness; it is because he
feels that this beauty of the shore is nothing to him next to that beauty he
loved and that he is losing, the "incomparable beauty" of the sea, that companion of past days and weeks. Yet, and this is what already opens a background for "La Belle Dorothée," the magnificence of the sea is surely of a
completely different nature from that of the land and its "promises": an
analogy of the stormiest depths of the soul, moreover "its "mirror," says a
famous poem ("L'Homme et la mer," *Les Fleurs,* XIV), its "image" in which
the spirit finds, not without a strange pleasure, its chimera and its bitterness.
Listen to "Déjà!" (*OC* 1:337–38), which is unambiguous: "I alone was sad,
inconceivably sad. Like a priest whose divinity is torn from him, I could not,
without a distressing bitterness, free myself from this so monstrously seductive sea, from this sea so infinitely varied in its terrifying simplicity, that
seems to contain in itself and to represent by its games, its allures, its rages,
and its smiles, the humors, agonies, and ecstasies of all the souls who have
lived, who live, and who will live!" (338). "Agonies," "ecstasies": again we
find here the vocabulary of the "Phares." The sea is the movement of the
spirit that from the heart of its dereliction throws itself woefully and grand-
ly on the rocks of inaccessible "eternity"; it is Delacroix, not Boudin, not
Fromentin; it is the religion of which one is the priest, not the aesthetic experience of the red umbrella next to the almost blue hair. This page, "Déjà!,"
makes one suspect that this immense presence, which, in "La Belle
Dorothée," "beats the nearby sand," is going to leave a mark one way or another—if not in the very poem, at least in an idea of painting, of art, of poetry, which might have sought to be born or reborn in this supposedly happy
moment of writing.

And indeed! Even "already" in the poem it seems to me that a thought is sketched out that risks diverting Baudelaire from his pleasure in the beauty and the truth of sense experience.

This second level surfaces through a fiction in this painting that seemed to be interested only in perceptions. Dorothy has a "little sister," we have learned, but we already knew that if at noon she goes through town, which is deserted in the heat, it is "perhaps" that she is meeting "some young officer" for whom her beauty matters as well, although he will not have simply the "thoughtful" eye of the artist for her body. This indication might appear to signify nothing but the young woman's likable venality that goes hand in hand with an imagined simple relation to the life of the senses, that does not divert our attention from sensible appearance, leaving the text to its surface effects, to its prominent relations of color to color. But to think in this way would be to miss a passage toward a completely different kind of foreboding and aspiration.

There is, indeed, the fact that this officer comes from France; he knows Paris, which Dorothy is curious about; he is going to talk to her about its luxury, make her want it, make her dream that she could go there one day. And it is true that Dorothy does not for the moment seem to think seriously about it. "Admired and cherished by all," she is happy on her island, where, moreover, the task of buying back her sister detains her. But a thought is no less at work in Baudelaire, of such a future, in France, in Paris, for the young woman or others, a painful and even tragic future. At work? To have no doubt about it, it is enough to remember another poem, a poem in verse this time, "A une Malabaraise." This page is not, like "Déjà!," from the same period as "Dorothée," for it was written as early as 1841, twenty years earlier. But it was the moment when Baudelaire was staying on the islands. And one cannot distance it from "La Belle Dorothée," since the woman from Malabar it evokes, it is said, was called Dorothy; she was the foster sister of his hostess in Mauritius, Madame Autard de Bragard, the "Creole lady." Moreover, Baudelaire describes this Dorothy in an even more allusive way that strongly recalls what he is going to say about the other one. Both have the same beauty in their black color; both are grace itself, with, in the older of the two texts, a nuance, perhaps, of nonchalance in her unconcern. And both are happy.

In the case of the young woman from Malabar, it is explicit that Baudelaire worries about her future, that he feels threatened. I will cite the final lines of the poem, which are not among the most beautiful, but are of the greatest importance, for a doubling is sketched out there—between a happy, cherished woman and a woman who is a victim—that is going to dominate his entire work yet to come and to assure its spiritual quality. Baudelaire asks,

> Pourquoi, l'heureuse enfant, veux-tu voir notre France,
> Ce pays trop peuplé que fauche la souffrance,
> Et, confiant ta vie aux bras forts des marins,
> Faire de grands adieux à tes chers tamarins?
> Toi, vêtue à moitié de mousselines frêles,
> Frissonnante là-bas sous la neige et les grêles,
> Comme tu pleurerais tes loisirs doux et francs,
> Si, le corset brutal emprisonnant tes flancs,
> Il te fallait glaner ton souper dans nos fanges
> Et vendre le parfum de tes charmes étranges,
> L'oeil pensif, et suivant, dans nos sales brouillards,
> Des cocotiers absents les fantômes épars! (*OC* 1:174)

[Why, happy child, do you want to see our France, / this over-populated country that suffering mows down, / and, confiding your life to the strong arms of mariners, bid a grand farewell to your dear tamarinds? / You, half-clothed in frail muslin, shivering over there under the snow and hail, / how you would cry for your soft and honest leisure, / if, the brutal corset imprisoning your sides, / you had to glean your supper in our mire / and sell the perfume of your strange charms, / your eye pensive, following, in our dirty fogs, / the scattered phantoms of absent coconut palms!]

What he has in mind does indeed give reason to worry. In fact, it is truly a risk of death and, moreover, the risk of a distressed soul. Dorothy over there on the island is happy and she is even "strong and proud"; she advances "harmoniously," assured of her right to be at peace with her mind as with her heart. In Paris, she would no longer be anything but a prostitute of the big city, the "woman of pleasure" dirtied and contaminated by a civilization as selfish as it is brutal; soon suffering from tuberculosis, soon thrown in the street. The worry is great in "A une

Malabaraise." There is no reason to think that this worry has disappeared from Baudelaire's mind when he evokes Paris in the other poem about a Dorothy on her island.

What does this preoccupation, this fear, that I thus make out in the background of "La Belle Dorothée" mean? And why would we have to be careful about it in a reflection whose object is the relation of poetry to perception; that is also to say, to some simple and straight painting, that of which this poem might appear to give an example as much as an allegory?

IV

Here it is: it means that there is already beginning, in this Baudelaire who paints, who gives himself over to relations of color, seeking to perceive only the sensible apparent, wanting to free himself thus of the aspirations and heartbreaks of the dream, the turn of thought that puts an end to this hedonist temptation.

I will recall, first, that Baudelaire had at first wanted to write "La Belle Dorothée" in verse, since he had proposed to include this poem in *Les Fleurs du Mal*. On 15 December 1859, he told Poulet-Malassis: "when I have done *Dorothée* (memory of Mauritius), *La Femme Sauvage* (sermon to a mistress), *Le Rêve*, and finally the letter-preface to Veuillot . . . *Les Fleurs du Mal* will be ready" (*COR* 1:635). But around Christmas of 1861, when he announces to his friend Houssaye that the poem is "done," it is from that moment a "Dorothée" in prose.[1] This, to my mind, already is meaningful and very much so. For this period, in Baudelaire's oeuvre, is nothing less than that of his "Tableaux parisiens." "Les Petites Vieilles," for example, was published in September 1859; "Le Cygne" in January 1860; "A une passante" in October 1860. Put differently, never as much as then was Baudelaire's verse the bow of his soul, the music that swells with all his intuitions, all his nostalgia, and we should not be surprised that Baudelaire, "saintly soul" as much as "perfect chemist," was unable to lift the minor project of "La Belle Dorothée" to this spiritual altitude.

On the other hand, is it completely impossible to discern the place in which "La Belle Dorothée" could have inscribed itself in the "Tableaux parisiens" if other ideas and images had not deflected its conscious intention, even if they may have revealed its hidden worry? No, to be sure, and the fact that we ask this question means that this whole section of *Les Fleurs du Mal* appears in a new light, in which its genesis is also discovered.

For Dorothy, as effaced as she might be from the book, is indeed present in the "Tableaux parisiens," and in what a central, unforgettable way to all readers of "Le Cygne": she is nothing less, in fact, than the woman he "thinks" of when he has advanced to the heart of his meditation in that great poem. Let us recall the concluding line of "A une Malabaraise," which sought to convey exile by a striking contrast of the orange-tinted green of over there and the colorlessness of here: in the Parisian fog the young woman, "her eye pensive," would one day believe she glimpsed "the scattered phantoms of absent coconut palms." When Baudelaire now invokes "the Negress, grown thinner and consumptive" who in "Le Cygne" emblematizes his new thinking of the other, he sees her seeking, "her eye haggard"—"haggard" from this moment on and no longer only "pensive" (one step further into distress)—

Les cocotiers absents de la superbe Afrique
Derrière la muraille immense du brouillard (*OC* 1:87)

[The absent coconut palms of superb Africa / behind the immense wall of fog.]

This return of the grand image, with the same meaning obvious, is enough to show that the prostitute of "Le Cygne" is none other than the Malabar woman fallen to the depths of misfortune that Baudelaire at twenty years of age had asked her to fear. What he had dreaded for the young women of the isles, lured by the metropolis, actually happened. It is from seeing on these women in Paris—Jeanne Duval is almost one of them—so many marks of degeneration, and first of all the degradation of the beauty of yesteryear, that he learns to feel that compassion that is the poetic event of these last and most beautiful of his poems.

That event wins out over the hedonist imaginings that his simple carnal desire still bears him along to dream, in the wearied moments of his final seasons: thus, when one of these moments of fatigue and nostalgia for a "Dorothy," a memory of the islands, the pleasure of his less worrisome years lays claim to him, it is certainly not in verse, not in the grand verse of "Le Cygne" or "Les Petites Vieilles" that he could paint the painting that would have permitted him to dream as Fromentin painted, with simply the fortunate color of the sensations born from fruit, flowers, and young bodies. The project of "La Belle Dorothée" is effaced from this alexandrine that mobilizes the mind like water evaporating from a hot plate. The little poem is returned to prose for one of its modest uses, although it will not be disregarded, the use that, beside higher projects, "lyrical movements of the soul" and "starts of consciousness," can adapt itself to the "undulations of reverie." "La Belle Dorothée," the prose poem, exists. But by its very existence, which is only prose, and minor prose, it signifies the limit of Baudelaire's capacity to give himself over peacefully to the pleasure of sensorial perceptions.

Another poem, in the "Tableaux parisiens," reveals the almost necessary transmutation that the sensual musing will undergo under the double pressure of nostalgia for the Ideal and of the impetus of emotional solidarity.

It is the sonnet "A une passante" (*OC* 1:92–93). This great poem, as we can now discover, has many connections with the modest prose poem. Like Dorothy, the "passing woman" advances in a street; like Dorothy, she has statuesque legs; like the young woman from the isles, she swings her skirt. But the woman passing by is in mourning, "une douleur majestueuse" (a majestic grief); she does not seduce by promising simple pleasures, but she causes one "to dream simultaneously, but confusedly, of voluptuous pleasure and of sadness," as in *Fusées* (*OC* 1:657). And in this sonnet color has given way to a blackness and a lividity that are so intense they require the red of passion as a complement in a painting that could only be Delacroix's, not Fromentin's. Unlike the latter, Baudelaire cannot give himself over to "gentle and calm contemplation." It is only in quickly abandoned moments that for him color can be perception and nothing else. Always, irresistibly, it becomes again the sign that speaks a transcendence, the mirror in which the storm of another sky is caught.

Part III

Questions of Genre

Baudelaire Sonneteer

Flare to the Future

Rosemary Lloyd

C'est un cri répété par mille sentinelles,
Un ordre renvoyé par mille porte-voix;
C'est un phare allumé sur mille citadelles,
Un appel de chasseurs perdus dans les grands bois!

Car c'est vraiment, Seigneur, le meilleur témoignage
Que nous puissions donner de notre dignité
Que cet ardent sanglot qui roule d'âge en âge
Et vient mourir au bord de votre éternité! (*OC* 1:14)

[It's a cry repeated by a thousand sentinels, / an order relayed by a thousand loud-speakers; / it's a beacon lit on a thousand citadels, / a cry from hunters lost in the wild woods! // For this is truly, Lord, the best testimony / of our dignity that we can leave, / this ardent sob that rolls down the ages / and comes at last to die on the threshold of your eternity!]

Flare and fanfare, light and sound, *Les Fleurs du Mal* mark a point at which this ardent sob that rolls from age to age changes, to some extent, its nature and its direction. Celebrated poets, so Baudelaire tells us in a draft version of the preface he contemplated including in his volume of poems, had long since divided up amongst themselves the most flower-strewn provinces of the poetic domain (*OC* 1:181), and if he does not explicitly add, as Valéry claims: "I'll do something different" (Valéry 1957, 1:600), he nevertheless makes that determination perfectly clear. "It is clearly visible," affirms

Valéry, "that Baudelaire sought out what Victor Hugo had not done and that he abstained from all the effects in which Victor Hugo was invincible" (1:602). And Valéry concludes: "There are in the best lines of Baudelaire a combination of mind and body, a blend of solemnity, warmth and bitterness, of the eternal and the intimate, an extremely rare alliance of will power and harmony, that distinguish them from Romantic poetry just as clearly as from Parnassian poetry" (1:610). But if that distinction can be found above all, as far as Romantic poetry is concerned, in the muscular energy of Baudelaire's poetic form, and, with regard to Parnassian poetry, in the intensity of his modernist vision, they nevertheless do not mark an absolute cleavage between Baudelaire and those around him: on the contrary, this distinction allows, or rather demands, the creation of several new directions, directions paved moreover with memories of ancestral poetic voices.

When Mallarmé rushed to bring his audiences at Oxford and Cambridge in 1894 the most astonishing of news—"Such a thing has never before been seen," he claims: "They've laid hands on poetry" (Mallarmé 1945, 643)—he suggested that poets had courteously waited until Victor Hugo died before offering those *vers libres* whose appearance struck him as an unprecedented event in human history. For the ironic and faunesque Mallarmé to manipulate the facts a little to astound his public is not in the least surprising: who better than he could transform a fact of nature or history into its vibratory near-disappearance (368). He was certainly not unaware that *vers libres* had been in preparation lo these many years, in the poetry of Hugo himself, of course, but above all in that of Baudelaire. No one had seized more clearly than he the intimate alliance of the beautiful and the bizarre, just as no one else, with the possible exception of Edgar Allan Poe, had understood to the same extent that "rhythm and rhyme respond to humanity's immortal need for monotony, symmetry, and surprise" (*OC* 1:182), those elements essential to successful free verse. And what poetic form is richer in both symmetry and surprise than the sonnet? It is this movement from the sonnet toward free verse that I would like to begin to study here. Graham Robb has already insisted in his study *La Poésie de Baudelaire et la poésie française, 1838–1852,* on the crucial role played by the irregular sonnet in *Les Fleurs du Mal.* As Robb affirms, the irregular sonnet constituted in itself a provocation that was even stronger than the choice of an unusual subject. It is not simply a question of astonishing the Philistines, according to Robb, who sees in it more the need to integrate these variations into the repertory of French poetry (237). What interests me is more generally the sonnet, whether regular or irregular, and the way in which the experiments Baudelaire carries out on this form prepare the way for the apparently more striking prosodic changes that mark the end of the nineteenth century.

What then did the nineteenth century expect of the sonnet, the form Verlaine was to call that "Chose italienne où Shakspeare a passé / Mais que Ronsard fit superbement française" [Italian thing through which Shakespeare has passed and that Ronsard made superbly French] (Verlaine 255)? I have to admit that the expression "où Shakspeare a passé" takes my breath away. Banville, in his little treatise on French prosody published on 9 March 1872, admits not the slightest doubt on the subject:

> The Sonnet always consists of two quatrains and two tercets. In the regular sonnet, the following rhyme with each other:
>
> 1. the first and fourth lines of the first quatrain and the first and fourth lines of the second quatrain;
> 2. the second, and third lines of the first quatrain; the second and third lines of the second quatrain;
> 3. the first and second lines of the first tercet;
> 4. the third line of the first tercet and the second line of the second tercet;
> 5. the first and third line of the second tercet.
>
> If you introduce into that arrangement any modification whatsoever,
> If you write two quatrains with different rhymes,
> If you begin with the two tercets and conclude with the two quatrains,
> If you use crossed rhymes in the quatrains,
> If you make the third line of the first tercet rhyme with the third line of the second tercet,—or indeed the first line of the first tercet with the first line of the second tercet,
> If, in a word, you deviate by however little from the classic type of which I have just given two examples,
> The Sonnet is irregular (Banville 1978, 173–74).

Which makes one want to say with Mallarmé: "he did that." And Banville, to his credit, recognizes that even if the regular sonnet is always to be preferred to the irregular, "the irregular sonnet has produced master-pieces, a fact easily verified by reading the most romantic and the most modern of all the books of this time,—the wonderful book titled *Les Fleurs du Mal*" (Banville 1978, 174). If from the beginning of his poetic career Baudelaire had promoted the sonnet, despite the somewhat dilapidated air of the form that Sainte-Beuve had restored to favor, it was because, or so he claimed in a letter to Armand Fraisse, he perceived in it "Pythagorean" beauties and a variety of tones that he was also to seek in the genre of the prose poem. "Because the form is restricting," he argues in an unforget-table formula, "the idea bursts forth all the more intensely. Everything suits the Sonnet, buffoonery, gallantry, reverie, philosophical meditation. There is in the sonnet the beauty of well-worked metal and mineral" (*OC* 1:676). And he adds, in a comparison I consider no less important: "Have you ob-served that a segment of the sky, glimpsed through a basement window, or between two chimneys, two cliffs, or through an arcade, etc. gives a more profound idea of the infinite than a vast panorama seen from a mountain summit?" A glimpse, a fleeting impression, a lightning bolt followed by darkness, the sonnet therefore corresponds to the drawing, in that it allows the poet to jot down aspects of modernity, that is to say, "the transient, the fleeting, the contingent," while the form's resemblance to "well-worked metal" allows it to seize that other half of art which is "the eternal and im-mutable" (*OC* 2:695). And yet, we all know what the poet E. A. Robinson calls "these little sonnet men / Who fashion, in a shrewd mechanic way, / Songs without souls, that flicker for a day, / To vanish in irrevocable night" (quoted in Preminger 1974, 783), and as Charles Cros has fully succeeded in showing, it is perfectly possible to write sonnets which contain no ideas whatsoever:

> Je sais faire des vers perpétuels. Les hommes
> Sont ravis à ma voix qui dit la vérité.
> La suprême raison dont j'ai, fier, hérité
> Ne se payerait pas avec toutes les sommes.
>
> J'ai tout touché: le feu, les femmes et les pommes:
> J'ai tout senti: l'hiver, le printemps et l'été;

J'ai tout trouvé, nul mur ne m'ayant arrêté.
Mais Chance, dis-moi donc de quel nom tu te nommes?

Je me distrais à voir à travers les carreaux
Des boutiques, les gants, les truffes et les chèques
Où le bonheur est un suivi de six zéros.

Je m'étonne, valant bien les rois, les évêques,
Les colonels et les receveurs généraux
De n'avoir pas de l'eau, du soleil, des pastèques.
(Quoted in Delvaille 1971, 80–81)

[I can write perpetual verse. Men / are delighted by my voice, which tells the truth. / The supreme reason I have, proudly, inherited, / I wouldn't sell for all the gold in the world. // I have touched everything: fire, women, and apples: / I have felt everything: winter, spring, and summer; / I have found everything, no wall having stopped me. / But Chance, tell me then what name to call you? // I amuse myself by looking through the shop windows / at gloves, truffles, and checks, where happiness is one followed by six zeros. // I'm surprised, given that I am just as good as kings, bishops, colonels, and tax inspectors, / that I have no water, no sun, and no watermelons.]

But the fact that a constricting form can, in the hands of a player as gifted as Charles Cros, contain no idea at all, does not stop a Baudelaire from attempting to pack that same form with ideas to the bursting point. Moreover, as the English poet John Keats remarked in reference to Shakespeare's sonnets: "I never found so many beauties in the sonnets—they seem to be full of fine things said unintentionally—in the intensity of working out conceits"(Keats 1987, 40). In other words, the struggle with the conceit leads in and of itself to beauty. As the Shakespeare scholar Helen Vendler notes: "Whenever Shakespeare sets up Procrustean beds of such exact framing, one knows that something is about to burst loose" (Vendler 1997, 138); the same, I would argue, can be said of all great writers of sonnets.

Before looking more closely at some of the formal experiments Baudelaire carries out in using the sonnet form, I would like to mention briefly an element that might well appear more vital to the form than the prosodic rules emphasized by Banville. After all, the very pattern of the sonnet seems to favor that duality so often noticed in Baudelaire, and to make it conform quite admirably to the bipolarity of Baudelairean thought, since the sonnet is based on the *volta*, or turn of the ninth line, signaling not only the shift in harmony between the two quatrains and the tercets, but also a change in thought, voice, or mood. "From our quarrels with others we make rhetoric," says that great creator of sonnets the Irish poet Yeats: "From our quarrels with ourselves we make poetry." Thus Ronsard divides himself in two in order firstly to put the woman at the center in the quatrains of "Quand vous serez bien vieille" [When you are very old] and then to resume a masculine voice in the tercets: "Je serai sous la terre" [I will be under the ground], just as Du Bellay raises in his quatrains the question, "Las, où est maintenant ce mépris de Fortune?" [Alas! Where now is that scorn I felt for Fortune?] in order to reply in the tercets: "Maintenant la Fortune est maîtresse de moi" [Now it is Fortune who holds sway over me]. "Ce ne seront jamais ces beautés de vignettes" [It will never be the beauties depicted in vignettes], protests Baudelaire, who finds at last in his tercets "Ce qu'il faut à ce cœur profond comme un abîme" [What is needed by this heart as deep as an abyss] (*OC* 1:22). In the case of Baudelaire it is not a question of mechanically applying a standard formula; I would say rather that he sees in it a spring that he can suppress, or whose function he can delay until later in the poem, or whose nature he can alter in the course of the poem, but in a Baudelairean sonnet that twist is always potentially there, even if it does not eventually appear. What seems to be essential for Baudelaire is that the reader, prepared by a prior knowledge of the sonnet or by indications in the text itself, expects the *volta* and enjoys the way in which the poet plays with that very expectation.

At first sight, for instance, one discovers this classic distinction in "Bohémiens en voyage" between the prophetic tribe that dominates the quatrains and the cricket that sings in the tercets, between those who leave and the one who stays behind; but already in this sonnet that seems to deploy the tension inherent to the *volta,* we realize that the passage from the tribe that sees to the cricket that watches is disturbed by a movement that returns unexpectedly to "ces voyageurs, pour lesquels est ouvert / L'empire familier des ténèbres futures" [these travelers for whom is open the familiar empire of future darkness] (*OC* 1:18). "I have tried more than once," confesses

Baudelaire in reviewing the Exposition Universelle of 1855, "to lock myself into a system [. . .] But a system is a form of damnation that drives us to perpetual abjuration; we're always obliged to invent another, and the weariness this inflicts is a cruel punishment. And my system was always beautiful, vast, spacious, convenient, clean, and above all smooth; at least so it seemed to me. And always something unexpected and spontaneous, produced by the vitality of the universe, would crop up and prove the falseness of my childish, old-fashioned knowledge, the deplorable offspring of utopia" (*OC* 2:578). Could it therefore be the case that the universal vitality that animates Baudelaire's sonnets bursts asunder even the mechanism that is the most natural or at least the most inherent to the form? "So true is it that there is in the manifold productions of art something that is always new and that will for all eternity escape from the rules and analyses of the school!" (*OC* 2:578), remarks the poet of *Les Fleurs du Mal*, the poet who has never ceased to vaunt "the value of the unexpected" (*OC* 2:390).

"Because the form is restricting, the idea bursts forth all the more intensely." But one has merely to inspect Baudelaire's sonnets in the light of this apothegm to perceive in it an idea analogous to those expressed by Mallarmé concerning Henri de Régnier's use of free verse. In a letter written at the end of April 1888, Mallarmé puts his position absolutely clearly: "I don't believe," he affirms to Régnier, "that the new combinations of the poetic line, since it was restructured, are infinite; and you have had the opportunity and the honor of having fashioned a number of unforgettable ones, truly delicious lines, of the kind that the alexandrine hasn't yet given us" (Baudelaire 1973, 190). And in his study entitled "Crise de vers," he insists on this capital point by saying: "the poet who possesses acute tact always considers this alexandrine as the definitive jewel, to be brought out, like a sword or flower, only rarely and only when there is some premeditated motive for doing so. Touching it only with modesty, or playing around it, he grants it neighboring chords, before producing it superb and unadorned" (Mallarmé 1945, 362). Indeed, *Les Fleurs du Mal* reverberates with chords that are close kin to the sonnet, for Baudelaire, so it seems, delighted in playing around the form rather than giving it, in Mallarmé's terms, "superb and unadorned." After all, the collection's first sonnet, both in the edition of 1857 and in that of 1861, proves to be irregular both in the quatrains, where each stanza has a different set of rhymes, and in the tercets, which end with a couplet: the sonnet in question is of course "Correspondances." In other fourteen-line poems, we find the quatrains sharing the same rhymes, but, whereas the first stanza follows the regular model *abba,* the second transposes them into a *baab* pattern:

> Je te donne ces vers afin que si mon nom
> Aborde heureusement aux époques lointaines,
> Et fait rêver un soir les cervelles humaines,
> Vaisseau favorisé par un grand aquilon,
>
> Ta mémoire, pareille aux fables incertaines,
> Fatigue le lecteur ainsi qu'un tympanon,
> Et par un fraternel et mystique chaînon
> Reste comme pendue à mes rimes hautaines. (*OC* 1:40)

[I give you these lines so that, if my name / comes safely to shore in those far-off times, / and sets human minds to dreaming, / a ship favored by the northern wind, // the memory of you, like some vague fables, / will weary the reader like the beating of a drum, / and through a fraternal and mystical chain / will remain hanging from my lofty rhymes.]

"Bien loin d'ici" reverses the order of the tercets and the quatrains; "La Fin de la journée" presents tercets rhyming *aba bba:*

> «Mon esprit, comme mes vertèbres,
> Invoque ardemment le repos;
> Le cœur plein de songes funèbres,
>
> «Je vais me coucher sur le dos
> Et me rouler dans vos rideaux,
> O rafraîchissantes ténèbres!» (*OC* 1:128)

["My spirit, like my spine, / ardently begs for rest; / my heart full of funereal dreams, // I will lie on my back / and roll in your draperies, / O refreshing darkness!"]

And in "Les Aveugles," too, the tercets have only two rhymes:

Ils traversent ainsi le noir illimité,
Ce frère du silence éternel. O cité!
Pendant qu'autour de nous tu chantes, ris et beugles,

Eprise du plaisir jusqu'à l'atrocité,
Vois! je me traîne aussi! mais, plus qu'eux hébété,
Je dis: Que cherchent-ils au Ciel, tous ces aveugles? (*OC* 1:92)

[Thus they pass across the limitless blackness, / that brother of
eternal silence. O city! / While around us you sing, laugh, or bel-
low, // deep in love with pleasure to the point of atrocity, / look!
I too drag myself along! But, more dazed than they, / I ask:
"What are they seeking in the Heavens, all these blind people?"]

If the ill muse of "La Muse malade" can inspire only an irregular sonnet,
in which the quatrains offer crossed rhymes rather than embraced rhymes
and the tercets propose three couplets, "La Muse vénale" is nevertheless not
going to adopt a regular appearance in order to sell herself. Indeed, the
rhymes may remain the same in each of the quatrains, but they present this
abnormality that the first and fourth lines of the first quatrain rhyme with
the second and third lines of the second quatrain, and the second and third
lines of the first quatrain rhyme with the first and fourth of the second. If
the tercets begin regularly enough with a couplet, the third lines of the first
tercet, which according to Banville should rhyme with the second line of the
last tercet, rhymes instead with the last line. As if to makes amends for this
crime of *lèse-prosodie*, Baudelaire suggest parallels that are conceptual rather
than phonetic between the words that in a standard sonnet would have
rhymed: between on the one hand "palais" and "marbrées" and, on the
other hand, "violets" and "azurées."

This particular sonnet takes advantage of another procedure favored by
the binary division of the form. Du Bellay, for example, raises in the quatrains
of "Las! où est maintenant ce mépris de Fortune" [Alas! Where now is that
scorn I felt for Fortune?] questions which will find a reply in the tercets. This is
a technique which also seems very much at home in the Shakespearean sonnet:

Unthrifty loveliness, why dost thou spend
Upon thyself thy beauty's legacy?

Nature's bequest gives nothing, but doth lend,
And being frank she lends to those are free:
Then beauteous niggard, why dost thou abuse
The bounteous largess given thee to give?
Profitless usurer, why dost thou use
So great a sum of sums yet canst not live?
For having traffic with thyself alone,
Thou of thyself thy sweet self dost deceive:
Then how when Nature calls thee to be gone,
What acceptable audit canst thou leave?
    Thy unused beauty must be tombed with thee,
    Which usèd lives th'executor to be. (Vendler 1997, 61)

In "La Muse vénale," the questions posed by the quatrains certainly find an answer in the tercets, but whereas the verbs in the quatrains are in the future—*auras-tu, ranimeras-tu, récolteras-tu*—and are moreover placed at the head of lines that rhyme together, as if to offer a kind of mirror to the rhyme—the verb in the tercets is in the present: *il te faut.* Moreover, the ternary rhythm created by the three verbs of the quatrains is repeated in the three verbs of the tercets: *il te faut jouer, chanter, étaler.* We might note in passing another example of a sonnet that asks a question, but whereas the Shakespearean example I have just quoted uses the final couplet to provide the answer, "Semper eadem" asks the question in the first two lines and uses the remaining twelve to answer: "'D'où vous vient, disiez-vous, cette tristesse étrange, / Montant comme la mer sur le roc noir et nu?' /—Quand notre cœur a fait une fois sa vendange, / Vivre est un mal" (etc.) ["Whence comes, you were saying, this strange sorrow, climbing like the sea on the black, bare rock?" When once our hearts have harvested their vintage, life is full of pain] (*OC* 1:41).

"De profundis clamavi," a poem first published in 1851, can be seen as a *quatorzain* that constantly questions the "rules" that all writers of sonnets ought to obey. If the rhymes in the quatrains are embraced, each quatrain has different rhymes, and the tercets are composed of couplets, a procedure that, unlike the habitual formula, offers no promise of closure: in this poem, the reader feels that the last six lines could very well form a quatrain followed by the first two lines of another quatrain, which, of course, serves to reinforce the message of the final line, with its evocation of a time that hardly passes at all: "Tant l'écheveau du temps lentement se dévide!" [So slowly does the skein of time unwind] (*OC* 1:33).

If the regular sonnet accords to both the octave and the sestet a particular unity, an independence, and an internal coherence, "De profundis clamavi" resolutely refuses any such packaging. The scissions already formed by the rhyme pattern merely throw more clearly into relief those scissions arising from the images. Thus, the first quatrain finds its reflection in the second tercet, where the "I" who speaks reappears, where we find, if not a cacophony as severe as that created by the words "l'unique que," at least a kind of stuttering in "Je jalouse," and where the line "Qui peuvent se plonger dans un sommeil stupide" [Who can plunge into a senseless sleep] takes up again several of the terms or ideas of the last line of the quatrain: "Où nagent dans la nuit l'horreur et le blasphème" [Where swim in the darkness horror and blasphemy]. Equally, the second quatrain offers several parallels with the first tercet: we might note the impersonality of the description, the stress placed on the cold and the darkness, the repetition of the word *soleil.* I would emphasize that in this poem Baudelaire abstains from the rich rhymes that he nevertheless delighted in using at this period of his life. Such rhymes, which draw attention to the end of the line and thus support the idea of a certain periodicity, would obviously not be appropriate in a poem that insists on a temporal movement whose main characteristic is precisely not to offer such divisions. On the other hand, the poem proves to be very rich in alliteration and in internal rhymes (the internal rhymes of *ruisseaux* and *écheveau,* for instance, that reinforce the rhyme of *Chaos* and *animaux* and thus turn attention away from the end of the line and toward the center). The very irregularity of this *quatorzain* corresponds therefore to its subject, throwing into sharper relief the suffering and powerlessness of the narrator.

With "La Musique" Baudelaire pushes even further the possibilities of the sonnet form, associating for the first and last time in *Les Fleurs du Mal* alexandrines and five-syllable lines. In each of the quatrains the five-syllable line rhymes regularly and even banally: *voile* (noun) rhymes with *voile* (verb) and *toile* with *étoile,* in a rhyme that brings out the pun in the other rhyme of the first quatrain: *mer /éther (et terre).* The alexandrines of that quatrain, however, offer a different rhyme: *gonflés /amoncelés,* while in the tercets there are four crossed rhymes followed by a couplet. This last provides the only example of an alexandrine that rhymes with a five-syllable line, and this repetition at such a short interval serves to reinforce the idea that the line expresses, breaking the flow and preventing any lyrical surge at the end of the poem. It's a technique that recalls *(mutatis mutandis)* the poem "Denial" by the English poet George Herbert:

> When my devotions could not pierce
> >   Thy silent ears;
> Then was my heart broken, as was my verse;
> >   My breast was full of fears
> >   And disorder.
> >   . . . .
> Therefore my soul lay out of sight,
> >   Untuned, unstrung;
> My feeble spirit, unable to look right,
> >   Like a nipped blossom, hung
> >   Discontented.
> O cheer and tune my heartless breast,
> >   Defer no time;
> That so thy favors granting my request,
> >   They and my mind may chime,
> >   And mend my rhyme.
> (Herbert 1994, 64)

We should also note that at the beginning of Baudelaire's poem the five-syllable lines suggest speed and joy, and that the fall of the final line is prepared and intensified by the broken rhythm of the penultimate line: "D'autres fois, calme plat, grand miroir" [At other times, dead calm, great mirror].

The antithesis at the center of the poem—music as source of inspiration and joy, offering the possibility of escape from the self, on the one hand, and, on the other, the dull reflection of the listener's black mood, preventing all escape—this antithesis which seems perfectly adapted to the contrast offered by quatrains and tercets, is on the contrary exactly what makes possible the sense of shock, the surprise that Baudelaire considers essential to any great work of art. Indeed, since music can sometimes seize the poet like a sea, it would be ridiculous to stop that inspiration banally at the end of the second quatrain, and Baudelaire is careful to avoid falling into any such trap, with the result that this movement of joy continues by means of enjambments as far as the second tercet:

> Le bon vent, la tempête et ses convulsions
>
>   Sur l'immense gouffre
> Me bercent. (*OC* 1:68)

[The good wind, the tempest and its convulsions // rock me / on the immense abyss.]

But it would be perfectly legitimate to ask what causes the abrupt fall on the word *bercent,* which ought on the contrary to be associated with happiness and continual movement. It seems to me—and I admit that other readings are perfectly possible here—that the word *gouffre,* highlighted moreover by its position at the rhyme, has arrived unexpectedly with all its "démoniaque cortège" (demoniacal procession) as our poet will say elsewhere (*OC* 1:281). After all, in the poem entitled "Le Gouffre," Baudelaire confesses: "mon esprit, toujours du vertige hanté, / Jalouse du néant l'insensibilité" [my mind, constantly haunted by vertigo, / envies the void its failure to feel] (*OC* 1:143). The word *gouffre* seems to perform here a role analogous to those of the word *forlorn* in Keats's "Ode to a Nightingale":

>   The same that oft-times hath
>   Charm'd magic casements, opening on the foam
>   Of perilous seas, in faery lands forlorn.
>
>   Forlorn! the very word is like a bell
>   To toll me back from thee to my sole self."
>   (Keats 1987, 190)

In "La Musique," the word *gouffre* appears to have provoked the same sense of vertigo, the despair aroused in Baudelaire by "l'espace affreux et captivant" [the horrible and captivating space] (*OC* 1:142). If this reading is viable, then the sonnet's *volta* could be said to come at the end of the twelfth line and to create a striking tension between the enjambment and the rhyme: the poem's meaning pulls us on to the word *bercent,* whereas the position at the rhyme of a word as steeped in implications and suggestions as *gouffre* forces us to pause on it.

The very irregularity of "La Musique" plays an essential role in the poem's total effect, to use the terminology of Edgar Allan Poe. The five-syllable line is all the more effective because the reader anticipates an alexandrine; the displaced *volta* delayed until the penultimate line is all the more striking in that we expected it at the end of the ninth line; and the couplet that ends the poem offers a conclusion that is all the more final, so to speak, because in a regular sonnet, or at least a regular Italian sonnet, a final couplet is avoided.

"Brumes et pluies," a poem that reveals yet another technique, exhibits analogous links between form and meaning: here the quatrains are in couplets, but as if Baudelaire wanted to insist on the boredom induced by the "endormeuses saisons" (soporific seasons) he is evoking, he repeats the rhymes, so that the first two lines of the first quatrain rhyme with each other and with the first two lines of the second quatrain, while the third and fourth lines of the first quatrain rhyme with those of the second quatrain: "Boue / loue / joue / s'enroue" et "cerveau / tombeau / renouveau / corbeau." What is more, these are not even *rimes suffisantes* but mere assonances, exactly what is needed to envelop the heart and mind of a poet "d'un linceul vaporeux et d'un vague tombeau" [with a hazy shroud and a vague tomb].

I would like to conclude this overly brief glimpse of several aspects of the use of irregular sonnets in Baudelaire with another fourteen-line poem that draws its effects from the contrast between its irregularity and what one expects of a sonnet. The poem in question is "Le Vin des amants," where, as Claude Pichois has pointed out, a sensation of speed is produced by the use of the octosyllabic line (*OC* 1:1056). This sensation is increased, moreover, by the couplets of the quatrains, which enhance the sense of forward movement, where crossed or embraced rhymes with their echoes, delays, and backward glances would have tended to slow down the movement of the thought. The speed and joy of the beginning, also signaled visually by exclamation points, stop abruptly at the *volta*, which in this case is situated at the ninth line. The quatrains speak of the lovers' identity, since both are tortured by an unrelenting fever and both are following the far-off mirage into the crystal blue of morning (*OC* 1:110). But the horse on which they ride is that of wine, and, if we know that the spectacles of wine are great, illuminated by the inner sun, we also know their sequels: "Mais combien sont redoutables aussi ses voluptés foudroyantes et ses enchantements énervants" [But how redoubtable, too, are its crushing pleasures and enervating enchantments] (*OC* 1:379). The word *mollement* (feebly) which opens the tercets (and which I've always admired in Flaubert's sentence: "Emma se dégageait mollement du bras de Rodolphe" [Emma feebly broke away from Rodolphe's arm]) abruptly slows down this movement and inaugurates a series of words which are relatively difficult to pronounce and even more so if one is drunk, words that are further remarkable by a proliferation of the letter *l*. The lovers who had set out astride wine, riding the Pegasus of porto, now find themselves "balancés sur l'aile / Du tourbillon intelligent" [carried on the wing / of the intelligent whirlwind], having abdicated their own intelligence to accept delirium. They no longer form a couple, since their delirium is parallel and, as we all know, parallel lines meet only at infinity. Moreover, the "nous" (we) of the quatrains is replaced here by the "elle" (she) created by the alliteration and the rhyme (*aile/parallèle*) as it is replaced in the second tercet by the first person singular, "ma sœur" (my sister) being invited to flee no longer toward the paradise of our dreams, but rather to the paradise of *my* dreams. And if the reader were tempted to see in the fact that the poem ends on the word *rêve* (dream) any justification for an optimistic reading, I would emphasize that the rhyme and the alliteration do not allow us to forget that a dream that has to be pursued "sans repos ni trêve" (without rest or respite) quickly becomes a nightmare, and I would draw attention to the following line in another well-known poem: "Certes je sortirai, quant à moi, satisfait / D'un monde où l'action n'est pas la sœur du rêve" [Certainly I for my part would happily leave / a world in which action is not the sister of dream] (*OC* 1:122).

Amid this impressive variety of irregular or libertine sonnets, Baudelaire scatters here and there sonnets that are regular, as if he wanted to remind his reader of the rule. "Parfum exotique," a poem that appears to date from the 1840s, can provide an example of this jewel one should bring out, according to Mallarmé, only rarely and for some premeditated reason. The rhymes follow the pattern *abba abba ccdede*; the key word *odeur,* which appears in the first quatrain, is taken up again in the first tercet; the main verb of the quatrains, *je vois,* is also the main verb of the tercets; the rich rhymes draw attention to the end of the line, culminating in the tour de force of "tamariniers" rhyming with "mariniers." In his last great study

of Poe, Baudelaire seems to adopt the beliefs expressed by Poe with regard
to rhyme:

> Poe attached enormous importance to rhyme and [. . .] in the
> analysis he made of the mathematical and musical pleasure that
> the mind extracts from rhyme, he deployed as much care and
> subtlety as in all the subjects which have a bearing on his craft as
> poet. Just as he had shown that the refrain is capable of infinitely
> varied applications, so he sought to rejuvenate, to redouble the
> pleasure of the rhyme by adding to it that element of the unex-
> pected, the *bizarreness* that is like the indispensable condiment
> for all beauty. (*OC* 2:335–36).

The strangeness of the libertine sonnet, thrown into relief and intensified by a regular sonnet such as "Parfum exotique," the infinite variety that
Baudelaire was able to reveal in his fourteen-line poems, and the obvious
desire to rejuvenate this fixed form did not go unobserved by the poets who
followed him. Here I would like to quote yet again Mallarmé, who seems to
me to sum up the situation perfectly when he says, speaking of the traditional poems of *Le Parnasse contemporain:* "Yet the Parnassians' precaution
is not without point: it provides a reference point between the Romantics'
utterly audacious remodeling of poetry, and freedom; and it marks (before
versification dissolves into something identical with the primitive keyboard
of language) an official game, or rather a game bound by a fixed rhythm"
(Mallarmé 1945, 491). A reference point, the traditional sonnet has also
been that, between Baudelaire's bold reforging of the possibilities of this
form and the freedom of the *vers libres* or, indeed, of the experimental sonnets being written in the early days of *vers libre*.

Verlaine, having bought at the age of fifteen a book he thought was entitled *Fleurs de mai,* also enjoyed playing with the possibilities opened up by
Baudelaire. Thus, as Huysmans's Des Esseintes notes, he provided sonnets
that remind one of goldfish, swimming with their tails held higher than
their heads, but observing the contrast between the two sections:

> Tout enfant, j'allais rêvant Ko-Hinnor,
> Somptuosité persane et papale,
> Héliogabale et Sardanapale!

Mon désir créait sous des toits en or,
Parmi les parfums, au son des musiques,
Des harems sans fin, paradis physiques!

Aujourd'hui plus calme et non moins ardent
Mais sachant la vie et qu'il faut qu'on plie,
J'ai dû refréner ma belle folie,
Sans me résigner par trop cependant.

Soit! le grandiose échappe à ma dent,
Mais, fi de l'aimable et fi de la lie!
Et je hais toujours la femme jolie,
La rime assonante et l'ami prudent. (Verlaine 26)

[As a child I would dream of Koh-i-noor, / of Persian and Papal sumptuosity, / Heliogabalus and Sardanapalus! // My desire created under golden roofs, / amidst perfumes, to the sound of music, / endless harems, physical paradises! // Today I'm calmer but no less ardent, / but knowing life and knowing one must give in to it, / I have had to rein in my fine folly, / but without resigning myself too much, however. // So be it! The grandiose escapes my teeth, / but fie on the amiable and fie on the dregs, / and still I hate the pretty woman, / the assonating rhyme and the prudent friend.]

He can be found in "Nevermore" offering quatrains, each of which has only a single rhyme, as if he wanted to insist in this way on the ineluctable nature of the memory, or taking pleasure in the creation of a "Sonnet boiteux," based on a thirteen-syllable line, and in which the first line announces quite clearly the failure of the rhymes in the last tercet:

Ah! vraiment c'est triste, ah! vraiment ça finit trop mal.
Il n'est pas permis d'être à ce point infortuné.
Ah! vraiment c'est trop la mort du naïf animal
Qui voit tout son sang couler sous son regard fané.

Londres fume et crie. O quelle ville de la Bible!
Le gaz flambe et nage et les enseignes sont vermeilles.
Et les maisons dans leur ratatinement terrible
Epouvantent comme un sénat de petites vieilles.

Tout l'affreux passé saute, piaule, miaule et glapit
Dans le brouillard rose et jaune et sale de sohos
Avec des indeeds et des all rights et des haôs.

Non vraiment c'est trop une martyre sans espérance,
Non vraiment cela finit trop mal, vraiment c'est triste:
O le feu du ciel sur cette ville de la Bible!
(Verlaine 1969, 258–60)

[Ah! Truly it's sad, ah! Truly it ends too badly. / People should-
n't be allowed to be so unfortunate. / Oh! Truly it's too much
the death of the naive animal / who sees all its blood flow away
beneath its faded gaze. // London smokes and screams. Oh what
a city of the Bible! / The gas flames and swims and the signs are
scarlet, / and the houses, terribly shrunken, / horrify you like a
senate of little old ladies. // All the dreadful past leaps, whim-
pers, meows and yelps / in the pink and yellow and dirty fog of
Sohos / with indeeds and all rights and aohs. // No truly it's too
much of a martyrdom without hope, no truly it ends too badly,
truly it's sad: / oh the fire of heaven on that city of the Bible!]

   The Belgian symbolist poet Grégoire Le Roy provides several variations on the sonnet in his volume *La Chanson du pauvre.* "Echos de valses"
alternates octosyllables and lines of ten syllables, whereas "Soir intense,"
with its nine-syllable lines, seems to provide three quatrains followed by a
sixain:

   C'était un soir d'étranges extases,
   Un soir où les roses trop écloses
   Se mouraient d'épanouissement,
   Comme meurent les roses des vases.

C'était un soir où même les choses
Semblaient mourantes étrangement
Et comme lentes, évanouies,
D'être, en ce soir, trop épanouies.

Et nous vîmes tomber des pétales
Dans l'attente amoureuse des heures
Et nous gardons à jamais au cœur,
La langueur de ces heures fatales.

Car jamais tes lèvres de bonheur
Ne seront plus douces ni meilleures
Qu'en ce soir de trop lentes extases
Où les roses, trop épanouies,
Se mouraient d'extases inouïes,
Ainsi que les roses dans les vases. (Delvaille 1971, 247–48)

[It was an evening of strange ecstasies, / an evening when the overblown roses / died of blooming as roses die in vases. // It was an evening when even the objects / seemed to be strangely dying, / and, were as if slow, swooning, / from having on that evening bloomed too much. // And we saw the petals fall in the amorous expectation of hours / and we will forever keep in our hearts / the languor of those fatal hours. / For never will your lips of happiness / be sweeter or better than on that evening of overly slow ecstasies / when the roses, too overblown, / were dying in unheard-of ecstasies / like the roses in the vases.]

"One after another, deliciously," Mallarmé wrote to him, with his great gift of the apt phrase which in his letters sometimes, as here, borders on pastiche: "I have read them, those little poems whose tone is so perfect and which are almost silent in their adamantine condensation or a swooning suspense" (Mallarmé 1969, 315–16). One has the impression on reading this extended sonnet that the poet is too close to swooning after the second quatrain to find the *sizain* straightaway.

Jean Moréas allows himself other liberties with the sonnet, as can be seen in "Et j'irai . . ." with its eleven-syllable lines:

Et j'irai le long de la mer éternelle
Qui bave et gémit en les roches concaves,
En tordant sa queue en les roches concaves;
J'irai tout le long de la mer éternelle.

Je viendrai déposer, ô mer maternelle,
Parmi les varechs et parmi les épaves,
Mes rêves et mon orgueil, mornes épaves,
Pour que tu les berces, ô mer maternelle.

Et j'écouterai les cris des alcyons
Dans les cieux plombés et noirs comme un remords,
Leurs cris dans le vent aigu comme un remords.

Et je pleurerai comme les alcyons,
Et je cueillerai, triste jusqu'à la mort,
Les lys des sables pâles comme la mort. (Delvaille 1971, 163)

[And I shall go along the eternal sea, / that foams and moans in concave rocks, / twisting its tail in the concave rocks; / I shall go along the eternal sea. // I shall come and place, O maternal sea, / among the seaweed and the wreckage, / my dreams and my pride, glum wreckage, / for you to rock them, O maternal sea. // And I shall listen to the cries of halcyons, / in the skies, leaden and black as remorse, / their cries in the wind sharp as remorse. // And I shall cry like the halcyons. / And I shall pluck, sad to the point of death, / lilies of the sand pale as death.]

No doubt, this is merely a finger exercise, wonderfully Poe-like, but in which the idea nevertheless does not seem to leap forth. It would perhaps be legitimate to find an experiment from the pen of Jean Lorrain more interesting, even if, like Moréas in "Et j'irai," he does not quite succeed in making of the sonnet something more than a landscape with little real depth:

Les rêves du clair de lune,
Frimas blancs dans la nuit brune
Neigent au bord de la mer.

Sur la falaise, qu'assiège
Un sinistre vent d'hiver,
L'écume éparse dans l'air
Se mêle aux flocons de neige.

Au pied des rocs descellés
Des plaintes et des cris vagues
Montent dans l'ombre et les vagues,
Au sanglot de vents mêlés,

Et blêmes, échevelés,
Des fronts implorants de femmes
Tournoient au loin sur les lames. (Delvaille 1971, 157)

[The dreams of moonlight, / white frost in the brown night, / snow by the side of the sea. // On the cliff, besieged / by a sinister winter wind, / the foam scattered in the air / mingles with snowflakes. // At the foot of shattered rocks / moans and vague cries / climb into the shadow and the waves, / mingling with the sob of the winds. // And pale, disheveled, / imploring brows of women turn far off on the billows.]

I would like to give a final example of these irregular sonnets that so proliferated toward the end of the nineteenth century. This time, it is a sonnet, or, if preferred, a fourteen-line poem that is somewhat more successful than those we have just seen in introducing into that constricting form a certain suppleness and a measure of thought:

Le bleu marin, doré de ciel, déroule ses soies lentes
Comme pour un manteau de Vierge byzantine,
Puis ce sont de gracieux rubans, irisés d'eau câline,
Que nulle âpre respiration du vent ne tourmente.

Les crêtes saphirines des vagues sont fondues
De tendresse, au sein de la brillante étendue
Soulevée à peine en paresseux mouvements
D'ailes frissonnantes—comme d'un ramier dormant.

C'est le Pardon joyeux et l'oubli des orages,
Le baiser unissant les éléments candides
Si intimement que—vertigineux mirage—
La mer semble un ciel doux, onduleux et liquide,
Où—telles des nuées—les navires oscillent
Et le vrai ciel paraît une mer immobile.
(Delvaille 1971, 275)

[The navy blue, gilded by the sky, unfolds its slow silks / as if
for the cloak of a Byzantine Virgin, / then there are gracious
ribbons, turned to rainbows by the affectionate water, tormented by no rough breath of wind. // The sapphirine crests of
the waves are melted / with tenderness in the heart of the brilliant expanse / scarcely lifted in lazy movements / of shivering
wings—like a dove asleep. // This is the joyous Pardon when
storms are forgotten, / the kiss that unites the candid elements, /
so intimately that—vertiginous mirage— / the sea seems a gentle, undulating, liquid sky / where, like clouds, the ships oscil-
late / and the real sky seems a motionless sea.]

The sonnet's author is Marie Krysinska, unjustly neglected in today's
canon. If Baudelaire's irregular sonnets have left traces that are clearly legible on these poems, it is above all in the desire they all reveal to make the
mechanism of the form more supple, rather than in an ambition to use
those very constraints to intensify the central idea. The case is entirely different, I hardly need say, for a Rimbaud or a Mallarmé, or even for a
Régnier, all of whom seem to share Baudelaire's conviction that the constricting form possesses enormous intrinsic advantages.

   Because the form is constricting, does the idea burst forth more intensely? Perhaps one should reply with Mallarmé: "it's not with ideas that
one makes poems, my dear Degas, but with words." But perhaps, too, one
could reply by quoting the contemporary poet Jean-Charles Vegliante,
who in his collection entitled *Sonnets du petit pays entraîné vers le nord*,
asks the question: "Sans forme, qui nous consolera?"[Without form,
what will console us?] Any study of the *vers libres* of the 1880s and 1890s

shows that they draw much of their strength and suggestive power from the gap created between their structures and the reader's expectations of what constitutes poetry. Looking at the sonnets of the time offers a useful starting point and focus for such a study, because the base from which the sonneteers start out is so well defined. I hope to have shown that it is precisely in the gap between what one expects and what one receives that one finds poetry.

Prose and Prosody

Baudelaire and the Handling of Genres

Jean-Christophe Bailly

Translated by *Jan Plug*

T HE "book" that is absent but surrounded by all the pages that prepare, sound, pursue, or deny it: one will find nothing of the like with respect to Baudelaire's prose poems. They appear and are gathered together quietly, so to speak, and what perhaps surprises us most about their invention is that it is neither preceded nor followed by any effect of announcement. Such discretion does not mean that with this new form Baudelaire revolutionized literature on the quiet or in a roundabout way: the dedicatory letter to Arsène Houssaye proves sufficiently that he was conscious of the singularity of his enterprise; but it is surely not out of false modesty that he there describes his endeavor as in part aborted or deviated. However, we who can unravel right up to ourselves the entangled texture of the modern he gave birth to know that with the prose poem he deposits the question of genre in its center, and that he bequeaths it to us.

The prose poem reveals this question of genre raised by the escape of the poem outside its prosodic rule and lexical customs; it is the most obvious emergence of it. But, like a cloud of milk one adds to a cup of tea and that colors it completely, Baudelaire's entire oeuvre is invested in it. Neither the verse poems, which rear up against and become distended within what Mallarmé will later call the "hereditary instrument," nor his

124

critical prose, nor, of course, the fragmentary form of the *Fusées* can be thought outside of what the intrusion of prose in prosody comes to turn upside down. And the question is so crucial and generic that even the genres Baudelaire did not practice, such as the novel, are dragged for us to figure at the heart of the problematic it institutes.

Yet, one will find nothing in Baudelaire that could be compared to the theoretical fever that circulated, concerning genre, in the circle of the Jena romantics, a half century earlier. Baudelaire neither knew nor shared Friedrich von Schlegel's or Novalis's paradoxical formulas crossing the recognized separations in order to transcend them in formally permeable *ideas* of genre, or their intuition of a kind of genre of genres that ends up by sublating all these ideas in a superior unity to come, and there is nothing in him that recalls them, not even the atmosphere of such a speculation. But in him everything takes place as though he had tried, on a strictly practical level, to put into play that emancipation of the poem or that other prose at which the "little poems" are the attempts. It will be Walter Benjamin's historical role to propose to us to make the connection ourselves beginning with his oeuvre—to such a point that between his early essay on *The Concept of Aesthetic Criticism in German Romanticism* and his later writings on Baudelaire, it is, via genre, a true genealogy of modernity that his oeuvre confronts us with. Let us say that on the side of the romantics of the *Athenaeum* we have the theoretical slant (the slant on which the fragment itself functions as a state of form),[1] and that on Baudelaire's side we would have the effectuation of it. A mountain without a summit that on one side is still lit by the last morning fires of German Idealism and that on the other is already lit by the gas lighting of the big city. From the one to the other, in fact, the absolute had to agree to roll in the mud of the suburbs and measure itself against the registers of objects of the industrial age. This fall, the Baudelairean version of what Novalis (in a letter to Friedrich von Schlegel dated 12 January 1798 and cited by Benjamin) called "enlarged poetry" (*erweitere Dichtung*), fulfills it.

The dedicatory letter to Arsène Houssaye might very well not have wanted to assert itself as the discovery of a theoretical continent and true new world of phrasing; after so many other commentators, it is dense enough in its concision for me to stop there—by illustrating that this density and speed are obviously not unrelated to those of the prose poems themselves. As we know, Baudelaire invokes a model at the threshold of his book, and it is *Gaspard de la Nuit,* Aloysius Bertrand's only book, published in 1842, a year after the untimely death of the young poet from Dijon. Perhaps it is advisable to look at it more closely than is usual or, at least, listening to Baudelaire, to take it seriously as an origin. The poems composing the six books of the collection are in prose, indubitably, a prose, moreover, that is extremely supple and sober, with a slightly magical lightness. But, as is often the case with an origin, the rupture is only half consummated with the form from which the new work has disengaged. The difference that jumps out between these prose poems and Baudelaire's (other than that capital one of the era and the urban type that are evoked—but I will of course come back to that) is the abandonment of strophic structure. Internally organized like songs of equal length and interconnected according to the riskless order of a strictly composed collection, each poem being a bit like a plate in a volume of engravings, Aloysius Bertrand's poems do not, like Baudelaire's, constitute a fantasy—the word is his—in which each fragment can exist by itself. The Baudelairean broadening is thus carried by the internal form—a prose completely gone out of verse—and by composition—a composite collection of diverse formats and even tones. The medieval connotation of Aloysius Bertrand's book allows us this image—every poem in *Gaspard de la Nuit* is like the square of a medieval garden, while with Baudelaire we must leave this *hortus conclusus* to penetrate into a land lying fallow, into a sort of vague literary ground. But beyond the almost complete abandonment of all cadence and according to the very slope that its escape toward the prosaic opens, the Baudelairean prose poem comes to verge on another brief form, that of the story. Baudelaire himself must have thought about this proximity, since in the outline in which the list of the prose poems, still in the state of a plan, figures, one finds twice, between brackets after the title, the indication "perhaps a story." It would no doubt be fruitless or scholastic to want to separate the prose poem and the story normatively, but what we must remember is this encounter, in the bed of the prosaic, this proximity that, however, does not and should not go all the way to fusion: whatever the hold over it by the fictional pulsion, there must be something in the prose poem that holds it back and acts in such a way that it does not purely and simply go about abolishing itself, something that does not abolish what comes to it from the poem. Thus, much more than a fixed genre disposing of its laws, codes, and standing, the prose poem appears as a form in the process of becoming, as a displacement that leaves the text unstable, as

though wandering between an origin that it must at once leave and not entirely lose and a destination at once to be glimpsed and not united with. This
all the more so since the story is not the only pole toward which the prose
poem is led. In fact, everything that stems from descriptive and critical
prose, everything that can be related to the essay provides another, perhaps
still closer, encounter. With such discontinuous and superimposed movements ("La Chambre double," from this point of view, being at least triple:
short story, short essay on art and time, and prose poem), it is a question of
rebounds, ricochets, billiard balls. Is it a certain passage of the aesthetic
writings that transforms itself into a "prose poem" or, conversely, a certain
passage of *Le Spleen de Paris* that converts itself into a fragment of aesthetic
theory? And can't we consider that in many respects *Le Peintre de la vie
moderne* itself also approaches, and very truthfully, that is, on the level of its
very writing, that "musical prose without rhythm and rhyme" that the dedication to Arsène Houssaye defines as a dream and a tension, as an active element that we know in fact disrupts the totality of the Baudelairean text?

Just after having defined this dreamed-of prose as "supple and uneven
enough to adapt to the lyrical movements of the soul, to the undulations of
reverie, to the jolts of conscience," a virtual prose in which we can recognize, precisely foretold and as though recognized, the Proustian sentence,
for example (everything taking place as though Baudelaire discreetly confid-
ed to the future a task to be accomplished or a breakaway to be caught up
with), just after this, which is the nucleus of the dedication, Baudelaire
moves without transition, with an astonishing and almost technical calm,
onto what will be the point of impact of his aim: "It is most of all from the
frequenting of enormous cities, it is from the crossing of their innumerable
relations that this obsessive ideal is born." To attempt, as he put it above, to
do with the modern city, with Paris, what Aloysius Bertrand had "applied to
the painting of ancient life, so strangely picturesque," to attempt a *description,* such is the program of the prose poems, a program that establishes
Baudelaire (need it be said?) in an incredible lucidity, since he makes of
himself the connection between the formal innovation he proposes and the
epochal form that rules it, the effect of which is to suggest to us that his endeavor is neither more nor less than that of the institution of a symbolic
form.

The formal movement of this endeavor is double: it implies that voyage
between the genres that we have spoken of, but it equally implies that what

was latent in the regular poem finds in the new form the surface of its fulfillment. Here I am thinking above all of that lexical rupture for which
Baudelaire's poetry is the experimental ground or the trial laboratory, a rupture that is already a rift caused by the prosaic in the resistant matter of the
alexandrine. This is what Benjamin writes: "*Les Fleurs du Mal* is the first
book to have used words not only of prosaic but of urban origin in lyric poetry,"[2] and he cites in passing a few of those words that disturb the tone
and hierarchical position of the genre: *quinquet* (oil lamp), *wagon* (truck,
wagon), *omnibus* (train, omnibus), *bilan* (balance sheet, assessment), *réver-
bère* (street light), *voirie* (road maintenance). The occurrences of these
terms or of similar words are obviously even more numerous in the prose
poems, but, most of all, they are at home there: their introduction into poetic material no longer stems from what Benjamin, speaking of *Les Fleurs du
Mal,* defines as being a *putsch* (143). From such a point of view, the prose
poem becomes the place in which the tension proper to Baudelaire's poetry—that is, this telescoping of the lyric by the trivial and of correspondences
by the urban theme—is assuaged. This does not mean—far from it—that
the prose poems fall over entirely and unanimously to one side, but at least
indicates that they have, on this side, more range and freedom, and, also, on
the level of their production, less tension. Into the very definition of the
"obsessive ideal" in fact passes a certain gentleness, passes the phantom of a
pure malleability. And thus the passages closest to the collection give the
impression of having been written "off the cuff" or in that neglected sublime
Baudelaire liked to identify in painters, as though their very matter had been
diluted in the water of Constantin Guys's watercolors.

Such a relative relaxation does not mean that there is anything at all in
these prose poems that could be likened to distraction or that borrows from
the genre of physiology, so in vogue in their time (and let it be said in passing, Claudel's famous formula talking about "a mixture of Racine's style and
of the journalistic style of his time" is scarcely appropriate to save us from
such an error). Simply, this dreamed-of prose that Baudelaire finally says he
did not achieve opposes to a fixed or at least scanned time a fluidity and a
possibility of dilation that the regulation and even the prosodic deregulation
of the poem forbids it from reaching; it constitutes another aim.

The violence of what he achieves by jumping outside of the tension
proper to the poem, in which the intrusion of the prosaic does not manage
to stop being a transgression, Baudelaire condenses into an allegory. It is

that of the loss of the halo in the prose poem that carries that very name. We know its motif, and it is clear and radical. In the phrase by which the fallen poet tells about the accident that brought him down to earth, the entire contradiction of *Les Fleurs du Mal* relaxes in laughter: "my halo, in an abrupt movement, slipped from my head into the mire of the road (*macadam*)." And in such a way that we can imagine that this dialogue is really, despite its caricatural aspect, an interview between two faces of Baudelaire himself: on the one hand, the lucid narrator who is only the witness and confidant of the affair, on the other, the poet he has stopped or wanted to stop being, but who, in a much more pregnant way than his cheap double, continues to lurk in him. In the course of this dialogue, we remember, the loss of the halo is immediately converted into a gain, and the immediate form, immediately accessible, of this gain is the joy of the incognito. Having climbed down from his imaginary pedestal, the poet is literally depos(it)ed in the crowd in which he will be able to lose himself, and we, we have witnessed in a few lines a true metamorphosis: the chrysalis having fallen like the halo, there springs up a new poet already ready to laugh at his old colleagues, but ready most of all, instead of believing that he flies or glides, ready to walk like anyone at all on the tarmac (*macadam*)—the modern and trivial English word here having almost the value of a password.

Certain aspects of the prose poems respond to the radicality of this allegory, and these aspects are those in which derision is brushed up against. Thus, the brief hyperfocalized poem that is "La Soupe et les nuages," a title—and a narrative—that, all the same, one would be at pains to imagine in the table of contents of *Les Fleurs du Mal;* thus again "Les Bons Chiens," where, to sing "the calamitous dogs" with a fervor that, moreover, is not feigned, Baudelaire revokes the high style with almost coarse accents, letting one think that the voyage of genre includes a detour through bad genre: "Stand back, academic muse! I have nothing to do with that old prude. I invoke the familiar, the city-dwelling, the living muse."

However, everything is not so simple or smooth (we suspected as much), and the conversion of which "Perte d'auréole" tells retains, beyond the sarcasm, something theoretical about it. The rhetorical brake that is continually at work in *Les Fleurs du Mal* in fact remains active in the prose poems, even if it acts differently there. No doubt, it can no longer exert itself as a continuous pressure on the verbal flood, no longer having at its disposition the regular and fatal brake of verse, but one senses its presence no less, and this presence, although unequally divided among the different poems and facets of the collection, contributes to giving the form for which they try that hybrid character that has so often been noticed. I am thinking less here of a given involuntary rising up of the alexandrine or of a given effect of tonal handling than of a sort of exclamatory unction that appears as a weakening of the design, and I will take as an example "Le Thyrse," that poem that begins so well by supposing that the ancient and sacred object is only a simple stick, but that ends so poorly, with a very pompous dedicatory eulogy to Franz Liszt. It would be ridiculous, however, to probe the whole of *Le Spleen de Paris* in this way, by distributing good and bad points. What is at stake here, beyond all criteria, is the work of a form, the work of the adventure of a form: how it comes, what it comes to, how it yields itself to, or, on the contrary, resists, what it gives rise to. To understand the nature of these resistances is not to judge Baudelaire; it is to accompany him in his movement, to the extent that it is effectively deployed.

At bottom, the poet crowned with a halo of "La Perte," "drinker of quintessence" and "eater of ambrosia," is but the inferior and comic version or the terrible parody of the tragic figure of the poet as it appears from the edge of *Les Fleurs du Mal* in "L'Albatros": for this giant who can no longer glide above the waves, the ship's deck is the equivalent of the tarmac, the surface, of a fall into the real, but this time disastrous and no longer salvatory. No doubt, the "vast birds of the sea" have nothing of the ridiculousness of the pretentious poet, who, for his part, is only a kind of crested crane. But in the crossing of these two figures and at the speed of a hurried passerby cutting across the crowd a new Baudelairean dream takes shape: that of a poet who would be entirely the poet of prose, who would still know how to be, on bare ground and among humans, the "winged traveler," one who, without halo and having lost the azure, would however still, and perhaps even finally, have access to the aura. Baudelaire wanted to be this poet frankly and with bravado, but to get there he had to defy himself. Baudelaire could only see or foresee the ultimate movement of the fall and the farthest reach of the prose, but one can guess that he sensed there equally an abandonment and perhaps even, as he indicated to Manet about his art, a decrepitude. It seems that Baudelaire could not resign himself to what Mallarmé later would call "the illocutionary disappearance of the poet"[3] and that he suddenly rowed violently against the flood that carried him toward this disappearance.

We do not have the clear sign of such a mistrust, and if Baudelaire shifts in relation to the prose poems, it is with respect to their success, which he seems to judge imperfect, not to their ideal, which continues to be for him a "mysterious and brilliant model." But it is the very substance of the prose poems that conveys this sign to us, to the extent that a glimmer of the sublime that it does not manage to depose still flickers within it. Baudelaire quite often, and more often in turn than any other poet, is also the "painter of modern life," but there is, despite everything, something forced in his gesture that puts him in a bad position, and the strongest thing about his genius, what places him right in the middle of the nineteenth century as a hearth that irradiates it completely, is no doubt this open contradiction between what he senses and what holds him back from yielding to it.

To what point this "Baudelairean problem" (which one would find identical in his relation to painting, in what tears him between the last fires of the great genre revisited by the genius and "prose" of modern painting, between Delacroix and Guys),[4] does not concern him alone is testified to by his entire lineage, beginning with Rimbaud, Verlaine, and Mallarmé, even if it is strange or at least significant that in "Crise de vers" no mention is made of the prose poem, prosaic tension intervening, according to this fundamental text that does not cite Baudelaire a single time, except by the bursting open of verse itself, under the form of free verse. It is not my intention here to explore this lineage—that would be the subject of a book up to Apollinaire, who revives it with a force much too underestimated, a book that would analyze the entire tension between the prosaic and what some thinkers (Agamben or Berman) have called musaic. Nor is it my aim to enter very far into this highly complex text that is "Crise de vers," since it would only be a question of retaining an echo of it that applies to the understanding of Baudelaire.

In the way that Mallarmé saves verse from its ruin or fatigue, especially in the reasons he invokes for restoring it, despite everything, as a vibratory model that is at bottom unsurpassable but not turned toward the past from which it comes, something perceptibly makes a sign toward the impeccable handling of Baudelairean verse, but still more seems to trace from a distance, even if it is in other terms, Baudelaire's contradiction, and also to foresee ours.

For Mallarmé, it is to the degree that it "pays for the defect of languages" ("imperfect in that there are a number of them"[5] that verse, unpredictably,

saves itself and becomes, by this defect, the "superior complement." Verse
owes this position not to some authority, to a legitimacy of genre, and of a
national genre, but to its law, which is simple: "this prosody, such brief
rules, all the more uncompromising." In other words, as absolutely specific
and sonorous form, verse strains from the paper toward its notion, because
it is the memory of itself, the elimination of chance. This tension proper to
verse and to it alone does not qualify it as "genre," but as oeuvre—not in the
greedy sense of Hugo, of the Hugo machine, but in the sense of an absolute
that bypasses the defect of languages like the chance of individuality. Not to
throw verse out, but to throw it differently—this is how one could understand Mallarmé's endeavor, as respects the poems as well as "Un coup de
dés," where chance is incurred. But as soon as it is thrown, the die falls
again, and Mallarmé was the first to know this. We can see that the throw
that does not return, coming under the book like a shadow or phantom, the
angel of literature itself, resembles that "obsessive ideal" Baudelaire defined
as out of reach of his prose. There is, in the one case as in the other, a taking
aim at a target that conceals itself, but also the movement of engendered
form that becomes frantic.

It is here, facing this chance, this returned chance, that verse straightens
up, old this time, and that rhetorical prestige plays anew, with nostalgia in
Baudelaire, with irony in Mallarmé, only Rimbaud perhaps managing to
eliminate nostalgia. But what is sure, as far as we may have been able to go in
the freeing up of genres and in the direction of that "enlarged poetry" that
Novalis conceived two centuries ago, is that we have not got out of this tension, not because the charm, in the Greek and strong sense of *charis,* not because the *charis,* then, of prosody (or of "musaic") would take hold of us
(which it does at any rate), but because that of which prosody is the delayed
echo belongs to language itself. What a called-for genre of genres covets is
not a simple mixture or an ultimate sublation, it is a language—that is to
say, the purest acting of language, without veil. And the prosodic belongs to
this unknown language like an integrated shadow: by accepting and accentuating the "defect of languages," that which, verse or not, recalls prosody,
recalls also the most secret layer of language, that layer in which it is still the
phoné that listens and speaks, that layer in which, in the most intimate connection to this voice, language stands beyond signification, in a disclosing of
the world of which it is the echo. Now, this "lost paradise" of language accompanies the human being in time, not as a memory, but as an indication

on the watch beneath language, preserving it. Rather than as a song, we should think of it as a sort of continuous bass; it is this bass that the prosodic lets be heard, not at all as a sonorous or musical value, but as the sign of the truth of naming. And from this moment we can understand the "gentle native tongue" spoken to the soul in secret, not as something evanescent, but as what has made this sign vibrate from the beginning of things.

Still in "Crise de vers," Mallarmé opposes, without our knowing exactly which way he is leaning, two manners of speaking. The one, which includes "in the subtle paper . . . for example the horror of the forest or the mute thunder scattered to the leaves," the other, which would go looking for "the intrinsic and deep wood of the trees." It seems to me that between these two manners resides the gap I have wanted to talk about and that the modern endeavor might be defined as the one that moves away from the side of this "intrinsic wood," effacing itself before it, having deposed everything: the poet, myth, the oracle, hymn, song, verse, and even prose no doubt—everything except what would still remain of language in which everything abandoned would be included. It appears to me, and this is my conclusion, that Baudelaire's oeuvre, in its historical position, opens the path that goes toward this wood, but that it does so by keeping "the mute thunder scattered to the leaves" from which, however, it distances itself, giving it, although it opens and is opened to modernity, the characteristic of a farewell: a morning, accordingly, but an autumn morning.

Contingencies and Discontinuities of the Lyric *I*

Baudelaire as Poet-Narrator and Diarist

Sonya Stephens

ECENT theoretical criticism has focused upon narratological questions, enabling crucial distinctions to be made with respect to textual voices and these, in their turn, have led to an increasingly nuanced understanding of autobiographical writing. In these critical debates, the question of the lyric persona has, until the past few years, been largely neglected, despite the relevance of such critical developments for an appreciation of the complexities of lyricism and its voices.[1] In the light of such debates, consideration of Baudelaire's prose poems and of his *Journaux intimes* raises particular problems, since *Le Spleen de Paris* seems often to be resolutely antilyrical and the diaries to be something other than is declared by this generic title. Indeed, as Claude Pichois points out, the title of *Journaux intimes* is *factice*, since Baudelaire never kept such a diary,[2] but even in recognizing the problematic status of the title and its facticiousness as here applied, he finds justification for it "insofar as the notion of the private includes or confirms the veracious." Béatrice Didier is more categorical in her rejection of this title and its so-called autobiographical status: "There is no justification for this title, nor for an autobiographical interpretation. It is because critics have been led astray in this way that these texts have been seen as an abortive work recounting the failure of a life" (Didier 1973, 57). It is precisely the problematic status of the self, or *moi*, in these forms of writing which is the focus of this essay, a *moi* created by and in the texts and which is the voice of the *intimus*. This essay does not, however, seek to propose new biographical or psychological interpretations, nor indeed to plead in favor of an autobiographical interpretation, but rather to demonstrate the functioning of a certain kind of writing of the self, with recurring patterns and common constraints and with the intimacy of the lyric subject as well as the ludic complexity of myriad other selves.

To speak of the *moi* of these texts is itself problematic, not only because theory insists on a disconnection between the *moi* of the subject and the "I" of discourse,[3] but because the challenges of writing and reading that "I" are different in poetry, narrative, and the diary form. Lyricism, like first-person narrative, can simulate the presence, subjectivity, and orality of the autobiographical voice, for, as Philippe Lejeune has suggested, "the poet has at his disposal all the resources that language can offer; he can use, in the form of a confession or an elegy, all that characterizes autobiographical writing: first-person discourse, retrospective narration, and pact with the reader" (1977, 245). The question of *pact* is here particularly significant, since it emphasizes the expectation of the reader. In the *journal intime,* as in lyrical poetry, the center and the proper "content" of the writing process is the writer himself or herself, the direct and immediate expression of the *moi.* In prose poetry such expectations are troubled, made problematic, first by the fact that there is no generic tradition to draw upon, no generic blueprint to shape such expectations (apart, perhaps, from those belonging properly to the distinct genres which compose the oxymoron that is prose poetry); secondly, and perhaps more significantly, the "I" seems less present, somehow less reliable than the lyric "I," often presenting itself at a further remove in the role of *narrateur-témoin,* or even totally eclipsed by the others of the prose poems. In a way quite distinct from lyrical verse and autobiography, Baudelaire's *Journaux intimes* and his prose poetry de-center the "I," staging a "vaporization of the self" by constantly bringing the lyrical subject into question and by placing it in perpetual opposition to both the Other and to difference.

This consciousness of the Other is, first and foremost, present in the very elaboration of the two projects, in Baudelaire's reference to "model" texts to which he simultaneously stresses a debt and from which he asserts his difference. In borrowing from Poe the title of one part of the *Journaux intimes, Mon cœur mis à nu,* Baudelaire is at one and the same time naming the model text and, in subscribing to this model, taking up the challenge that goes with the title: to write a work that would keep the promise it makes. Such a work is, according to Poe, impossible to write:

> If any ambitious man have a fancy to revolutionize, at one effort, the universal world of human thought, human opinion, and human sentiment, the opportunity is his own—the road to immortal renown lies straight, open, and unencumbered before him. All he has to do is to write and publish a very small book, the title of which will be simple—My Heart Laid Bare. But—this little book must be true to its title. [. . .] But to write it—*there* is the rub. No man dare write it. No man will ever dare write it. No man *could* write it, even if he dared. The paper would shrivel and blaze at every touch of the fiery pen.[4]

But, this is not the only challenge to which Baudelaire rises, for a second model text is also invoked, and one which is explicitly mentioned at the time Baudelaire first describes his autobiographical ambitions in a letter to Madame Aupick. It is to be "a great book" in which Baudelaire will heap his every resentment, a work which will make Rousseau's *Confessions* seem pale in comparison (*COR* 1:14). Here again Baudelaire takes up a stiff challenge, for as Rousseau clearly states, his is "an undertaking for which there is no precedent and which, in its execution, will know no imitators" (1:9). Three months later, Baudelaire is still nurturing this ambition and speaks again to his mother of the project, which he describes as "a great book about myself, my *Confessions*" (2:182). As Claude Pichois has pointed out, then, Baudelaire's project is defined as "a response to Jean-Jacques's *Confessions*" (*OC* 1:1471), as well as in terms of its difference from the earlier work. This, in its turn, plays upon Rousseau's own conception of himself as different from all other mortals: "I alone. I feel my own heart and I know men. I am unlike any of those I have met; I dare believe, indeed, that I am unlike any other living man. If I am no better, then I am at least other."

In Baudelaire's case, as in that of Rousseau, it is clear that the difference of the work seeks /serves to confirm the difference of the self. What is interesting is that the prose poetry enterprise is defined in ways remarkable for their similarity to the autobiographical project.

> It was in leafing through, for at least the twentieth time, Aloysius
> Bertrand's famous *Gaspard de la Nuit* [. . .] that I had the idea of
> attempting something similar and applying to the description of
> modern life, or rather of *a* modern and more abstract life, the
> procedure he had applied to the depiction of ancient life, which
> is so strangely picturesque. (Baudelaire 1991, 30)

In the conception of the prose poetry project, the "model" is acknowledged only to be challenged. Baudelaire's *Confessions* are, for example, to constitute "a unique book" (*COR* 2: 141), "something quite different from Jean-Jacques's famous *Confessions*" (2:302). The prose poems, likewise, "will remain very far from my mysterious and brilliant model," and will be "something singularly different" (*OC* 1:276).[5] In both cases, however, he will seek to inscribe in his writing the experience of "a particular modern life" and "an abstract life," in other words, a life that is in some way reasoned. In both cases, Baudelaire sets out to write something which ties writing to being—the writing of the self and the self as writer—in which he will distinguish himself from the Other while defining the self in relation to that Other.

Far from engaging in the act of confession in the *Journaux intimes*, Baudelaire speaks incessantly of others in order to demonstrate his difference: "I want constantly to make it clear what a stranger I feel in relation to the world and to its beliefs" (*COR* 2:305). In the same way, in *Le Spleen de Paris*, the title of which seems to confirm the prevalent spirit of *Mon cœur mis à nu*, the unity and the limits of the self are determined in relation to others. The textual structure that results from this is necessarily fragmentary, since it depends on accidents of thought or on the chance encounters generated by *flânerie*. In an early entry in *Mon cœur mis à nu* Baudelaire underlines the contingent and discontinuous nature of the project: "I can begin *Mon cœur mis à nu*, anywhere, anyhow, and continue with it day by day, following the inspiration and the circumstance of the day, just as long as that inspiration is intense" (*OC* 1:627). It is a journal, then, in the true sense of the word, driven by the logic of approximate chronology, by "a daily frenzy," and by Baudelaire's desire to "date" his anger (1:667). The same circumstantial inspiration, and the same derision, are at work in *Le Spleen de Paris*, for, as Baudelaire explains in a letter to Sainte-Beuve, he hoped to show "a new Joseph Delorme, whose rhapsodic thoughts would follow each and every accident of his *flânerie* and who would draw from each encounter an un-pleasant moral" (*COR* 2:583). The structure of the work is indeed acciden-tal, born of discontinuities, "both head and tail, alternatively and reciprocally." And, as Baudelaire tells us, "we can interrupt wherever we wish" (Baudelaire 1991, 30). The lack of structure is, in both the diary and the prose poems, part of the conception and design of the project; the snakelike tortuous fantasy of the prose poems is a mirror for the *journal intime,* itself described as "a great monster dealing with everything" (*COR* 2:443).

For Béatrice Didier, however, this is the very antithesis of a *journal intime,* a form which "responds to a search for unity, to a fear of dissipation" (1991, 116). How can Baudelaire seek, then, to write a great work about him-self or to describe "*a more modern and abstract life*" without placing the self at the center of the enterprise? For this self is difficult to discern among all the people who feature in the space of the apparently private text: woman, Girardin, the Légion d'honneur, the Dandy, imbeciles (including Clément de Ris and Castagnary), magistrates, civil servants, newspaper directors and the literary riffraff ("la canaille littéraire"), Durandeau, Mathieu, Nacquart, George Sand, Voltaire, Molière, Renan, Feydeau, Octave Feuillet, Scholl, Nadar. The list goes on and includes both the crowd and the elite. Similarly, the prose poems stage the spectacle of contemporary life, and it would be possible to draw up a list of ideas and individuals representing a similar cross-section to the one cited above: literary figures, madmen, loathsome concubines, magnificent imbeciles, priests, children, dogs, moralists, and medical men. Indeed, the poet himself comes close to constructing such a list in the first part of the prose poem "A une heure du matin." As he comes into contact with all these types, themselves representative of ideas and opposi-tions, a wide range of themes begins to take shape in the "diaries:" theology, God, Progress, the vote, the death penalty, slavery, nineteenth-century cus-toms, torture, pleasure, love and misunderstanding, commerce, music, the-atre, intoxication, and beauty. All of these are important contemporary themes and present significant philosophical questions; all of them are also Baudelairean preoccupations. But, then, as he says in perhaps the most quot-ed entry of all in *Hygiène:* "In order to find subjects *Know Thyself . . .* (A list of my tastes)" (*OC* 1:670). The self can, in other words, reveal itself by what Baudelaire says are "his opinions on" (1:682) or "what he thinks of" (1:684) any given question, thing, or person—and this despite Baudelaire's avowed lack of conviction, or rather determined by what he describes as "a few convictions in a loftier sense, and which are beyond the comprehension of my contemporaries" (1:680).

In order to give a sense of this more modern and more abstract life, it will not, then, be enough to offer an account of the private self. This self must be portrayed in its encounters with others, with other selves; it must externalize itself and confront the outside world.[6] This confrontation is clearly staged in "L'Etranger," a poem that reminds us of Baudelaire's conviction of being "étranger au monde et à ses cultes." It is a poem that emphasizes alterity and solitude, that opposes two selves which contest a territory that one might call a "patrie morale." The stranger is "extraordinary," incomprehensible, other, but the way in which he responds to his interlocutor demonstrates that he understands perfectly well the context and discourse of the other. But, he refuses both of these and locates his own values in an intangible elsewhere. This encounter with the other affirms the alterity of the "I," but it is a productive and creative alterity for as long as the poet can ensure his mastery of it. As Baudelaire makes clear in "Les Foules," such mastery of the other is an art. The poet "enters, when he so desires, into the character of each individual" (Baudelaire 1991, 44), and yet is always aware of his own individuality, for this intoxicating "universal communion" is also "singulière."[7] Unlike "the selfish man, who is as tightly sealed as a strong box, or the lazy man, who is as self-contained as a mollusk," the poet knows how to exploit the other without jeopardizing his self; he even constrains the crowd by imposing that self upon it: "For him alone, everything is vacant; and if certain places appear to be closed to him, that is because in his eyes they are not worth the bother of visiting" (*OC* 1:291). He seeks out excitement and inspiration in the external events and individuals. This is, in Hegelian terms, antilyrical since the lyrical poet must constitute a subjective and circumscribed world, enclosed in the inner self. Baudelaire's poet of "Les Foules," however, has, on the contrary, "a taste for disguise and masks, a hatred of home life, and a passion for travel." A similar entry in *Mon cœur mis à nu* testifies to the same affliction: "The Sickness of the horror of home life" (1:689).

Like all journeys, however, this voyage beyond the self is not without its dangers. From the privileged position of observer, the "moi" of the prose poems, who is almost always a poet, refracts, through the prism of his consciousness, that which Baudelaire refers to in *Fusées* as "the multiplication of numbers" (1:649). This proliferation of others is intoxicating; Baudelaire describes it as "religious" or "pantheistic." The self is at once subsumed in the proliferation of others and yet is capable of somehow imprinting itself upon that mass of otherness: "I am everybody. Everybody is me. Vortex" (1:651). Caught up in this eddying frenzy, the poet is transported by the crowd, carried along in a rapid and irresistible movement, as in "Le Vieux Saltimbanque." Rather than constraining himself by a technique which would restrict his desires (the insatiability of the other, or "non-moi") by imposing what Baudelaire might call "la concentration du moi," the poet runs the risk of "vaporization." This can be seen in "Le *Confiteor* de l'artiste," where "in the grandeur of reverie, the sense of self soon fades" (Baudelaire 1991, 33), or in *Le Poème du hachisch:*

> It sometimes happens that the personality disappears complete-
> ly and that objectivity, which is the characteristic of pantheist
> poets, develops within you so abnormally that the contempla-
> tion of external objects makes you forget your own existence,
> and soon you merge with them completely. (*OC* 1:419)

In "A une heure du matin," this "vaporization" is more negatively experienced as a form of contamination. The poet feels the need to impose a solitude which he has been unable to maintain in the crowd, and this he does by barricading himself into his room and double-locking the door. The recapitulation of the day's events is revealing. In this prose poem, we are confronted with a genuine *journal intime,* a diary of events of a kind not to be found anywhere else in Baudelaire's writings. The encounters of the day are listed and each exchange cataloged and contested by a poet-diarist who is striving to recover his sense of self through a self-ironizing perspective on the events. The contours of that self become blurred, however, by a hypocrisy and perverseness which progressively undermine the difference between the self and the others.

> Let's recapitulate the day's events: saw several men of letters [...];
> argued generously with the editor of a review [...]; greeted
> twenty-odd people, fifteen of whom were unknown to me; dis-
> tributed an equal proportion of handshakes and did so without
> taking the precaution of buying gloves; to kill time during a

shower went up to see a female mountebank [...]; paid court to a theatre director [...]; boasted (why?) about several scurrilous acts I've never committed and pusillanimously denied several other misdeeds I performed with joy, delight in boasting, crimes against human dignity; refused to do a friend an easy service and gave a written recommendation to a complete ass: oof? is that the lot? (Baudelaire 1991, 41)

This passage from the prose poem, more akin to a diary than any passage in the *Journaux intimes,* expresses the fear of dissolution of the self and poses writing (whether it be in the form of such a recapitulation or of the later prayer for poetic inspiration) as the only solution. Baudelaire here has recourse to a form of immurement and introspection common to diarists, for such immurement in the home, in the room where the diary (or poetry) is written, becomes, as Didier points out "a reflection of the enclosed space in which the soul is inscribed" (1991, 124). This self-confession enables the poet to escape the indeterminate in order to exist in and by writing. In "A une heure du matin," the status of the narrative-lyrical-autobiographical voice remains fundamentally ambiguous. The "I" is an indecipherable mix of autobiography and fiction, referring simultaneously and indissociably both to a historical, biographical figure, to the poet as person, and to a figure that is entirely constructed, or fictive—a figure of the poet become character in an allegorical fiction of poetic creativity.

The concentration ("la centralisation") of the self and the mastery of the Other which are explicit in "Les Foules" might appear to be in complete opposition to the vortex and the vaporization expressed in "A une heure du matin." In fact, the two poems are representative of a bipolar creative tension which itself expresses the paradox of a self that is unable to come to terms with itself in either multitude or solitude and is realizable only in the conjunction of the two, in interdependence. This interdependence is a metaphor for writing, for a particular way of writing the self which is reminiscent of Baudelaire's notion of modernist "art pur": "a suggestive magic containing both subject and object, the world beyond the artist and the artist himself" (*OC* 2:598).[8]

The dynamics of the exchange between subject and object are reproduced in the very act of writing, since the writing subject must strive to impose some distance between himself and the object, to offer an intellectual appraisal, while the object (and the self as object) is the refuge of sensitivity and passion. This distinction has been made by Crépet and Blin with respect to the different sections of the *Journaux intimes,* but it is a distinction that could equally be applied to the internal shifts of *Le Spleen de Paris:*

> In *Mon cœur mis à nu,* Baudelaire gives free rein to violence, coarseness, personal attacks, cries of hatred and despair, and the appetite for revenge, while in *Fusées,* however disenchanted and world-weary the author appears to be, he remains a psychologist and an artist, a moralist and a man of wit. In short, he stands back from himself and, more often than not, expresses himself in a more "detached" way. [. . .] Over all, the same change of register is discernible between *Fusées* and *Mon cœur mis à nu,* a change from sadness to anger, from pessimism to bitterness, from complaint to rage, and from casual sarcasm to insult.
> (Cited by Pichois, *OC* 1:1378)

Pure introspection, religious or lyrical mediations, a chronicle of encounters and relations with the other ("le non-moi"), political or polemical *fusées,* the *Journaux intimes,* like the prose poems, reveal the poet's modes of being and his methods of writing the self, affirming as well a form of *intimus* which seemed to be lacking. In sketching out just a few ways in which the prose poetry project connects with the *Journaux intimes,* this essay has sought to demonstrate that all the encounters of such writing are organized in relation to an ever-present "Je," which consistently underscores that the texts, the characters, and the ideas exist only in their relation to the self of the writer. Despite the fact, then, that these texts are structured around the fragmentary and around multiplicity, that they are born of kaleidoscopic proliferation,[9] or "the junction of innumerable connections," they are nevertheless unified to some degree by the fact that the kaleidoscope is "endowed with consciousness," the consciousness of the perceiving subject. It is in this way that the entries in the *Journaux intimes* and the prose poems, however disparate and fragmented they may seem, find a sort of unity. It is a unity which can exist in even the most fragmented of genres, since it relates to the very act of writing and what it means to write.[10] There is, then, a unity on two distinct levels. First, the coherence of the two works is assured, even in what Didier has called "an aesthetics of the discontinuous" (1991, 58) by the dominant (if not always explicit) concerns about the writing enterprise. Secondly, the encounters with the other are paradigmatic of the relationship between the writing self and external reality, but it is an external reality which is important only inasmuch as it focuses on self-knowledge (and the way in which that is translated into "singular" works). As Baudelaire makes clear in "Les Fenêtres," "What does external reality matter, if it has helped me to live, to feel that I am and what I am?" (Baudelaire 1991, 87). The others that pass through the prose poetry or the *Journaux intimes,* the figures that define the emotions and attitudes of the poetic subject, are but fleeting simulacra of the first person and of its relation to itself and to writing.

PART IV

Reformulations

Modernity's Curse

Susan Blood

MODERN art, according to a longstanding school of thought, is autonomous art. It no longer serves an end beyond itself, whether political, religious, or ethical. Its privileged subject matter is itself; it reflects upon its own processes. Modern art is original, not imitative, it is not anonymous, but bears the mark of an individual signature. Baudelaire's poetry is often cited as exemplary of this type of modern art.

Critics who have contributed to the theory of aesthetic autonomy frequently call attention to another characteristic of modern art—those who practice it are not happy. According to Roland Barthes, Voltaire was the last of the happy writers, which is another way of saying that Voltaire was not modern. Rousseau, the "anti-Voltaire," was the first unhappy writer, "the first to write with *ennui*" (to cite Maurice Blanchot),[1] and in this sense truly modern. Blanchot does not see Rousseau's persecution complex and his paradoxical conception of writing as mere indications of madness or moral insufficiency. Rousseau's unhappiness is deeply implicated in the modernist adventure: "I have always suspected that we owe literature itself to his profound and elusive character flaw. Rousseau helps literature come into its own by freeing itself from antique conventions and acquiring a new integrity" (Blanchot 1959, 63–64).

By the mid-nineteenth century, the unhappiness of certain writers is no longer considered an incidental feature of the literary vocation. Poetry, in particular, is understood to be an accursed practice. Verlaine's anthology of *Les Poètes maudits* (1884) attests to this heightened awareness. It is fair to say that Baudelaire is responsible for giving the curse on poets a theoretical resonance, and that with his 1852 essay on Edgar Allan Poe he crystallizes the concept with his treatment of the term *guignon*. *Guignon* refers to bad luck, either in life or in games of chance, and as such gives the notion of the curse an aura of triviality, which I will discuss later. Baudelaire mentions Rousseau elliptically in his list of persecuted writers, and adds Hoffmann, Balzac, and, of course, Poe to their number. Baudelaire's own poem "Le Guignon" dates from the same period as the essay (1849–51), thus inviting the supposition that he applied the portrait of the unhappy writer to himself.

The period during which Baudelaire was elaborating his theory of *guignon* is worthy of remark.[2] It roughly coincides with the national crisis that took France from the 1848 Revolution to the coup d'état of Louis-Napoléon in 1851. Ross Chambers and Dolf Oehler, among other critics, have pointed to this period as a time of trauma, and have argued that the modernist aesthetic originates with this experience.[3] The argument has the advantage of explaining the troubling fact that in 1846 Baudelaire denied the existence of *guignon* in his *Conseils aux jeunes littérateurs*. We could assume that Baudelaire's reversal of position corresponds to the experience of political trauma, and that the *poète maudit* may be nothing more than the traumatized subject par excellence. As seductive as this hypothesis appears, I am not going to pursue it here, and for two reasons: First, if literary modernism originates in trauma, the trauma had already begun with Rousseau, and its specific connection to the 1848–51 period therefore needs to be rethought. Second, despite Baudelaire's apparent change of position on the topic of *guignon,* there are interesting points of analogy between the 1846 essay and the later poem. For the rest of this essay, I would like to examine these analogies and define how they contribute to a particular theory of human agency.

Baudelaire's *Conseils aux jeunes littérateurs* offers a volatile blend of economic and ethical advice. The combination is traditionally bourgeois, suffused with an optimism and eclecticism that are alien to high modernism. The essay begins with Baudelaire's insistence that he wishes to be helpful to his younger colleagues. He consistently treats literary activity as a practical profession, not as a vocation, and the values he advocates are the bourgeois virtues of utility and civility. There is no trauma here. The mistakes Baudelaire claims to have made—"a certain sum of blunders"—have all been absorbed and transformed into wisdom—"the fruit of experience" (*OC* 2:13). It is in the name of this wisdom that Baudelaire denies the reality of *guignon.* "Those who say 'I have *guignon*' are those who have not yet had enough success and who are unaware of this fact" (13). There is no ontological issue at stake in the difference between success and failure. The failed writer is neither untalented nor cursed, nor even unsuccessful. The failed writer simply has not had *enough* success. As Baudelaire presents it, success is an economic concept—it marks the border between intrinsic and market value, the point at which quality can be translated without apparent difficulty into quantitative terms. There is no sense that intrinsic and market value are fundamentally at odds with one another. The implication seems to be that a failed writer could become a success by accumulating success, much as a poor person could become rich by accumulating wealth.[4]

The complexity in Baudelaire's argument comes when he tries to explain *how* a failed writer might go about accumulating success. After reassuring his reader that such accumulation is possible, he reveals a terrible, hard truth: "If you have *guignon,* it is because you are lacking something" (*OC* 2:14). The statement is shocking because we have been led to believe that anyone could become a successful writer, that no intrinsic limitations lie in the way of success. Now Baudelaire seems to be advocating the harshest of positions—to paraphrase: if you fail, it is because you deserve to, and you aren't even allowed the grace of believing that you might simply have bad luck. This scenario seems to suggest, contrary to what Baudelaire has just claimed, that success and failure are nothing but measures of intrinsic value, that the failed writer is deficient in some way and could never, therefore, become successful. Curiously, however, this is not the conclusion that Baudelaire draws. The failed writer is lacking in some [objective] quality, but this is no excuse for giving up the literary enterprise. Here is where Baudelaire's ethics intervenes, with a twist. He advises young writers to study what they are lacking, not in order to improve the quality of their writing, but to determine how best to sell themselves. Baudelaire's argument on this point is surprisingly complicated, and I would like to analyze its contours in detail.

First, Baudelaire concedes that all humans are victims of circumstance, and that no one is simply an infinitely free agent: "I take into account the fact that the human will is enveloped in a thousand circumstances, all of which have their legitimate causes; they are the circumference in which the will is confined" (2:14). This is the sop he gives to writers who feel they are laboring under a curse. Human will is limited by an envelope of circumstances. But these circumstances cannot completely paralyze human agency, because they are both too numerous and too unstable: "this circumference is moving, living, whirling, and changes its circle and its center every day, minute, and second. As they are thus swept along, all human wills cloistered within this circumference vary their interplay each instant, and that is what constitutes freedom" (2:14). Freedom, thus defined, is a function of the indeterminate relationship, or "play" (Baudelaire uses the expression "jeu réciproque"), that exists between the human will and circumstances. Such free play is possible because the circumstances, as I have mentioned, are manifold, and also because they are not only objective in nature. They are composed partly of objective things and partly of "all human wills." The individual human will is circumscribed by other human wills, which themselves are more or less reified or free. This intersubjective reality both acts upon the individual will and may be acted upon by it.[5]

Baudelaire's emphasis on the intersubjective tissue that may be taken for an objective limitation enables him to claim that there is no essential distinction between freedom and fate: "Freedom and fate are two opposites; seen up close and from a distance, it is a single will."[6] By looking at circumstances from the right perspective, one will see in them the trace of a free will, which may be nothing other than a point of equilibrium of many human wills. The individual who believes in *guignon* treats as reified this point of equilibrium which in fact is quite mobile: "That is why there is no such thing as *guignon*. If you have *guignon,* it is because you are lacking something: get to know this something and study the interplay of neighboring wills in order to displace them more easily" [pour déplacer plus facilement la circonférence]. Young writers will be able to sell themselves if they learn how to "play" an *objective* failing into an *intersubjective* success. Writing, understood as a category of human action, thus is given a double valence—it involves both work and play, production and promotion, self and other. A single act of writing can therefore succeed and fail simultaneously. This involves more than the banal possibility that a bad work can be a commercial success. Baudelaire is hinting at a deeper entwining of success and failure, in which one becomes the other.

My contention is that the poem "Le Guignon" can be read as such an act of writing, and that, seen from the right perspective, it does not contradict, but illustrates the earlier essay. Critics have often quarreled over the unity of the poem, a fact which may be symptomatic of its "double valence."

While the poem's title clearly asserts the existence of *guignon,* the poem it-self gives no clear clue as to what *guignon* might be. Critical discussions have revolved around whether *guignon* is an individual or a universal problem: is Baudelaire claiming that he alone is cursed, or is the curse in some sense basic to the human condition? There are other points of apparent contra-diction, or disjunction, that could be mentioned in addition to this: does the poet's *guignon* result in a failure to write, or in a failure to find an apprecia-tive audience? Is *guignon* an objective or a subjective problem? Does it relate to work or play, production or promotion, self or other? The poem seems to change its answer to these questions, most markedly in the passage from the quatrains to the tercets. The "turn" of the Petrarchan sonnet appears here as a radical shift of focus, one which I suggest corresponds to the kind of liter-ary strategy Baudelaire outlines in *Conseils aux jeunes littérateurs.* To see how this strategy works, I would like to examine the poem more closely.

> *Le Guignon*
>
> Pour soulever un poids si lourd,
> Sisyphe, il faudrait ton courage!
> Bien qu'on ait du cœur à l'ouvrage,
> L'Art est long et le Temps est court.
>
> Loin des sépultures célèbres,
> Vers un cimetière isolé,
> Mon cœur comme un tambour voilé,
> Va battant des marches funèbres.
>
> ⎯⎯ Maint joyau dort enseveli
> Dans les ténèbres et l'oubli,
> Bien loin des pioches et des sondes;
>
> Mainte fleur épanche à regret
> Son parfum doux comme un secret
> Dans les solitudes profondes. (*OC* 1:17)

[To lift up such a heavy weight, / Sisyphus, would take your courage. / Although our hearts are up to the task, / Art is long and Time is short. // Far from the famed burial-places, /

Towards an isolated cemetery / My heart, like a muffled drum, /
Goes beating funeral marches. // Many a gem sleeps buried / In
darkness and oblivion / Far from pickaxes and plummets; //
Many a flower releases with regret / Its perfume sweet as a secret /
In deep solitudes.]

It is common knowledge that "Le Guignon" is composed, almost exclusively, of borrowed text. With the exception of the first two lines, the quatrains
are a translated fragment from Henry Wadsworth Longfellow's "A Psalm of
Life" (1839).[7] The tercets of "Le Guignon" come from Thomas Gray's *Elegy
Written in a Country Churchyard* (1751). Clearly, as many critics have com-
mented, this piecemeal composition places the aesthetic unity of
Baudelaire's poem in question. Even more peculiar, however, is the fact that
a poem which presents itself as emblematic of the modern poet's predicament should be so unabashedly unoriginal. Baudelaire confesses having pla-
giarized in other poems of *Les Fleurs du Mal,* but, since there is not space
here to argue the point, let me simply assert that his borrowings in "Le
Guignon" are unique—they are much closer to the original text, much
more extensive, and contribute much more to the "message" of the poem as
a whole. Baudelaire seems to feel no need to struggle with these predeces-
sors, or at least his struggle leaves no trace of anxiety. This is all the more remarkable in a poet who defended himself in terms of an imperative for
self-distinction (how not to be Lamartine, Hugo, Musset, etc).

The only original lines of "Le Guignon" are an apostrophe to Sisyphus:
"Pour soulever un poids si lourd, /Sisyphe, il faudrait ton courage!" This first
statement of the poet's curse is already fraught with uncertainty. The "poids
si lourd" is never clearly defined. It seems to locate *guignon* in the realm of
objective reality, in something external to the subject who is crushed by its
weight. But in the declaration "Sisyphe, il faudrait ton courage!" we can also
read a subjective predicament, the admission of a failure of will. Baudelaire's
words, "if you have *guignon,* it is because you are lacking something," remain
an appropriate commentary on the situation. It is important that Sisyphus
should stand as an emblem of human freedom, as the figure who lies outside
the poem's presentation of *guignon.* The myth of Sisyphus is, after all, one of
the fundamental myths of cursed humanity. But Baudelaire seizes the figure
of Sisyphus in his freedom, from a point of view that enables freedom and
fate to be perceived together—that is, from a point of view where *guignon*

disappears as a meaningful concept. The acts of Sisyphus are thus conceived as both successes and failures, as having the "double valence" I have tried to define in Baudelaire's *Conseils*.

By turning away from Sisyphus, the poet is admitting to a failure of will. It is at this point that the borrowing from Longfellow begins: "Bien qu'on ait du cœur à l'ouvrage, / L'Art est long et le Temps est court." Longfellow's poem reads as follows:

> Art is long, and Time is fleeting,
> And our hearts, though stout and brave,
> Still, like muffled drums, are beating
> Funeral marches to the grave.

I would like to make two observations here. First, the opening of Baudelaire's citation of Longfellow, "Bien qu'on ait du cœur à l'ouvrage," directly contradicts what the poet has just told us, that he is lacking Sisyphus's courage. Second, Baudelaire inverts the order of Longfellow's lines, telling us first that he is stout-hearted, and second that it makes no difference, since Art is long and Time is fleeting. Both these details contribute to a lightening, even a trivializing, of the poem's tone. The admission of failure is quickly denied and then put down to a fatality inscribed in the order of things. When Longfellow says, "Art is long, and Time is fleeting," the tone is sadly serious. When Baudelaire says, "L'Art est long et le Temps est court," one has the impression that he is happy to have found a good excuse for himself. Longfellow's citation of Hippocrates's aphorism, "Vita brevis, ars longa," sounds like the statement of a marmorial truth; Baudelaire's citation of Longfellow has an automatic quality, as though he were repeating a lesson he had memorized without fully understanding it. In summation, the turn to Longfellow constitutes a lightening of the poet's burden, it represents a first lifting of the "poids si lourd" of individual responsibility.

At this stage, the poet's problem still appears to be that he cannot work, that there is not enough Time in the world to bring to fruition some ambitious aesthetic idea. In the next turn of "Le Guignon," however, even this burden is lifted. The poem suddenly abounds in the representation of aesthetic objects, jewels and flowers, as Baudelaire turns from Longfellow to Gray. The lines borrowed from Gray's *Elegy* are the following:

Full many a gem of purest ray serene
The dark unfathomed caves of ocean bear.
Full many a flower is born to blush unseen,
And waste its sweetness on the desert air.

In Gray's poem, of course, the jewels and flowers do not represent works of art. They stand, instead, for beautiful souls who die without being able to realize the work that is in them. But Gray's symbolism is unsteady, and the failure to find recognition is fused with the failure to realize one's life's work. My contention is that Baudelaire exploited this unsteadiness, and that in his poem the jewels and flowers appear under a double aegis: they symbolize both the success of the work and the failure to be recognized. To the extent that they proclaim failure, they proclaim it happily. Jean-Pierre Richard went so far as to claim that the "magical" tercets of "Le Guignon" show us definitively "a happy Baudelaire" (1955, 95). The regret that Baudelaire adds to Gray's sweet flower—"Mainte fleur épanche à regret / Son parfum doux comme un secret"—is not simply a sign of unhappiness; it indicates as well an excess of riches, an aesthetic superabundance.

How, then, are we finally to interpret the poet's *guignon*? I would like to filter the preceding reading through comments that Jean-Paul Sartre makes in *Qu'est-ce que la littérature?* concerning aesthetic autonomy and literary engagement. Sartre's basic contention is that poetry cannot be engaged because poetic language is not instrumental. He devotes the first chapter of his book to an elaboration of the poetry/prose distinction, claiming for poetry the autonomous characteristics that I have associated with modernism. The privileged relationship between poetry (since the nineteenth century) and modernism has frequently been noted,[8] and Sartre is following this convention. But he feels compelled to nuance conventional wisdom in a footnote devoted to the concept of *guignon*. In the footnote Sartre argues, as I have, that modern poetry is defined by its accursed character, which he takes to be an affirmation of failure. The affirmation of failure can be thought of as a kind of aesthetic formalism, since human action is thereby deprived of its transitive, instrumental quality: "failure alone, by arresting like a screen the infinite series of [man's] projects, returns him to himself in his purity" (1948, 42). The failed individual enjoys a kind of pure self-presence, appearing as in a photographic still. For Sartre, this stillness is mythic. Hector and Achilles, for example, are mythic figures because their battle arrests the forward-moving action of the Trojan War, transforming it into "stunt or dance" (1948, 41). Up to this point, Sartre's analysis of *guignon* seems consistent with the theory of aesthetic autonomy.

In further elaboration, however, Sartre's treatment of *guignon* breaks with the conventional theory by marking a kind of minimalist engagement of poetry with the world. This engagement is of nineteenth-century vintage and involves a certain breakdown of the poetry/prose distinction: "With the advent of bourgeois society, the poet joins forces with the prose writer to declare that society intolerable" (41). The poet's critical commentary on society takes a particular form—poetry engages with the world as a mode of resistance in which the poet's actions are turned against themselves.[9] This self-reflexive, self-negating impulse is not simply autonomous, since its goal lies outside itself. That goal is to reveal the self-destructing character of human action on the largest of scales. Sartre explains this minimalist engagement in the following terms: "[The poet] is the man who pledges to lose" (43).

In Sartre's analysis (and here he is not far from Baudelaire's *Conseils*), the failure of poetry is also its success, since it involves a paradoxical appropriation of the world. When language fails to serve as an instrument for some world-oriented goal, then the world makes itself felt with a singular intensity. "When instruments are broken and obsolete, when plans are undone and efforts are useless, then the world appears with a terrible, infantile freshness—without supports, without roads. It has the maximum of reality because it is crushing for man; and, just as [successful] action generalizes, defeat returns things to their individual reality" (42). The nameless, crushing weight of the world is not without analogy to the opening line of Baudelaire's "Le Guignon." Although there is no way of proving such a contention, I would even argue that Sartre has Baudelaire's poem in mind. Just as Baudelaire's sonnet turns Sisyphus's burden into an aesthetic flowering, Sartre's reasoning transforms the weight of the world into a birth of poetry: "poetic language," he writes, "arises from the ruins of prose" (42). The failure of instrumental language, which at first seemed to put poetry at risk, ultimately leads to a sublime affirmation of poetry. The world attains a "maximum of reality" as it becomes the instrument of this affirmation.[10]

The coincidence of failure and success in the poetic project as Sartre outlines it here involves more than a conflicting relationship between life and art. Sartre's poet is not the clichéd *poète maudit*, who fails in life but succeeds in the art of poetry. In the clichéd view, artistic success offers a compensation or a consolation for the failures of life. What Sartre suggests, however, is that poetry *itself* is threatened with failure, that its success is wrested from its own failure, and that its character is not merely compensatory. This is consistent with Baudelaire's treatment of the poetic curse in "Le Guignon": "L'Art est long et le Temps est court" implies that art may never take place. Such a critical situation defines the condition of modern poetry, but in Sartre's argument it goes a step further to bear witness to the human condition at large:

> [The poet] is convinced that all human activity is a failure and manages to fail in his own life in order to bear witness, through his singular defeat, to human defeat in general. He thus challenges [human activity] . . . which the prose writer does as well. But the challenge of prose is made in the name of some greater success, while that of poetry upholds the defeat that all victory conceals. (43)

The slippages that mark Baudelaire's poem, between poet and poetry, individual and collective destiny, are all present in Sartre's analysis. This presents problems for the historical scenario, in that modern poetry attests to the most universal (and therefore historical) of concerns. The critical energy of modern poetry is finally brought to bear upon all of human action, and not merely upon the exploits of nineteenth-century capitalism. All of human action is presented as having two sides, as concealing defeat within victory, failure within success. From this standpoint, the struggle between Hector and Achilles does not simply arrest the action of the Trojan War but reveals the twofold nature of that action—Achilles's military victory is also his moral defeat, his sublime *agon* with Hector contains the shadow of his absurd death by Paris's arrow. This is *guignon* in a heroic mode, and it ultimately coincides with the intuition of modernism. The courage of Sisyphus in Baudelaire's "Le Guignon" is similarly sublime and ridiculous. Perhaps this is how we should understand Walter Benjamin's puzzling statement in reference to Baudelaire: "The hero is the true subject of modernism."[11]

(S)(m)othering Baudelaire

Margaret Miner

> My dear mother, if you really possess maternal genius and if
> you're not yet worn out, come to Paris. . . . You don't read my
> letters attentively enough. . . . Your letters contain numerous er-
> rors and false ideas. . . . There was in my childhood a time when
> I loved you passionately; listen and read without fear. I've never
> told you this much about it before. . . . Oh! do read me attentive-
> ly, try hard to understand.
> —Letter to Madame Aupick, 6 May 1861 (*COR* 2:150)

Justly famous, this letter from Baudelaire to his mother is best known as a
moment of revelation, a lyrical confession of the poet's childhood adoration
for his mother and his lasting dismay at the rifts that later widened between
them. One senses that the strain of producing this particular piece of confessional lyricism was extraordinarily high: even more than other missives
Baudelaire sent to Madame Aupick over the years, this one amplifies the
eloquence of abjection in the jagged rhythm of its distressful sincerity and
its tender, practiced, blackmailing emotionalism. But this letter might lay
claim to another kind of celebrity as well, for in the cracks between its suicide threats, its nostalgic reminiscences, and its winding requests for money,
it clings to an unexpectedly direct and sustained inquiry: how should
Baudelaire's mother read what her son has written? In its immediate context, this formulation of the question is perhaps too broad; the 6 May letter
suggests that Baudelaire was especially worried about how his mother was
interpreting their recent correspondence and less concerned, possibly,
about how she had read his other, published writing. Yet the letter also

alludes to Madame Aupick's inattentive ignorance regarding Baudelaire's literary reputation and her fearful, uncritical submission to a priest in Honfleur who felt that *Les Fleurs du Mal*—the second edition of which had appeared only three months earlier—should be burned.[1] And the pleading, accusing insistence with which Baudelaire interrogates his mother about her reading—its timid incompetence, its urgent necessity, its uncertain ties to "maternal genius"—ultimately gives rise to larger questions. Not just how should Baudelaire's mother read his work? But rather how should any mother read Baudelaire's work? How is Baudelaire's writing open to maternal reading?

Baudelaire criticism has frequently edged around these questions. Not that critical work on Baudelaire has avoided focusing on mothers: from Jean-Paul Sartre's declaration that Baudelaire "thinks of himself as *son by divine right*" through Claude Pichois's analysis of Baudelaire's own "creative difficulty" and on beyond Barbara Johnson's claim that "the drama of separation/individuation from the mother . . . can be seen as *the* topic of Baudelaire's poetry," motherhood has been a perennial source of debate within Baudelaire studies.[2] The mothers thus considered have been variously characterized (profaned, desired, devoted, widowed) and distributed over a variety of registers (literal, autobiographical, mythological, metaphorical), but they have all been at least partly constituted from wisps and shadows and slivers of maternity represented in Baudelaire's writing. Just as images of Madame Aupick have been pieced together from her son's morselized responses to her uncollected letters, other Baudelairean mothers have been assembled from fleeting, distorted representations and fitted into odd-shaped spaces apparently reserved for them in Baudelaire's writing.[3] It is as if Baudelaire criticism, although not always an obedient child of the modernist commitment to the coherent wholeness of its subject, has nonetheless hoped for a smooth path into that subject's preoccupation with motherhood, so as to learn more easily to walk over the shards that always roughen the way toward origins. The present study partly shares that hope, but it also assumes that loose fragments can help to break as well as cause a fall. To recover (from) the splintering maternity with which readers of Baudelaire are threatened ("You don't read my letters attentively enough . . . Oh! do read me attentively, try hard to understand"), it clutches at a snippet of *Richard Wagner et Tannhäuser à Paris* and several bits of *Le Spleen de Paris,* piecing together the mother-child relation between poetry and criticism that emerges along the uneven edges where these fragments meet. Thus cushioned against a full-length fall into the general puzzle of motherhood, the following pages take a deliberately piecemeal, peekaboo approach to something enormous and vital that, in Baudelaire's work as perhaps everywhere else, eludes fully coherent representation.

A few days before Baudelaire wrote his confessional letter to Madame Aupick, the publisher Dentu brought out an expanded edition of Baudelaire's essay on Richard Wagner; a month earlier, Baudelaire had sent his mother the first serialized version of the essay, begging her to return it as soon as possible for corrections. Unaltered by either maternal reading or editorial revisions, however, is a passage in which Baudelaire suddenly interrupts his main argument so as to assert that criticism must always follow after art. He makes this point three times in less than a page, with rising emphasis. The first formulation, already grandiloquent, evokes the process that turns an artist into a critic, an unavoidable transformation that may or may not also be a self-transformation: "It would be a completely new event in the history of the arts for a critic to turn into a poet, a reversal of every psychic law, a monstrosity; on the contrary, all great poets naturally, inevitably become critics" (*OC* 2:793). The second formulation, more succinctly hyperbolic, nuances its representation of the transformative process: "It would be miraculous for a critic to become [devînt] a poet, and it is impossible for a poet not to contain [ne contienne pas] a critic." Predictably subject to the so-called natural laws governing both history and the psyche in Baudelaire's first assertion, the poet in this second statement is subjected to a stranger kind of imperative. Here, *devenir* becomes *contenir* in midsentence, and in the hollow thus formed between two propositions there grows something like a critical embryo. Pregnant by and with rhetoric, the "great poet" eventually gives birth to the little critic. And this happens on a world-historical scale in Baudelaire's third formulation, given over to delusions of phylogenetic grandeur: "Poetry existed, affirmed its presence first, and it engendered the study of rules. Such is the uncontested history of human work."

It would be easy to exaggerate the profundity of this passage from *la grandeur poétique* to *la grossesse critique,* not least because of its context in *Richard Wagner:* even the limited reading Baudelaire had done among Wagner's prose works would put any impressionable writer in the mood to play around with metaphors of fertility. Baudelaire's triple-layered evocation of the birth of criticism out of the body of poetry nonetheless complicates the critical reader's position with respect to Baudelaire's poetic mothering. In the middle of the evocation (just after the first stage), one reads that if poets inevitably bear critics, it is in the (presumably elusive) hope of discovering "the obscure laws by virtue of which they have produced [their works]" and hence generating "a series of precepts whose divine goal is infallibility in poetic production." Thus pressured from inside, the half-finished evocation begins at once to raise questions, forward offspring that emerge, Athena-like, straight from the cerebral folds of the essay and ready for critical action. If poets mother critics so as thereafter to produce further generations of poetry, who mothers poets in the first place? That is, where do poets learn to mother? Among others, the famous and ferocious maternal model of "Bénédiction" comes unnervingly to mind. Themselves typically abused in childhood, can Baudelairean poets ever be good enough mothers for critics? How exactly does Baudelaire's poetry mother its critical readers? Does Baudelaire's simultaneously overstated and elliptical formulation of this mother-child relation (poet gives birth first to critic, then to more poetry) imply an incestuous mother-son alliance between poetry and criticism for the conception of a hybrid—something like prose poetry, for example—with the attendant complications of illegitimacy, subalterity, Sophoclean fatality, and psychoanalytic resonance?

To begin considering such questions means first trying to confront some basic implications of the Baudelairean critic's position as child or, more precisely, his position as a male child potentially aligned with the law of poetic production but as yet (forever?) unable to invoke it for himself. Apparently born to serve as a living reflection of "the obscure laws by virtue of which [the poet] has produced [his writing]," a reflection the poet himself systematizes and projects over his future work, the critic would seem to be caught in a sort of pre-Oedipal relation of unstable dependency. Barely separated from the poetic matrix he reflects and is reflected in, the critic would appear to remain abjectly mired in the murky threshold between mother and other, unable to maintain either an objectively distanced or a subjectively self-absorbed perspective. But to the extent that any distinct portrait of the maternal poet is visible from this critical borderline position, it would seem to represent some version of the phallic mother, nurturing the infantile critic in a vaguely stifling embrace while preempting his future authority over the finely delineated precepts of poetic law. One might thus propose to figure the maternal Baudelairean poet less as a mother than as a (s)(m)other, with a proliferation of parentheses preceding the /o / and turning its arrival into an exclamation—O!—of welcome or nonrecognition or both. By layering consonants before the other like baby blankets, one hints at a liminal scene of collusion and disconnection in which both poet-mother and child-critic struggle abjectly both for and against "des lettres en couches."

Among the numerous times and ways such a scene is played out in Baudelaire's writing, one might turn to a small group of prose poems, beginning with "La Corde." It might be said that this prose poem sets out to illustrate the kind of artistic maternity theorized in *Richard Wagner* and arrives at something similar but with provocative twists. Here, the theorist addresses the reader indirectly, his autobiographical narrative contained inside the quotation marks with which another narrator surrounds it. In two of the text's three published versions, the only break in this citational *enceinte* is a four-word interjection ("my friend told me") through which the quoting narrator emerges into the first line, interrupting the quoted speaker almost before he has begun (*OC* 1:328). Since the interruption is long enough to signal the porousness of the boundary between the quoting and the quoted but not to show much else about their connection, it reveals above all the unclearly divided space in which the narrative unfolds. The text is dedicated—also in two of its three versions—to Manet, but the dedication bobs up indeterminately between the two narrators, like a placenta joining them but not clearly belonging to either.

What does become clear is that the storytelling painter, however uncertain the status of his cited *I*, is angling to speak from what might pass for a maternal position. Having befriended a neighborhood waif who works as his model, the painter might appear to position himself as a surrogate father by obtaining permission to substitute his art studio for the boy's grim "paternal hovel" (*OC* 1:329). But what the painter particularly emphasizes is his nurturing attachment to the waif, a maternal bond that deepens throughout a description of their shared studio as a "paradise" flowing with variegated paints and amorphous pleasures. Marvelously pliant in the beginning, the child identifies himself with the desire of the painter to the point of all but dissolving into any number of illusory images—from a little gypsy to a little Jesus— that float from canvas to canvas. But when the growing boy takes a first clumsy, inarticulate stab at independence by stealing sweets, the painter's artfully constructed maternity threatens to collapse under the child's nascent criticism. Unable either to stay nestled in the painter's fluid paradise of image-making or to articulate his separation, the abject child critic writes himself out of his predicament with the sickeningly literal, diacritical exclamation point formed by his dangling corpse. Upon discovering this, the painter obscurely realizes that he is, after all, still smothered (add parentheses as desired) in the child's critical dependence, and he observes with a kind of lexical and grammatical irony that "to *unhang* him [le dépendre] was not as easy a job as you might think" (239, emphasis mine). The painter's cradling gestures, as he continues to evoke the scene, become exaggeratedly maternal: "I had to support it [the body] entirely with one arm, and, with my other hand, cut the rope" (330). Such a dramatically symbolized severing of the umbilical cord does not, of course, disengage the artist: having brought a small critic into the world, however abortively, the painter now moves toward a future scheduled full of masterful artistic production: "It remained only for me to go back to work, even more intensely than usual, so as gradually to chase away that little cadaver who haunted the folds [replis] of my brain, and whose phantom exhausted me with its big, staring eyes" (331).

From blissful mother-child union through unpreventable crisis and on to decisively bereft maternity: in this first revision of the *Richard Wagner* scenario, the Baudelairean artist evolves into a mother who is always critically haunted, hence endlessly productive. One might recall that "maternel" rhymes with "éternel" near the end of "La Servante au grand cœur," which considers the possible return of spirits from beyond the grave. Relevantly, however, the ghost in question there is that of a *substitute* mother, a beloved nursemaid, blended into whose incorporeal substance there may be the spirit of the poet's dead father.[4] In the opening paragraph of "La Corde," where the painter-narrator is already accompanied if not authorized by the phantom of the other narrator, there is yet another phantom in evidence. To frame his story with a meditation on the nature of illusion, the speaker claims that "when the illusion disappears, that is, when we see the being or the event as it exists outside of us, we have a bizarre feeling, complicated partly by regret for the phantom that has disappeared, partly by agreeable surprise with regard to the novelty, the real event" (328). The specific ghost this narrator has in mind to lay is "l'amour maternel," since he feels that the neighbor woman's mercenary reaction to her little son's suicide will be sufficient to dispel any illusion that motherly love is "an obvious, trivial phenomenon, always the same, utterly unmistakable in nature" (328). In the ensuing narrative, however, this illusion is not so much exorcised as it is displaced onto the child's substitute mother: as tender and stifling as ever, "l'amour maternel" migrates to the painter-narrator and pushes him as expeditiously as possible beyond the othering /mothering /smothering of criticism to the precepts of perpetual creativity.

But the undead illusion of maternal love does not take possession of the narrator unaided, without material support. After he finished preparing the little corpse for burial, but before he went back to painting masterpieces, says the narrator, he was puzzled to receive a lot of letters. Arriving from every floor of his building and from every class of society, mixing every style of expression with every level of literacy, these letters all said the same thing, repeating the neighbor woman's request for the supposedly magical rope of her hanged child. The narrator seems to have been disconcerted by this abject barrage, but he does not appear dismayed exactly. His introductory paragraph prefigures his reaction to the letters that would later settle in layers over "that little cadaver who haunted the folds of [his] brain" when it alludes to the feeling of "agreeable surprise with regard to the novelty, the real event" that follows upon the disappearance of an illusion. In fact, the narrator claims he kept all these *lettres en couches,* as if aware that by puzzling over them and piecing them together he symbolically elaborates the critical laws—and guarantees the future production—of his oeuvre. Hesitating before such a narrator, who materializes a dead maternal illusion as a phantom perpetually pregnant with the paternal authority of criticism, one might well quaver with the Baudelaire of *Fusées:* "My mother is fantastic; one must fear her and please her" (*OC* 1:662).

Less frightening but no less fantastic are the supernatural mothers who bustle around in "Les Dons des fées." Terrifically busy organizing "the distribution of gifts among all the newborns [m.pl.] who have come into the world in the last twenty-four hours," these "bizarre Mothers of joy and pain" have to substitute, on top of everything else, for the baby boys' natural mothers, who are presumably still recovering from childbirth (1:305). When the newborns show up with their fathers, the fairies pitch in with a will but without much planning, doling out a random succession of "Gifts," "Faculties," "Lucky Chances," and "Invincible Circumstances" at top speed to whichever infant happens to be next in line. Variously compared to pawnshop clerks, school masters, government ministers, and courtroom judges, the fairies are more preoccupied with public administration than with quality day care, and they wear their maternal responsibilities lightly. The father of one neglected child is thus obliged to grab the nearest fairy "by her dress of many-colored vapors" in order to demand a gift for his little son. In the grand tradition of fairy godmothers, however, this "bizarre Mother" rises to the occasion and thus proves herself to be a great artist. Since all the gifts have already been given, she instantly recalls an obscure rule of supernatural jurisprudence, imagines a new gift—"supplementary and exceptional"—and endows the child on the spot with "the *Gift of Pleasing*" (*OC* 1:307; Baudelaire's emphasis).

Here a difficulty arises in this second, otherwise faithfully illustrated, replay of the critical birth scene from Baudelaire's Wagner essay. Unwilling to grasp that the little crisis has been resolved, the baby's father starts to criticize: "'But pleasing in what way? pleasing . . . ? why pleasing?' stubbornly demanded the little shopkeeper, who was undoubtedly . . . incapable of rising to the logic of the Absurd" (1:307). Herself unwilling to entertain picky questions about her masterpieces, the fairy flounces off with a retort about the pointlessness of discussing "the indisputable." Having at first paid only cursory attention to the gifts that constitute her works of art, the fairy gives only ersatz birth—not to an authentic, infant embodiment of critical reading, but rather to the childish questions of a father who prematurely articulates misplaced criticism. One suspects, therefore, that the fairy artist may encounter a hitch when it comes to the infallible production of more artworks: the paternal instance of criticism that she is supposed to fold back into her future creativity shows untimely resistance to such envelopment. Wavering along an abject line between cynical humor and serious critique, "Le Don des fées" ultimately has trouble (s)(m)othering either its artists or its critics thoroughly enough.[5]

Among the nondiscussable absurdities most unsuccessfully smothered by this text is the lucky baby's much discussed *Gift of Pleasing,* on the subject of which it is tempting to stay in dialogue with the inquiring shopkeeper. One question seldom posed, though, is how this magically endowed—some might say alienated—infant will please his natural mother, who has been excluded from affairs. Does the child now leave the fairy to her poetic endeavors and resume where he left off with his real mother? Does he conflate the maternal fairy with the human woman and proceed to treat his confused (or delighted?) natural mother as a creature so "fantastic" that "one must fear her and please her"? Is he too absorbed in pleasing the poet-fairy to bond with his other mother? Put otherwise, can this pleasing baby himself be pleased by either of his mothers?

This would seem to be the question made urgent not, perhaps, by "Les Dons des fées," but by "Le Désespoir de la vieille," which is also haunted by a mother too invisibly not absent to ignore:

> The shriveled little old woman [la petite vieille ratatinée] felt ever so joyful [réjouie] at the sight of that pretty child whom everyone was celebrating, whom everyone wanted to please; that pretty being, so fragile like her, the old woman, and, also like her, without teeth and without hair.
>
> And she approached him, wanting to make him nice smiles and funny faces.
>
> But the terrified child struggled against the caresses of the good, decrepit woman [la bonne femme décrépite], and filled the house with his shrieks.
>
> So the good old woman retreated into her eternal solitude, and she wept in a corner, saying to herself:—"Ah! for us, unhappy old females, the time is past to be pleasing, even to innocents; and we horrify the little children whom we want to love!"
> (OC 1:277–78)

A first look at this piece in the present context might suggest a darkly allegorical reading in which the poetic life cycle is reaching its end; no longer able to mother either a howling baby critic or a cooing newborn poem, the old woman would represent the outworn artist in a grandmotherly equivalent to "Le Vieux Saltimbanque." But except that she shares everyone's possibly knee-jerk interest in a "pretty child whom everyone was celebrating," nothing definitely marks this old lady as a former mother or mother substitute. Speaking through her tears in the last paragraph, the old woman uses instead language reminiscent of a faded lover if not a courtesan, lamenting that she can't even seduce an infant anymore: "Ah! for us, unhappy old females, the time is past to be pleasing, even to innocents; and we horrify the little children whom we want to love!" The "horrifying" nature of this encounter between the pre-Oedipal baby and the postmaternal crone may thus lie partly in the kind of mirroring that does *not* happen in the course of it. Staring at each other, neither sees anything like an image of a mother's desire.

Not surprisingly, then, the symmetrical economy for which this prose poem is often celebrated starts to give way under a bit of critical pressure. The baby is represented in the text with mildly expansive grammatical variety: he is evoked not only by a nice little panoply of adjectives ("pretty," "fragile," "terrified," "little") but also with neatly paired prepositional phrases ("without teeth and without hair") and burgeoning relative pronoun clauses ("whom everyone was celebrating," "whom everyone wanted to please"). But the old lady is for the most part associated with a sort of lexical depletion, as if verbal supplies for her are running low: not only must she reuse the baby's attributes ("fragile," "without teeth and without hair") barely refurbished with a repetitive "like her," but she must also make do with minimalist variations on a few conventional descriptors ("little old woman" [twice], "good old woman," "unhappy old female"). Although this insistent repetition fulfills its ostensible purpose by showing baby and crone to be images of sameness, it also paradoxically deepens the disparity between them.

But three adjectives escape repetition in the old lady's linguistically deprived description: "joyful" (réjouie), "shriveled" (ratatinée), and "decrepit" (décrépite). All three call to mind "Les Petites Vieilles," in which the latter two figure explicitly, while "réjouie" recalls the old women's laughing, little-girl eyes as evoked in the verse poem. "Ratatinées," which modifies "ombres" (shadows) in "Les Petites Vieilles," describes something wrinkled and shrunken, and this is linked in turn with the image of "maints cercueils de vieilles / . . . aussi petits que celui d'un enfant" [many an old woman's coffin / . . . as small as a child's], as if an old woman, "s'en va tout doucement vers un nouveau berceau" [goes off ever so gently toward a new cradle] (*OC* 1:89–90). Suggestively, in an etymological note on "ratatiné," the *Trésor de la langue française* gives an attested sixteenth-century usage in which *retatiné* means "*effacer* les plis" (*efface* the folds; emphasis mine), thus reinforcing the verse- and prose-poem images of a wrinkled crone on the verge of identification with or rebirth as a smooth-skinned baby. Wrinkled shrunkenness also characterizes "Les Sept Vieillards," who share their "décrépitude" (1:88) with the "femme[s] décrépite[s]" in both verse and prose, just as "Les Petites Vieilles" share the appearance of "un fantôme débile" (a frail phantom) with the fantastic repetition of old men.

The point is this: if the despairing old woman is sometimes very like the baby and sometimes very different from him, it is not because she functions or substitutes as his mother. It is instead because she is always on the way from ruinous age to earliest infancy and back again, mirrored in the baby at the critical turn where the poet who raises her must also mother a critic, at least in passing, so as to prolong the perfection of his art. Caught in "Le Désespoir de la vieille" near a moment of crisis, the old woman figures the endlessly, infallibly renewed subject of art, infinitely multipliable during the poetic evolution theorized and/or hallucinated in Baudelaire's Wagner essay. It is as if the old woman, *ratatinée,* is reborn from the *replis* (folds or wrinkles) of the artist's brain as he meditates on the productive precepts to be drawn from the wrinkled "bourrelets de l'enflure" (rolls of swelling) inscribed on his little critic's mutilated neck in "La Corde." The critical baby and the poetic crone may at times look similarly and equally fragile, but only the infant would seem to risk permanent hurt.

This still leaves the mother question from "Le Désespoir de la vieille" disturbingly unaddressed, however: when the small critic in that text "fill[s] the house with his shrieks," amplifying the fatal panic of the child in "La Corde," where is his mother? Is she deaf? What is she doing at the moment when *her* presence is critical? One possible answer is that she is neither deaf nor otherwise occupied—that she is in fact close by, alert—but that she seems deceptively mute and nearly invisible. The third-person narrator of "Le Désespoir de la vieille" appears even more literally than usual *im*personal: a nonperson excluded from the I-thou of grammatical, intersubjective dialogue and apparently reduced to a sort of function—semiotic or diacritical or both—with practically no independent, embodying voice of its own. But this narrator—she?—may be there nonetheless, intimately and absently, nursing both the aging poem and the infant critic along from the difference-generating hollows and folds and wrinkles in the textual matrix, like a mother who discreetly helps her little one make a critical choice of puzzle pieces. It is maybe this not-quite-mutely narrating mother who makes sure all the letters stay creatively and critically *en couches*, who (s)(m)others them with punctuating, parenthetical maternity. This would mean that the (dia)critical mother in "Le Désespoir de la vieille" stays friends with that other Baudelairean mother of criticism, the artist, and one might remember, in this connection, that other narrator of "La Corde," the narrator traceable only through an interjection to a "friend" and some quotation marks. Less effectively concealed than her counterparts in "Les Dons des fées" and "Le Désespoir de la vieille," perhaps because the child critic's horribly premature death has jolted her into the open, this narrator leaves a haunting little trail of signs to remind us that if the mother is sometimes hard to find in Baudelaire's work, it may be that she is hidden, like the quotation marks beside a letter, in plain sight.

Yet despite her unobtrusive power to tuck legibility like a blanket for us into some treacherous cracks within and between prose poems, there is no assurance that this occluded mother would herself be able, if pressed, to read Baudelaire's writing. Such is one implication of "Les Yeux des pauvres," the final variation on the *Richard Wagner* scenario to be considered here. Accentuating its ties to urban rebirth as well as poetic renewal, "Les Yeux des pauvres" evokes "a new café that formed the corner of a new boulevard, still all full of rubble and already gloriously showing its unfinished splendors"(*OC* 1:318). Cradled thus between a newborn restaurant and a half-born street is

> a good man of forty or so, with a tired face and a graying beard, holding the hand of a little boy and carrying in his other arm a little being too feeble to walk. . . . All of them in rags. Those three faces were extraordinarily serious, and those six eyes fixedly contemplated the new café with an admiration that was equal but diversely nuanced by their ages.
>
> The father's eyes said: "How beautiful! how beautiful! it's as if all the gold in the poor old world has come to stay on these walls."—The little boy's eyes: "How beautiful! how beautiful! but it's a place where only people who aren't like us can go in."—As for the littlest one's eyes, they were too fascinated to express anything other than a stupid and profound joy. (1:318)

Ragged, incomplete (where is the mother?), and amorphous (the baby is no more than a formless "being"), this assemblage of familial fragments appears unlikely to achieve live social birth into the new city taking shape around it. Verging on dismemberment, "those six eyes" are unable to unite in either analysis or criticism of their plight; the meager pile of admiring gazes falls on the café with as little critical force as bits of the rubble littering the street. It is only the narrator's verbal interpretation that introduces a hint of reproach into the stare of the father, who reputedly relates the café's wealth to others' poverty, and the little boy, who allegedly tries to express a sense of exclusion. But as he subsequently admits, this narrator is a biased interpreter, swayed by his desire both to extend the pleasure and avoid the shame of conspicuous consumption. Liminally seated just outside the café, sipping from an elegant glass within earshot of street singers whose lyrics suggest that happiness gives birth to charity, the narrator becomes aware of the maternal space in which he is neither wholly united with nor clearly separated from the childlike admiration in the "family of eyes" (319). "Tenderly" [attendri], the narrator dreams of mothering the inarticulate eyes into eloquent critics, thus simultaneously bringing into the world a well-conceived social order and a well-nurtured prose poem about it.

This narrator hesitates, however. Unlike the painter in "La Corde" or the shopkeeper in "Le Don des fées," the people watcher in "Les Yeux des pauvres" stops to look a little before leaping into a maternal subject position. Possibly daunted by the prospect of assuming idealistic, metaphorical maternity for a family in which the mother is so concretely, perhaps painfully wanting, the narrator turns to the woman seated beside him. As his beloved companion, he expects she will instantly share his conviction that the family needs figurative mothering; and as a woman, he implies, she will compensate more naturally than himself for the literal mother's absence. But he miscalculates on both counts, since the woman neither follows her lover's train of thought nor feels anything but impatience at the family scene before her. The disconnect occurs, according to the narrator, because the woman is unable or unwilling to read eyes; she deciphers no meaning in the six eyes turned toward the café and fails even to acknowledge the look her lover directs toward her. It is this last failure that particularly infuriates the narrator: by not reading his gaze, pregnant as it is with poems yet to be born once the embryonic family before him has been nurtured into a viable agent of criticism, the woman withholds motherly support from her companion's future creativity, from what would in *Richard Wagner* be called his "infallibility in poetic production." When the narrator exaggerates this woman's incompetence as a reader into "the most gorgeous example of feminine impermeability that anybody could meet" (317), one can almost hear Baudelaire peremptorily pleading with his mother: "if you really possess maternal genius . . . Oh! do read me attentively, try hard to understand."

Although it is possible that the woman in "Les Yeux des pauvres" really does lack maternal genius, nothing in the text imposes this as the only explanation for her nonmaternal behavior. In fact, the narrator never asks her to generate full-blown motherliness. When first gazing at the fragmentary family before him, the narrator realizes that the father "was doing duty as a maid and taking his children out to breathe the evening air" (1:318). Were she to cooperate with the narrator's maternal ambitions, therefore, the woman would in effect serve as a substitute for the children's father, himself a substitute for the nursemaid, who should properly have substituted for the missing mother. As if this triply or quadruply displaced maternity were not problematic enough, moreover, the narrator requests the woman's cooperation in an especially indecisive way:

> I turned my gaze toward yours, dear love, in order to read in it
> *my* thought; I plunged into your eyes, so beautiful and so
> bizarrely sweet, into your green eyes, inhabited by Caprice and
> inspired by the Moon, when you said to me: "Those people there
> are unbearable to me with their eyes open like carriage gates
> [avec leurs yeux ouverts comme des portes cochères]! Couldn't
> you ask the maître d' to make them go away?" (1:319)

Eagerly hesitant, unsure that he is adequately equipped to engender poetic immortality, the narrator reaches for a mirror. If he gazes at his companion's eyes, it is ostensibly to check his maternal makeup, to verify that his reflected image looks like a substitutable mother all ready for critical positioning in the family before him. Yet his mirror-grabbing, assurance-seeking gesture is also that of an insecure child, a little boy who wants to be sure that his mother is looking out for him. Attempting a partly idealizing and partly essentializing plunge deep into his companion's eyes, that is, the narrator hopes to (s)(m)other himself in his own infinitely poetic gaze, conflated with and maternalized by the motherliness assumed to be so naturally inherent in the woman's own gaze that she can substitute on call for a variety of other mothers or mother figures. And this maternalizing conflation, moreover, is simultaneously supposed to confirm the critical authority with which the narrator has already begun to infiltrate the gazes of the father and son standing opposite him.

It is little wonder, then, that the woman responds strangely. One can't be certain, from the narrator's account, that her eyes respond at all. Beautiful, capricious, unreflective, they might be the unreadable eyes of a child. Or, "bizarrely sweet" in their family resemblance to Caprice and the Moon, they might also be the eyes of a "bizarre Mother" from "Les Dons des fées," divinely unreliable in her substitute maternity. In any case, the woman's only reported response is in words—harsh words that preempt the narrator's discourse without apparent respect for his poetico-maternal project. Yet by drawing her clichéd comparison between the family of staring eyes and a row of gaping carriage entrances, the woman aptly points, as if despite herself, toward a useful critique of the narrator's situation.[6] Treated by the narrator mostly as books for him to edit or publicize, as mirrors to look at—as more or less reflective surfaces that may not necessarily open onto anything other than dead-end self-gazing—the various eyes of this prose poem might, as the woman intimates, fruitfully be reconceived as doors. Even if one can't see much of what lies beyond their daunting aperture, hints the woman, eyes like *portes cochères* are at any rate thresholds of movement, parturient spaces for poem-nourishing departures and separations. Sketchy, unkind, possibly unwitting, the woman's critique offers no assurance that she will ultimately be able to read any of the narrator's writing, and it gives him little immediate help as a baffled reader of her odd gaze; the narrator's attempted plunge below the hard surface of the woman's eyes remains uninterpretable. But her words still place the woman like an unsolved puzzle at the critical phase of the Baudelairean poet's work, the moment when fragments of his creativity must be integrated into principles of flawless poetic production. And this is why the recalcitrant companion of "Les Yeux des pauvres," as stifled as she seems by the maternal ambitions of her poet-narrator, may perhaps be the best representative of all Baudelaire's mothers, from Madame Aupick to the occulted mother substitutes of *Le Spleen de Paris*. Ill-represented (when she is represented at all) as an inept, unsympathetic reader, the Baudelairean mother nevertheless positions herself at the door to future reading. Herself in danger of suffocation from the press of poetic progeny she renders conceivable, she opens critical breathing room for new generations of the (s)(m)othered and the (s)(m)othering.

Suffering and Expenditure

Baudelaire and Nietzsche in Char's Poetic Territory

Van Kelly

R ENÉ CHAR'S poem "Baudelaire mécontente Nietzsche" (Baudelaire Irritates Nietzsche), which appeared in the 1972 collection *La Nuit talismanique,* begins with a contrast:

C'est Baudelaire qui postdate et voit juste de sa barque de souffrance, lorsqu'il nous désigne tels que nous sommes. Nietzsche, perpétuellement séismal, cadastre tout notre territoire agonistique. Mes deux porteurs d'eau. (Char *OC* 495–96)

[Baudelaire from his boat of suffering postdates and sees things with justice when he describes us as we truly are. Nietzsche, ceaselessly earthshaking, maps out all our strife-ridden land. My two water-bearers.][1]

Paulène Aspel noted in 1968 that Char had devoted pieces to Rimbaud, Camus, Heraclitus, and others, but not to Nietzsche, with whom the poet seemed to "entertain, to prolong an intimacy" (1968, 166).[2] "Baudelaire Irritates Nietzsche" thus fills gaps in a longstanding chronology of influences.

Other texts imply that Char's two "water-bearers," or provisioners, flank and complement Rimbaud at the confluence that defines modernity.[3] The essay "In 1871" clarifies Rimbaud's middle position in this series of partial intersections. Char associates Rimbaud's poetic revolution with the fall of the Second Empire: "A contemporary of the Commune, and with a similar vengefulness, he punctures like a bullet the horizon of poetry and of sensibility" (Char *OC* 727). Rimbaud breaks the dam standing against modernity, while Baudelaire and Nietzsche inhabit opposite sides of the divide: "Romanticism has dozed off and dreams aloud: Baudelaire, the entire Baudelaire, has just died after he moaned with true pain. . . . Nietzsche readies himself, but he will have to return each day a bit more lacerated from his sublime ascensions" (726). In "1871," Baudelaire lingers behind, straddling the divide between Romanticism and modernity, whereas Nietzsche, yet to arrive, represents futurity. "Baudelaire Irritates Nietzsche," by contrast, asserts that Baudelaire "postdates" rather than just completes a dying era.[4] In this version, he survives Romanticism's catastrophe and accompanies Nietzsche into the future.

Char's temporal perspective on Baudelaire and Nietzsche is thus paradoxical, as is the case for Rimbaud. There is a "before" life and an "after" life through philosophy or poetry. Char states enigmatically that "Nietzsche détruit avant forme la galère cosmique" ("Nietzsche, destroyed prior, forms the cosmic galley" ["Page d'ascendants pour l'an 1964," Char *OC* 711]). If Baudelaire postdates, Rimbaud is "ahead of the wave." He is temporally unfinished, "the first poet of a civilization yet to materialize" and cannot be defined precisely, but he is crucial to Char's poetic vein: "If I knew exactly what Rimbaud meant to me, I would know what poetry remains ahead of me, and I would no longer need to write it" (732). Char's characterization of Baudelaire, Rimbaud, and Nietzsche as radically forward-looking responds to what de Man sees as the prototype of modernity: "Modernity exists in the form of a desire to wipe out whatever came earlier, in the hope of reaching at last a point that could be called a true present, a point of origin that marks a new departure."[5] Commenting specifically on Baudelaire's essay *The Painter of Modern Life*, de Man notes that modernity has a predilection for ideas and representations that "illustrate the heroic ability to ignore or to forget that this present contains the prospective self-knowledge of its end" (158–59). This general propensity is quite evident in Char's poetry— "Action is virgin, even when repeated," (*Feuillets d'Hypnos*, no. 46, in *OC* 186)—but his *grands astreignants* (great models who include, significantly, Heraclitus and Georges de La Tour) also tend to annul duration and deny the erosion of newness within his own works, through the mechanism of an artistic, philosophical, and poetic community situated paradoxically as if it were entirely in the present, despite the passage of time. De Man argues his definition of modernity along similar lines: "This combined interplay of deliberate forgetting with an action that is also a new origin reaches the full power of the idea of modernity" (162).

Unlike de Man, Char incorporates Baudelaire hesitantly into his modern continuum, as the title "Baudelaire Irritates Nietzsche" implies. The displeasure or irritation signals a conflict, yet the qualities that Char attaches to Baudelaire and Nietzsche in the opening stanza of the poem seem complementary rather than mutually exclusive: lucidity amid suffering does not necessarily annul a vigorous struggle to conquer adversity. Char deepens the enigma when he mentions explicitly neither Baudelaire nor Nietzsche in the rest of the poem, creating thereby a gap that our interpretation of the poem must bridge: the title implies a conflict of influences, but the opening stanza implies their compatibility. This opening gambit or paradox creates more problems than it solves, but it conceals, too, the defense of a position on modernity which the rest of the poem plays out stylistically and allegorically.[6] What does Baudelaire's skiff of suffering, and Nietzsche's seismic mapping or registry, represent for Char?

Skiff of Suffering

Claude Pichois depicts Baudelaire as "plagued throughout his life by what he called his *guignon*—the evil spirit of misfortune and disaster," and Baudelaire is certainly an icon of personal misfortune in Char's view (Pichois and Ziegler 1989, xi). This offers the basic outline for an interpretation, yet the skiff of suffering which postdates and sees things with justice leads to a rich zone of Baudelairean imagery. Cargo's concordance to *Les Fleurs du Mal* lists no use of the word *barque* ("bark," as in Charon's bark or ferry), whereas *vaisseau/vaisseaux* (vessel/vessels) occurs nine times, *navire* (ship) four times, and the synecdoche *mâts* (masts) five times. The various usage of boat images form a neat dichotomy as well. In one set of Baudelairean poems, woman is represented as a ship on a trip toward pleasant, idyllic countries as in "La Chevelure," where the lover's hair, at first a "noir océan" (black ocean), becomes a "pavillon de ténèbres tendues" (shadow-filled sail), or in "Le Serpent qui danse," where she is compared to "un fin vaissseau / Qui roule bord sur bord" [a gossamer ship, / Swayed by ocean swell] (*OC* 1:26–27, 29). "L'Invitation au voyage" and "Parfum exotique" prolong this idyllic utopia. By contrast, the vessel, like woman in Baudelaire's world, has strong contrastive associations, and they are more pertinent to Char's "barque de   souffrance." "L' Héautontimorouménos" pointedly echoes the line from "Le Beau Navire," where desire, "[like] a beautiful . . . vessel putting out to sea," finds not an idyllic land but the victim or self-torturer's experience (*OC* 1:78). This establishes the double, antithetical register of the ship: symbol of pleasurable exoticism or hellish journey.[7] "Le Voyage" refers insistently to the suffering that inner enemies or complexes inflict. The soul, "un trois-mâts cherchant son Icarie" [a three-master seeking its utopia], encounters at home and abroad "le spectacle ennuyeux de l'immortel péché" [the monotonous spectacle of immortal sin].[8] Baudelaire concludes: "Amer savoir, celui qu'on tire du voyage" [Journey's bitter fruit], but he departs in Death's ship, heedless of good or evil. Suffering does not postpone the trip.

The elements associating vessel and suffering coalesce in Baudelaire's "La Musique," where the figure of the poet becomes a ship:

> Je sens vibrer en moi toutes les passions
> *D'un vaisseau qui souffre,*
> Le bon vent, la tempête et ses convulsions
>
> Sur l'immense gouffre
> Me bercent. D'autres fois, calme plat, grand miroir
> De mon désespoir. (*OC* 1:68, emphasis added)

[I feel tensed within me, like passion, all the lurch and tremblings *of a ship that suffers,* the downwind, the storm and its convulsions lull me over the vast abyss. In other moments, flat seas, endless mirror for my despair.]

Other poems drift from ideal toward spleen. In "L'Irrémédiable," all sense of adventure has disappeared from the image of the ship: "Un navire pris dans le pôle, / Comme en un piège de cristal" [A ship immobilized in polar ice, / As in a crystal trap] (*OC* 1:75). Char states, by contrast, that Baudelaire sees things justly despite suffering ("voit *juste* de sa barque de souffrance," emphasis added): in this sense his vessel encounters despair but elation, too, in a less fatal mix of spleen and ideal than in "L'Irrémédiable," something closer to the melancholic if harsh adventure in "La Musique" and "Le Voyage."

Char strongly connects creation and suffering. Poets of all eras, from his perspective, have purveyed harsh truths and have been persecuted (before and after 1857):

> Think about the suspicion and torture to which Villon, Baudelaire, Nerval, Rimbaud, Mandelstam, or Maria Tsvetaeva were subjected . . . Do not forget that poets have always received fireworks in the chest, their internal and external enemies having placed them in a target zone. (*Sous ma casquette amarante,* in Char *OC* 856)

For Char, poetry is conspiratorial yet triumphant: "From the Inquisition to modern times, temporal evil clearly did not get the better of Theresa of Avila nor of Boris Pasternak . . . The statute of limitations has expired there where poetry flares up, resides . . ." ("Arthur Rimbaud," *OC* 727–28).

When Char comments on the image of suffering offered by Baudelaire— "I am the wound and the knife, / The victim and the executioner"—he infers the lesson that "at such a degree of suffering and flight, the poet is brother to all the earth and its misfortune" (*OC* 858). Poetry espouses a lucid violence that resists all compromise with oppressors: ("One of the noble aspects of violence . . . is its ability to pay off the victim's debt and deliver him from that plague: false knowledge, the nursemaid of shipwrecks, of capitulations," *OC* 857.) Char echoes this ethical reading of "L'Héautontimorouménos" with a stylistic one. Competing moments of lucidity and frenzy inform poetry. Char finds the "ardent Nuance" (his own aesthetic ideal) in Baudelaire's poetry, too:

> Nuances and violence are in close combat. Through their mediation, the conflicts and tempers slowly but steadily counterbalance, and through them poetry disseminates, like water through limestone . . . Nuance and ardor raise and lower the horizon line, morning and evening, stimulating the spectrum. (*OC* 857)

Nuance is another form of violence, because it battles ardor to form poetry: "Poetry likes that double, mad violence and its double taste which listens at the doors of language" (*OC* 858), a violence in which Baudelaire's poetry shares. Char, significantly, interprets "L'Héautontimorouménos" not as a depiction of Baudelaire's psyche but as an allegory of poetry itself and of the poet's role in history.

The positive meaning of the skiff of suffering in "Baudelaire Irritates Nietzsche" becomes clearer: struggle is a necessary ingredient of self-accomplishment, and the good struggle (to write the poem or to resist oppression) elates the poet. Char associates the ship or the boat with the exhilarating struggle in his poem "Faction du muet," where the word *barque* confirms but diversifies the Baudelairean images of suffering. The shift from Baudelaire's *vaisseau, navire* and *mâts* to Char's bark may be explained partly by the effort to translate a marine image, reminiscent of Baudelaire's journey to the Indian Ocean, into a fluvial world centered around representations of the Sorgue, the river that flows through Char's native town. A *barque* is a smallish vessel, used on inland waterways or employed in seaports to unload merchandise from a larger ship. In "Faction du muet" (*Le Nu perdu,* 1971), the poet, reminiscent of his counterpart in Baudelaire's "La Musique," becomes a skiff gliding over the transparent riverbed of human experience. The journey enriches poetry, sometimes violently through the shock of life's contradictions, at other times sympathetically through identification with human foibles and tragedies: "Je me suis uni au courage de quelques êtres, j'ai vécu violemment, sans vieillir, mon mystère au milieu d'eux, j'ai frissonné de l'existence de tous les autres, *comme une barque incontinente au-dessus des fonds cloisonnés*" [I allied myself with the courage of some people, I have violently lived out my mystery among them, never aging, I have trembled to the existence of all others, *like a boat shifting above the cloisonné of a riverbed*] (*OC* 429, emphasis added). The experience of the Other stimulates the poet and energizes him. This kind of ecstasy contrasts with the desperation of Baudelaire's leave-taking in "Le Voyage"—"Plonger au fond du gouffre, Enfer ou Ciel, qu'importe?" [Plunge to the bottom of the abyss, whether it is Hell or Heaven]. Suffering often appears in Char's poems, but a mysterious exhilaration usually gives it tone. Something resembling exhilaration fills the poet's sails in Baudelaire's "La Musique" ("I feel tensed within me, like passion, all the lurch and tremblings / Of a ship that suffers"), though there is only partial satisfaction: Baudelaire's "good winds" die to reveal the "calm mirror" of his despair. Char and Baudelaire become allegorical vessels of Poetry, each "shivers" or "suffers" in the wind, but each to different effect.

Differing attitudes toward despair, self-doubt, regret, and remorse furnish Char's rationale for placing Baudelaire on the near side of modernity, as its precursor, rather than at its point of origin:

> Baudelaire is the most *humane* genius of all *Christian* civilization. His song incarnates that civilization in its conscience, in its glory, in its remorse, in its malediction, at the moment of its beheading, of its loathing, of its apocalypse. "*Poets,*" writes Hölderlin, "*are usually revealed at the beginning or the end of an era.*"[9]

This remark occurs in the essay "Arthur Rimbaud," but it is crucial to Char's view on poetic modernity, and it attaches a caveat to the reception of Baudelaire's work: Baudelaire brings a premodern era of poetry to its end and represents an apogee prior to modernity's clean slate and new inscription. What survives the tabula rasa is Baudelaire's empathy with human suffering, less sin and remorse which are foreign to Char, who would certainly be irritated by the sense of guilt and self-deprecation in the conclusion of "Un voyage à Cythère": "—Ah! Seigneur! donnez-moi la force et le courage / De contempler mon cœur et mon corps sans dégoût!" [Oh Lord! Give me the force and courage / to consider my heart and body without disgust!"] (*OC* 1:119). In moments of suffering, Char does not feel remorseful but anxious, as in "Baudelaire Irritates Nietzsche": "What is, our greatest cause of suffering? Worry" (*OC* 496); in other words, our anxiety lacks a religious, eschatological foundation in God's redemptive or damning gaze. Personal instinct or difference, rather than belief, founds resistance to the world's weight, to its thrusts and currents: "We are born in the same torrent, but we roll differently amid frenetic stones. Worry? Follow instinct" (496). Char sees suffering not as an apocalypse that reveals or subverts godhead, but as a self-affirmation and instinctive resistance to phenomenal change.

Baudelaire's sense of suffering as Char portrays it in "Baudelaire Irritates Nietzsche" implies a religious sense, even if that sense manifests itself as Cain's revolt against God. Char rejects the postlapsarian aspect of Baudelairean suffering, and through this rejection the figure of Baudelaire begins to migrate through the poem, after the initial stanza introducing the two precursors. Humanity is part of a purely materialistic universe: "Sons of nothing and destined to nothing. . . . What we hear during sleep is our

heartbeat and not the outbursts of our soul at leisure" (496). The only redemption and rebirth is in the poet's work. "The work, unique, in the form
of a broken shutter" is the sole agent of "the sense of its own renewal"
(496).[10] Suffering pervades the house of poetry with its broken shutter, yet
this results not in divine transcendence but only in the renewal of our participation in a world that is either a chaos or an impersonal determinism:
"Whether we defy order or chaos, we obey laws we have not intellectually
ratified. We approach with the step of a mutilated giant" (496). We struggle violently, as if Titans, against the assault of senseless material forces—
this is one of the lessons that underlies Char's fragmentary style—but here
mythology evacuates theology and relegates it to the realm of metaphor for
the blind forces of nature.[11] Char's poetry, which cultivates rupture and
discontinuity, cannot assimilate Baudelaire's "ardent sanglot qui roule
d'âge en âge" [ardent sob that rolls from age to age] and which dies—fu-
tilely or with redemption—at the feet of God's eternity ("Les Phares," *OC*
1:14).

Char willfully effaces the divine, but his fragmentary style also saps the
poetic conventions of wholeness and unity that typify Baudelairean verse
(the open-ended succession of quatrains and artists of "Les Phares," for instance, or the interweaving typical of the sonnet and pantoum). "Baudelaire
Irritates Nietzsche" typifies Char's fragmentary style. The poem consists of
eight prose stanzas, and the links from one to the next are "eluded" if not
"burned," to use Char's own terms for describing transitions.[12] His poetry
points through its form to the lack of an overarching principle, immanent
to the universe and to language, which would make the movement from
moment to moment and stanza to stanza self-evident. The poet presents
fragments without apparent coherence, or with a unity that the poet senses
incompletely, and the reader must join in this search beyond catastrophe for
renewed wholeness. Char confirms the idea that poetic modernity, in the
lineage of Rimbaud, is joined to the annulment of theology, since poetry is
"toujours en chemin vers le point qui signe sa justification et clôt son existence, à l'écart, en avant de l'existence du mot Dieu" [always in transit toward the point that signs its verdict and closes its existence, well ahead of the
existence of the word God].[13] Deprived of religious finalities, the poem
crafts and imposes an immanent linguistic justification upon the surrounding chaos or oppressive order of things. Char's poetry, by its form, indicts
the coherence of a universe it confronts and intends to conquer.

Char's version of poetic modernism is founded on the death of god, or, as Virginia La Charité says, "Poetry has the position that religion assigns to God" (1974, 57). Char suggests this again, but elliptically, in "Faire du chemin avec . . ." (*Fenêtres dormantes et porte sur le toit*, 1979): "Baudelaire, Melville, Van Gogh are haggard gods, not readings of gods" (*OC* 580)—that is, Baudelaire's poetry of misfortune and resistance to spleen inspires Char, but he rejects the detour through religious finality that *Les Fleurs du Mal* implies. Baudelaire survives the collapse of Romanticism but in a secular, de-Christianized form: "Baudelaire forges the wounds of the heart's intelligence into a pain that rivals the soul" ("Page d'ascendants pour l'an 1964," *OC* 711).

The Seismic Registry: Nietzsche

What then does Nietzsche carry on Char's journey? Nietzsche, too, signals the existence of oppression and suffering, since he plots Char's "territoire agonistique," but pain derives in this case from a voluntary struggle and from the swords of battle. Commenting on "Baudelaire Irritates Nietzsche," Paul Veyne interprets the "séisme nietzschéen" as the destruction of social conformity, or "valeurs établies," and this includes conformist institutions and conventional language.[14] Critics have also pointed out that Char appropriates Zarathustra's eagle to symbolize the poetic summit, sovereign independence, and human overcoming without the aid of God or gods (Aspel 1968, 180–81; Mathieu 1984–85, 1:121 n. 75). Char adopts Nietzsche partially because of the latter's rejection of the divine: "Creation—that is the great redemption from suffering, and life's growing light"; "Away from God and gods this has lured me; what could one create if gods existed?" says Zarathustra (Nietzsche 1968, 199), echoing the madman in *The Gay Science:* "Gods, too, decompose. God is dead. God remains dead. And we have killed him" (Nietzsche 1974, 181). Char's journey, too, is an ascension instead of the sea voyage that informs his interaction with Baudelaire. The ascension of man involves the annulment of God—"God, the arranger, could not but fail," Char declares—yet this lays the ground for a modern humanism, namely the cultivation of the "intermittent gods" who "pervade our mortal amalgam without ever going beyond us."[15] Char uses the philosopher-poet Nietzsche against the poet-philosopher Baudelaire, because in Nietzsche the philosophical and poetic project replaces religious teleology.[16]

As Aspel remarks, Char's "open attitude toward chance" echoes Zarathustra's claim that he has liberated the world from "the slavery of goals or ends."[17] Otherworldly redemption, or even blasphemy, gives way to an affirmation of the intrinsic value of the world and of the individual's path through it: "Let your will say: the overman *shall* be the meaning of the earth! I beseech you, my brothers, *remain faithful to the earth*," says Zarathustra, although it could just as well have been Char, so close are the thought and instinct (Nietzsche 1968, 125, author's emphasis). Although he praises Baudelaire and has more indulgence for pity than does Nietzsche, Char's version of self-renewal closely emulates Zarathustra's praise of going under in order to overcome adversity:

> Man, says Zarathustra, is a rope tied between beast and over-man—a rope over an abyss. A dangerous across, a dangerous on-the-way, a dangerous looking-back, a dangerous shuddering and stopping.
>
> What is great in man is that he is a bridge and not an end: what can be loved in man is that he is an *overture* and a *going under*. I love those who do not know how to live, except by going under.[18]

In "Baudelaire Irritates Nietzsche," Char likewise denies otherworldly redemption while he espouses renewal through strictly human creativity. The human condition demands neither faith nor salvation but self-reliance. Char emphasizes renovation and a despiritualized transcendence, where the beginning point is the self and the culmination a self refashioned through its agonistic contact with *this* world: "To die is to go through the eye of the needle after several burgeonings. One must traverse death in order to emerge in front of life," but "in a state of sovereign modesty" as an individual self-sufficient, content to live without the self-importance imparted by notions of divine providence or of revolt against divinity (*OC* 496). Ascension toward personal sovereignty and elation also entails a plunge into the deepness of the world. Nietzsche's dialectic of overture and going under harmonizes with Char's supreme indifference to the divine, unless divinity is redefined as the vitality of nature, the ceaseless shock and metamorphosis of contraries without any transcendence beyond process.

Nietzsche's depiction of secular agony differs fundamentally from Baudelaire's striving between spleen and ideal. For Char, as for Nietzsche, risk and endangerment are fundamental categories. Life is a dangerous crossing over the abyss. Poems from the collection *Fureur et mystère,* published in 1948 but written from roughly the Munich crisis onward, grant an important place to these ideas and explain why Nietzsche, for Char, is "perpétuellement séïsmal." The idea that going under may result in destruction and not rebirth is accentuated in the poem "Les trois sœurs," where the poet beseeches the earth to safeguard "that child on your shoulder," whose allegorical sense is not yet clear—endangered innocence? human vulnerability? Disaster strikes, however, and a volcanic eruption engulfs the child, yet the child is poetry and the cataclysm only ignites the olive tree on the slope, here a symbol of the poetic image itself and its renewal through creativity (*OC* 250–51). In "Seuil" (The Edge), the Nietzschean denunciation of metaphysics and the images of cataclysm conjoin. The human figure in the poem confronts "the gigantic fault line of the abandonment of the divine," which has broken down the "dam of humanity." The reaction to catastrophe is not a political philosophy, or a philosophy of the will, but a language: "distant words, words that did not wish to be lost, mounted a resistance to the exorbitant thrust" (*OC* 255). Paul Veyne interprets this as a rejection of the Nietzschean overman in favor of the poet who sees in language, and not in metaphysics, the only valid project (316–17), but the ecstatic, wide view of "Seuil" suggests a reform of the ontological environment: when the downfall of God threatens humankind, the poet steps forth to await new words but also to remake the universe out of the surrounding chaos. Being, and not just language, is at risk here, though language, to be sure, is the agent of salvation. The dawn after the catastrophe signals the birth of a new poetic language, but the consequences surpass language and poetry alone, indeed this enriched threshold alludes to all of life—"life, immense limit," as Char asserts ("Donnerbach Mühle," *OC* 252). The world is not an expiation for the sin of existence ("le châtiment du devenir," in the terms Bianquis uses in 1938 to translate Nietzsche's evaluation of Anaximander). It is, rather, "la justification de l'être" (Nietzsche's synthesis of Heraclitus: the sanctification of being), an apt description of Char's poet in "Seuil," who, his belt "full of seasons," stands before the flood to welcome the rebirth of poetry after the quake, amid change.[19] As Aspel says, "Char's poetry sings reality, 'noble' reality, and seeks to attain it beyond the very idea of the unknown, and one may accurately call this exaltation Dionysiac" (172; see also 182).

Char's poetry in general, takes noble endangerment as its unspoken ground.[20] From violent risk issue words with the hard edge and urgency that contemplation of death imparts, and this is the sense of the characterization in "Baudelaire Irritates Nietzsche": "Nietzsche, always earthshaking, maps out all our strife-ridden land" (*OC* 495–96). The devastated site, traversed by flood, volcanic eruptions, and tremors, produces, through struggle against the tragic sense of life, poetry at its most intense and its most exhilarating.[21] Against this background, and with reference to Baudelaire's remorseful apocalypse, Char espouses a Nietzschean "gaspillage sans frein," a relentless going under in order to overcome the world's resistance to poetry, philosophy, and justice.

The Anagogical Sense: Baudelaire's Return

The end of "Baudelaire Irritates Nietzsche," however, should cause hesitation. Baudelaire is not easily repressed; he returns despite Nietzsche's displeasure.[22] Once Char rehearses his two provisioners' itinerary, he suddenly cannot choose between the two. Poetic language trembles in the confrontation:

> Qui appelle encore? Mais la réponse n'est point donnée.
> Qui appelle encore pour un gaspillage sans frein? Le trésor entrouvert des nuages qui escortèrent notre vie. (OC 496)

> [Who calls out once more? But no answer is given.
> Who calls out once more for a relentless expenditure? The open treasure of the clouds that escorted our life.]

"Relentless expenditure" is the Nietzschean release of the poet's and Zarathustra's "wild dogs" (1968, 155), of his Dionysian urges toward fusion, toward the testing of limits, and toward devastated orders and sites. The closing sentence of "Baudelaire Irritates Nietzsche," however, could be read as an allusion to Baudelaire's prose poem "L'Etranger" (*Le Spleen de Paris*): "Well then, what do you like, extraordinary stranger?—I like the clouds that are passing! down there! down there! the marvelous clouds" (*OC* 1:231).[23] Char opposes this "open treasure" to "relentless expenditure," not as retention opposes prodigality, since the treasure, too, is opened up/"entrouvert," but as serene contemplation and recollection contrast with, and nuance, an ecstatic and tragic vision of life—in other words, as Apollonian serenity tempers Dionysian frenzy in Nietzsche's early works on the origins of philosophy and tragedy (one of Char's early contacts with Nietzsche's work).[24]

Char's "open treasure of the clouds" echoes the interplay of distance and intimacy that marks not just "L'Etranger," but Baudelaire's "Harmonie du soir," too, with its concluding metaphor of the sunset and a memory:

> Un cœur tendre, qui hait le néant vaste et noir,
> Du passé lumineux recueille tout vestige!
> Le soleil s'est noyé dans son sang qui se fige . . .
> Ton souvenir en moi luit comme un ostensoir! (*OC* 1:47)

> [A tender heart, that hates the vast black nothingness, / from the shining past collects all remainder! / The sun has drowned in its clotted blood . . . / Your memory glints in me as if a gilded monstrance!]

By contrast, a Dionysian sunset—one that insists on violence and expenditure rather than on retention and nostalgia—marks Char's "Le Visage nuptial": "The eagle's claw funnels high the blood" (*OC* 151), an aggressive painting of the crepuscule that clashes with the more serene, contained violence of "Harmonie du soir," where the clotted sun of the penultimate line is held by coming darkness just as the poet captures the ray of memory.[25] The union of disparate parts, and an inner distance or serenity essential to contemplation, are even more evident in "Correspondances," where the mix of elements moves toward unity, not toward clash and disintegration. A number of Baudelaire's poems do focus on dissolution ("Une charogne," "Le Masque," "La Destruction") or Orphic mutilation ("L'Albatros," "L'Héautontimorouménos"), but poems that accent disruption often occur against a background of calmness, as in "Harmonie du soir" and similar poems that convey Baudelaire's predilection for a simultaneous picture of spleen and ideal. "La Cloche fêlée" establishes the poet's flaw through such counterpoint: the soul's broken moaning ("râle épais") punctuates an Apollonian vastness ("faraway memories" and bells that sing through the mist). In "Baudelaire Irritates Nietzsche," Char's own conclusion among the "open treasure of the clouds," however, accentuates what suffering could not annul in Baudelaire's poetic vision, namely serenity and contemplation as in

"Recueillement": "Ma Douleur, donne-moi la main . . . / . . . Vois se pencher les défuntes Années, / Sur les balcons du ciel . . ." [My Pain, give me your hand . . . / . . . See the dead Years lean over / The balconies of the sky. . . .], a serenity set against (and despite) the frenetic search for pleasure taking place in the city streets below.

At the end of "Baudelaire Irritates Nietzsche," when Char evokes both the philosopher's "relentless expenditure" and the poet's "open treasure of the clouds," he reaffirms his need for a contrast between ecstatic violence and serene contemplation, distance and fusion. Char refuses to exclude from modernity either Nietzsche or Baudelaire, furor or mystery, fusion or distance, dismemberment or order. This poem is not a Nietzschean monologue. Baudelaire postdates Nietzsche: he remains a valid marker and companion on Char's poetic journey through the desert or through the archipelago, and he is not brutally annulled. Instead Baudelaire contests, by his *ennui* and pessimism, but also through his sense of passive contemplation, Nietzsche's harsh yet enthusiastic going under. Baudelaire is put under erasure but returns in Char's poetry as the supplement of suffering that maintains pity on the horizon, though this does not lead Char to remorse or to condemnation of the self's deep urges.

I have left for last the second strophe of "Baudelaire Irritates Nietzsche," because we must seek the true rather than the apparent place of each of Char's stanzas within the heterodox and fragmented order of his poem. This stanza demonstrates, too, Char's inclination to adopt a worldview more fundamentally Nietzschean than Baudelairean, though the Nietzschean element never governs uncontested. Encounter, conflict, and influence renew poetic language and assure its continuity: "Duty, before one takes another breath, to rarify and hierarchize people and things that impinge on us." Pollen, deprived of a future, "smashes into the rocky partition." Char allows Baudelaire and Nietzsche, suffering and untold generous expenditure, to inflect his poetry. Pollen, or the word, is thus triple—Baudelaire and Nietzsche interact with Char, constrain him momentarily with their own original limits, pollinate his poetry, open it to change and growth beyond his solitude. Char's praise for his provisioners is not funerary rhetoric or banquet praise—it is not eulogistic or elegiac properly speaking—so much as it is a creative stimulus for further poetry. Nietzsche justifies, in similar terms, his own search for models of thought and life among the Presocratics. "Let us leave the tombs in peace, but make ours whatever is eternally lively. Humanity grows only when it venerates what is *rare* and great." "Adopter un style de rêve ou de légende," says Nietzsche in a French version which Char had read (Nietzsche 1985, 168, 171; Mathieu 1984–85, 2:90 n. 4). The poet has taken this advice and crafted a dialectic of Baudelairean clouds and Nietzschean dam breaking, but within the hidden design of a Nietzschean genealogy of influences.[26] Char's choice of clouds to symbolize Baudelairean poetics should be read as an allusion *both* to strophic poems such as "Harmonie du soir" (where the pantoum relies on the obsessive return of sentences and images in order to evoke the memory of lost love) *and* to the prose poems like "L'Etranger," freed from rhyme and strophic measure. In *Le Spleen de Paris,* Baudelaire attains a modernity and a freedom from convention that tie more directly to Char's vein of formal experimentation.[27]

In Char's poetry, Baudelairean stasis, ambiguity, and suffering contest alternative moments of vertigo, frenzy, and empowerment. Baudelaire remains a veiled reference in Char, although Nietzsche retains preponderance as the more modern one, less attached to a past morality and style. "Dans la marche" (*La Parole en archipel*) anticipates "Baudelaire Irritates Nietzsche" and illustrates the bind: "We can only live in what is opened up, precisely on the hermetic dividing line of shadow and light," says Char. This is stasis, penumbra, calm before dawn or dusk. "But we are irresistibly thrown ahead. All our person aids and spins this thrust" (*OC* 411). Expenditure indicts stasis but cannot avoid its moment.

To Spear It on the Mark, of Mystical Nature

Michel Deguy

Translated by *Wilson Baldridge*

W HAT are we doing when we speak of Baudelaire?[1] Some are "Baudelaireans," research specialists as they are sometimes called, nineteenth-century scholars, experts on Charles Baudelaire's lifework and "searching" to know it better. Others—as in my case—like to speak "in the interest of poetry" so that, at the end of the next century, there will continue "to be poetry."

Sometimes they ignore one another, I am forced to note, when I read, in a recent article by Antoine Compagnon, this observation without reference which I published seven years ago: the *diminutive infinite* represented for Baudelaire by "twelve or fourteen [leagues] of *liquid in movement*" (*Mon cœur mis à nu*, XXX, *OC* 1, 45) is the set form of the alexandrine; hence, Baudelaire, in speaking of the sea, also speaks about poetry and encodes a proportion— the poem/poetry ratio as homologous to the finite/infinite ratio.

In other words, the perspective which I prefer to adopt in an assembly even of Baudelaireans is that of a *question* such as, "Where do we stand with poetry?"—a perspective whose means of elaboration, whose tone and discourse, if one prefers, are those of poetic knowledge. "What is *our* modernity?" and how do we measure its proximity and distance from that of Baudelaire—as did Michel Foucault in his 1983 seminar, characterizing it as "*ironic heroization of the present*, a game of freedom with the real for its *transfiguration*, an ascetic elaboration of self [. . .] which can happen only in *another* place (other than society or the body politic), in what Baudelaire calls ART" (*Magazine littéraire*, March 1993).

Making *revelation* out of *profanation* as did Baudelaire—that is, making
sense of the depth of life (see *Fusées* XI) using the Christian fable (in the
sense of *Fable* recently recalled by Starobinski)—has our simony trans-
gressed one step further beyond that of Baudelaire? Measuring this step is
what is difficult. For Baudelaire, there is homology between poetic revelation (of the depth or intensity of existence by means of an "ordinary spectacle," which may become its "symbol") and Christian Revelation, which
provides the parameters (in the sense that the Greek *parametron* may be
translated as *comparator*), parameters measuring the lot of humankind, *religious* parameters such as from heaven to hell, or from the angelic to the satanic. One recalls (for example) that, in "Duellum" (piece thirty-five of *Les
Fleurs*), the lovers as infernal couple eternalize their ardor, *post-coitum* as it
were, but one ought to say beyond sexuality and beyond youth, by turning it
into hatred, whereas at the other pole (*Fleur* numbered 121) the lovers,
"vying to use up their last blush of heat," die "exchanging a single gleam,"
which an Angel, faithful and joyous by definition, will rekindle in every mirror. There is a celestial version and an infernal version of the impossible
unison—impossible *unisex*—of humanity's twofold being. In one version,
the poet of *Les Fleurs du Mal* makes their strange nosegay blossom on
shelves above the lovers' *divans* of death; in the other version, like flowers
adorn the flayed skin of "Duellum"'s *mature* heroes, "embittered by love,"
twisting and turning in a Dantesque hell where "hate flares eternal."
Between the (Kantian) philosophical hypothesis of radical evil at the height
of the "Enlightenment" and our era of trivialized evil (Arendt), the poet of
the nineteenth century internalizes the original *privilege* of evil, preserving
Christian religious thought right down to the provocative litanies of Satan
and other "reversals of Christian values" which passed for scandalous or
laughable.

Asking *ourselves,* with Baudelaire's words, about the status of the depth
of life in his poetic experience, *we* must distinguish through our reading a
structure of that experience, a *like*-structure, a sort of homothety or internal, intrinsic analogy, and on the other hand its *meaning,* interpreted
through the relation preserved with the Christian tradition of truth; *we* distinguish the terms of the homology between a capacity and a content; up the
counterslope of de-Christianization, *we* must recover the homology between this profane revelation and Revelation. But in the end—today—it is
in order to ask ourselves whether there is still something to be derived from

the profanation of revelation and what kind of revelation to remake with this profanation. That is why my comments take in turn (or blend) a reflective remembrance of Baudelaire's religious atheism with a recapitulation of his *ars poetica,* disconnecting this homology between revelation and Revelation.

Reginald McGinnis (1994), in a penetrating study entitled *Sacred Prostitution,* speaks at one point of *water* as a "metaphor for the crowd" in Baudelaire. I shall open my comments by saying "yes" and "no": water is not a "metaphor for the crowd"—that is too tenuous. Water is made to stand-for (the crowd)—and not optionally. If we decide, as did Northrop Frye, to name all stand-fors "metonymies," then it is a metonymy. But metonymy is much more than metonymy. It is not about making identifications; man *is not* the city; the artist is not the prostitute; the crowd is not water, etc. A thing, a being, may stand for, with, in place of, its other; through such wording we must understand the solidarity, the coalescence, of *possibility* and *essence* within *rapprochement* or the "image." And an entire grammar of vocatives, optatives, destination, use of the familiar form, enjoins the special performative of this poetic *proposition*—a distant echo perhaps of the Gospel's *parabolic-imperative* ("be ye as children"), its *be-like.*

The poetic transaction offered through a comparison—or rapprochement—in the general form of A *or* B holds in reserve a possibility offered (and refusable) to future *recognition* (in other *circumstances* wherein the *relation* in question recurs). Thus the poem itself is an "expansion of infinite things"; a place where things not finite may be extended, expanded; an offered extension, expansion of things into things of things; or *an extension of possibility upon the world.*

Hence, to read Baudelaire is to situate such *figures* within a more radical and powerful play than the so-called rhetorical play of metaphor-metonymy. We might just as well call them *allegories,* or *prosopopoeias,* or still otherwise if only we reawaken the etymologies of these terms (and perhaps the sum total of the play of differences that come down to the same, or life, would be called "tautegoria"). Next—that is, at the same time—it is to meditate upon the principle that governs their traffic, their exchange: a principle of substitutability, of correspondence, of *reversibility*—a notion which, as Claude Pichois sketched out in his note for this poem numbered 45 in the 1868 edition, on the one hand concerns Joseph de Maistre, and on the other "corresponds" . . . to the "correspondences." Let me add that

Pichois seems to underestimate the "Catholic orthodoxy" of the term *re-versibility*—that is, the *theology* of the thing. He perhaps insufficiently exploits the output of this component of Baudelaire's *ars poetica,* that one could perhaps call a "poieme," coining the word upon the model of mytheme, theologeme, or philosopheme or seme, sememe, to designate a diacritical, analytic presupposition within a poetic *system.*

Now the play of equivalencies is governed by a principle that finds one of its heteronyms in the great Baudelairean term: *prostitution.* Comparison draws upon the resources of a general convertibility or "prostitution." The reversibility, or equivalence, between solitude and multitude, or between poet and crowd, poet and metropolis, or between poet and prostitute in the exchange twixt interior and exterior and, in general, the veering from one *extreme* to the other, has as its element, in the sense of medium and mediation, "prostitution." Such reversibility takes place in the religious exhilaration of Paris-Babylon, where the proteiform poet—by turns victim and executioner, whose "atomized" ego embraces the crowd—"meditating incessantly *through* the whirlwind of the big city" is subjected to and executes an initiatory obstacle course from solitude to solitude through the labyrinth/multitude, from empty unity to resolved unity, "from the atomized ego to the centralized ego." This "man of genius who wants to be *one,* hence solitary," goes by way of the alteration and gratification of the crowd, woman, the numerical other, deity, and by way of the *neutr*alization of the sexual duel retraced by the poem "Duellum," without the paranoia of "I-am-alone-and-they-are-everyone" ever winning out over "I-am-everyone" in this spiritual orgy of an ego saved by its ability to change places—that is, to turn-itself-into—such that one would like to be able to speak of "stitution" by isolating the common root of substitution, prostitution, restitution.

Two or three comments, at this point, concerning what pertains to the *ars poetica* (experience and method):

With the issue of intensity, or "excitability," or the *energy* whose motif haunts the poet's relation to Delacroix, and in general—if we recall its insistence in *Les Paradis artificiels*—that of a thing's turning-into-it*self* through its *more*-being, its being-more-itself, it is a matter of raising a common value to its maximum, comparatively to itself and superlatively, as to its truth; but said common value in its ordinary, distributed, shared capacity, does not afford a glimpse toward its property, its *same*ness, except to the artists who give its *hours* a *rush*. And thus, "prostitution" does not so much denote the commonplace capacity of what lends-itself-to-many (incessant flirting, powdering oneself here and there through more or less tenuous liaisons, friendships, *relationships*, in keeping with the trivial gray melodrama of the one and the many that makes up the usual state of things). Rather it functions as a reminder of "sacred prostitution," this mediation for and within the partition of heaven and hell, which is our deepest partition, from one shore to the other of whose excessive span we tumble quartered.

The oxymoron—"holy prostitution," for example—serves to join, to resolder at high temperature two realms overseparated by doxa; to comprehend once more a forgotten indivision, to retrieve something lost from the symbolic. And if doxa is oblivious to the chiasma of a more original co-adherence, the recrossing of exchanges between these two sides which a paradoxical syntagma such as "holy prostitution" apposes, then the poetic oxymoron comes, if you will, to paroxyze a paradox, be it "preciously" as they used to say in the days of the *agudezza,* by whetting the adverse sides of the *coincidentia oppositorum* to the point of a sharp-edged discord within thought, tracing unto itself the mind's intimacy.

The crowd/city (for example), an unstable environment, itself reversible, is instantaneously mutable into its opposite, from one extreme to the other, from charity/fraternity to violence/horror, like a cathartic theater in which compassion advances and horror recedes (here is the lovely lady passing by, here comes the horrible old lady), *rhythmizing* the *promeneur's* dancing curiosity.

However the reversibility, the correspondence (the sub-stitution) does not run "every which way." Sense is not just any consequence whatsoever of the equivalencies' versatility "in all senses." How does one distinguish "good" reversibility from a metastatic reversibility whereby the exchanges would cancel each other out?

Just as the Gospel's law of love (in itself "paradoxical" or *double bound* when *expressed,* as in Augustine's famous exclamation, *Ama et quod vis fac*) restricts the field of possibles because of the selected, "determined" *comparator* (be ye as *children*) to be interpreted (one recalls, too, that Breton felt obliged to theorize a *rising* sense of the *sign,* "ana," a deferent preferability within the reference—against the general license of comparability or analogy, against "automatic" or "free association"), so beings are what they are by standing *for,* or they turn into themselves by being turned into others, but on the condition that the *for,* or the *into,* be understood within a certain orientation, a certain *thought,* that of ritual victimization. A sacrificial victim is such if it can be taken-for, be sacrificed to, or sacrifice itself for, another that is its other. McGinnis says this for example: "The woman's saintliness does not result from naïve devotion but from her victimhood." The general equivalent, which ensures the circulation of valences, is ritual victimization. Quite generally, Baudelaire's poetics is "religious"; I was about to say, it is "indexed" with precision to (Christian) theology. Not only the poems—whose tenor, or almost a "provocation," our own de-Christianization or, as Starobinski would say, our uneducated amnesia of the Fable, chances to make us *not* take seriously—but many passages from the intimate journals, or the *Salons,* or the prose, declare it, a tiny portion of which I mention at times allusively. "Even if God did not exist, Religion still would be Holy and *Divine.* God is the only being who, in order to reign, need not even exist" (*Fusées* I).

To recognize figures of the archaic (sacred and Christian) within the modern, for example, in the old ragman or in assassin wine, is the work—thought and craft—of the poet: *"to spear it on the mark, of mystical nature."* Metamorphosing it one more time, poetry inherits the end [*purposiveness, finality*] of religious thought. "An ultimate ironic heroization," according to the citation from Michel Foucault; *ironic,* indeed, because Baudelaire does not believe but saves the letter. All is "ironic" because held within the as-though of a suspended faith in relation to precise, theological beliefs.

Now, in these times of *our* modernity, when knowledge no longer reckons with poetry, I shall suspend a conclusive coda on Baudelaire's suspended belief and return to the question of an *ars poetica*'s capacity for truth. In what way can the practice of poetry, reading and writing, interest our *savoir-vivre,* whatever people's relation to a religion might be; and what does Baudelaire say over and over to us, from this perspective? Two or three comments.

I start again from the "spectacle, *ordinary* as it may be, that one has before one's eyes," and from the *almost* supernatural *circumstance,* so named once more by Baudelaire. The poem is for the circumstance. *Parisian* for example. "Along the old outskirts," for example; or "As I was crossing the new Carrousel." So what is *that* little river? To what, one asks, does the deictic refer, for if there is something that *refers,* it is indeed the deictic. The river that runs by here, namely by the Carrousel, is indeed also the Seine—or the *basin,* "mirror," it is the same thing. *That* little river, actually perceived, inseminates the fertile memory.

The forked, duplicitous deictic points with deference toward two elsewheres: the nearby Seine and the absent Simoïs, in other words toward an "over-there" other than the "there" of my "here," this "there" of the Seine not far off in the background of the existing circumstance. The present, local, circumstantial relation between nearness and remoteness serves as a sighting device for a relation to a *very faraway very near* where the very remote makes itself nearest, *all the nearer. . .* And perhaps that is what is meant by "presence," which has to be reached, be "made," like that famous "silence" music desires . . .

Memory, the by-heart of one's heart awaiting citation, awaits, fertile, exuberant, the encounter; that "circumstance which will make the relation" (Prigogine), the relation to Andromache. Fertile memory is penetrated by this, here, a percept evoked *conjointly* by the demonstrative, a "lived experience," as one says, or e-motion. In a nearby poem (two pages before), cobblestones that trip the lyric subject awaken, set in motion, the verse; the *corner* (of the street, the gutter) makes swordplay and rhyme coincide, lances of circumstance. *Words* and *cobblestones* exchange through *likeness:* and here we take this opportunity to remember another Baudelairean narrator's famous stumbling over cobblestones—"dazzling"—in the Guermantes courtyard.

Poetry is a matter of sight and ear, or of vision and hearing. The aspect of the visible which interests such seeing, or, better yet, the visibility correlated to this type of attention, or intention, called poetic, is that middle ground where metamorphoses, where turning-into, "may take place," a middle ground of rapprochement or "image." Of course, "metamorphosis" has changed meanings, from Ovid to Proust or to Kafka, and it does not concern credulity toward "real" magic. It is about what Proust has in sight when the narrator witnesses the transfiguration of Madame Guermantes into a Nereid, or more ungenteelly of Madame Leroi into a frog. To have a certain air . . . It is a question of such and such a thing having an air of another, or "resembling" it; a question of a middle ground where likeness, family resemblance, rushes in. Andromache, I am thinking of you. Now in what medium can this likening, this dis-junction, operate? It concerns the ear, this time; a name, or word, *for* another, for a thing with—or like—another. Word-alchemy. "Fanciful swordplay," says Baudelaire, rhyming *rhyme* with a paronym of *crime*. There would be no reason not to restate the whole operation in terms of imitation—that overly discredited term—if imitation, which is neither identification nor subjective affinity, tells of the one swarming within the many, of what I hoped to denote by the phrase *commutuality of mortals*.

Allow me to digress a moment regarding these prepositions: the *for* of substitution and the *into* of change.

Suddenly I hear again passing (in "memory") this Cornelian distich Valéry admired: "Le ciel a-t-il formé cet amas de merveilles / Pour la demeure d'un serpent?" [Did heaven form this mass of marvels /for a snake's dwelling place?] And I sound out this *pour* (for) that is not so much final, "teleological," as adopting the value of the Latin *pro,* as in the phrase *to take for.* As though it were a matter of abridging in a flash an Ovidian metamorphosis, in this instance that of the global reversal of the marvelous into horror, of the charm or the spell cast, *for* this result theology asks us to consider as the effect of an original "catastrophe" that never ceases to have taken place, turning all the world's gold into base lead, etc. The distich oxymoron retraces becoming by short-circuiting the extremes, from marvel to monstrosity.

Poetic experience is a taking-for, taking *a* for *b,* not by error but rather thanks to a brief illusion, for a resolute transformation, *turning* error *into* incentive, wresting an opportunity gained from errantry (as did Quixote), "gaining some ground." Either to understand what happened, "what ever could have happened" since the catastrophe of the origin (all this possibility turned into fate by freedom)—or to reopen the possibilities, to multiply reality by possibility—a setting, or *re*setting, into place of things through each one's ability-to-be in place of others.

In other words: a mistake—or a chance of mistake—is turned into a take [*view*] by the operation of a poem. Poetic vigilance and the fervor of the poem favor misunderstanding. They play with and upon the perceptual error or "illusion of the senses"—willingly mistaking the cloud for a herd, but in order to turn "the mistake" into a *possible* truth. Because if I took X for Y, with and in words as with and in things, I then could either blush at it, laugh, and forget, or else exploit the delusion, going from a surprised credulity to a reflection that turns the confusion into ever-possible rapprochement, turning a reserve and resource of language into an operation at work within a work—with full knowledge of things and of language . . . that is what has been called an *objective chance,* circumstance turned into relation, appearance into apparition, coincidence into meaning, improvisation into providence.

In a tragic and agnostic, heroic and ironic fable whose principal devices would be those of recollection, prosopopoeia, and allegory, Baudelaire redramatizes the articulation between the poem and the Christian within the modern, as though everything had become a staging ("in the Spanish style," for example, or of an "unknown master") of great theologemes turning back into mythologemes and philosophemes. It is as though modernity were a permanent sacrificial crisis without a ritually assignable victim, in the effervescence of substitutions, in the remanence *and* oblivion of the crisis, as though nothing were left but universal prostitution without resolution, and a never-ending "fountain of blood." As though no transcendence, not even a quasi-transcendence, could emerge from the effervescence, not even in the mode of a satanic counterreligion.

"Christian" thought without Christianity, a sort of religious atheism, a thinking made of as-thoughs, suspends belief *in* that which gives it the means to be configured; a crafty mobility of exchanges between profanation and revelation, blasphemy and sanctification whose irony compels us not to lose sight of its literality—indeed even against Voltaire when the Enlightenment in its own way forgets the "meaning of the sacred;" for example, the meaning of pagan prostitution, which Joseph de Maistre's reading conserves.

Just as Christianity forbade at the same time Baal and Aristotle, sacrifice and prostitution, by treating them ironically and generalizing their meaning, so the modern poem exploits (shall we say one last time?) the transferability of "Christian figures" . . . as though the New Testament were in turn an *emblem*—an interpretant—of our condition, a purveyor of parables to be turned inside out for the benefit of the earthly kingdom.

What is the status of the "depth of life?" we ask ourselves again and again, when the meaning of the *occasion* (or circumstance) is to reveal (simply, I was about to say) the "analogies of experience," and when to exist finds within the spectacle its *analogon*, such that the instance of "poetic" reflection recaptures the fact that there is revelation—the autonomous moment of an epiphany of to-exist itself. "Diminutive of the infinite," this lovely expression with a Pascalian feel applies to humankind and the poem is the enduring enlargement of this diminutive.

But if this depth within and of the occasion which reveals it is the intensity of a meaning looping back upon the meaning of intensity, free from articulation with a system of meaning or *quasi*-theology, [then] the identity between the meaning and nonmeaning of every *thing* of which such an occasion is the circumstance runs the risk of washing existence up on the desolate shores of the Ecclesiast.

The dislodgment, by a homothetic or homological *mise en abyme*, within the *ordinary*, of a *depth* which the ordinary sets out to symbolize, does it yield anything more than the "richness" of life? Or more precisely the opposition, the antinomy (*nomos* of the *anti*?), without "reconciliation here below," between this inebriant profusion of what exists and the horror, the ill, of existing makes up the abyss of existing, whereof "Christianity" is the mediation, the *middle ground,* articulating in detail the polarities, unfolding the "meaning." Covetousness before window displays or the keenness of an imprisoned glance darting out through innumerable bars, and from the depths of its paralyzed omnipotence, so many *scenes,* figurations, that re-echo each other because they echo THAT (this condition) of which they are the example, the occasion, the repetition, the transposition . . .

This neuter, this THAT, of which we speak, whatever *it* may be, may be being (maybe it is being), but according to the most vernacular usage of *Being,* to be a being—in other words, the one Baudelaire calls "*mon semblable.*" What is it to be a counterpart? It is what it is by being-like, cast into the abyss between a "mass of marvels" (Corneille), this world which is given/refused (or for some created/destroyed), *and* someone living/dying to whom it is shown and withdrawn, offered and held back. Proximity of what is refused, dispossession of the gift, inaccessibility of what is approachable, insatiability of desire, etc., constitute the oxymoronic existentiality of thwarted being or, more calmly, what I have called *capacity.* Senseless? It is sense itself.

How does one make revelation out of profanation after having made profanation out of revelation? Or how does one invent a relationship between the unbelievable and the undeletable; that is, "un-delete what has become unbelievable"? The fable must retain its potential to be followed to a multivocal, equivocal, letter, captivating and deluding a reader who becomes a legatee of every promise of a connection to a promised land, so that interpretation may continue, endlessly, of what is and is not there in every sense of its figurative appropriateness. *A willing suspension of belief?*

The perfection of unbelief that it is a matter of achieving is in no way the liquidation of the great schemata of figuration, hence (I would say) of revelation, *of* existence; in no way the liquidation of all the emblems that mythology and history, savage thought, structural thought, and historical thought comprise to another end altogether than simply to collect their archives.

Taking my chances in a more personal tone with regard to belief, I shall advance, not far from concluding: I tend to believe (against the grain of current doxa) that the future of the poem, for us, is a movement of discredence, withdrawing (tearing itself away) from belief; it is a disenchantment more powerful, more ruinous, more depriving and ascetic than anything the ordinary usage of to disillusion-disenchant-recant may signify.

The operation may be called interpretation, or profanation, or translation. The poet is someone who seeks a re-use for the great theologemes that made and were our great beliefs, wandering now like the tombless dead, unappeased, unappeasing. The perpetuity of the fable is at stake, as well as the community of belonging to a culture prior to media-culture, the one that formerly still allowed the multitude to read the great painted images, to recognize in general the artifacts of their world: annunciation, incarnation, sacrifice, settings of the Last Supper, deposition, elevation, resurrection, dormition. . . . Inventive poetic profanation, the inspired simony of religious thought, converts the unbelievable into revelations of the *"depth of life"* in this earthly Kingdom unto "the end of the world"; converts it all into poems, if one allows this word to be taken, as just requested, upon the model of mytheme, philosopheme, theologeme . . . Farsighted (poetic) improvisation summons the ordinary to appear in the light of the memorable, in a reciprocal *trans*figuration between the invented configuration of new things and inherited figuration. A judgment may recognize therein a figure unhoped-for and expected; it can be of use again . . . and make us useful for something—assuming there still are things, that's the whole question.

A sketch by Claudel (it is in *Conversations in the Loir-et-Cher*) catches off guard the Western male (this husband whom Montesquieu passes judgment upon in his *Notebooks:* "All husbands are ugly"), sunken into his household armchair in the evening, muttering an abstracted retort to his wife, "and whom the newspaper swallows up again" (one would say, today, the television . . .).

Ruminating, retired, a self-serving solipsist, if this sort of *subject* is what the News procures and produces, then I dream of yet another addressee, another interlocutor for the poem, another user for what I called here poetics, a widened field where poet/poetry/poem fill roles while trading places (in what Mallarmé calls exchange of a reciprocity of proofs)—that field wide enough so poetry will not be alone there. As the vital and infinite middle ground of the relation (a Romantic might have said), or, more trivially today, as a locus of generalized translation, that field enables and activates the thoughtful and effective exchanges (theoretical and practical, one used to say) of the arts among themselves, both along their confines and with their exteriors.

Such a poetics calls for an inverse movement from the one Claudel lends to that bourgeois against whom Baudelaire already inveighed in his page on "the world that is going to end." It alerts and has one go outside the self. *To sally forth;* and it is not enough to go out so as to be outside. One must still, like Don Quixote, or the Surrealist escapade of late, go out and, in going out, go out; cross and in crossing, cross; fall and in falling, fall: to clear, precisely, a way for the double meaning of the poetic propositions, which are twice true or, as one used to say, allegorical.

To bring about a movement toward an emergency exit which in no way leads to the other world, to beyond the world, neither *"behind the world"* (Nietzsche) nor to the *immonde;* instead assembling counterparts/brothers, Baudelaireans, in the experience of their com-mutuality as mortals.—But perhaps music alone succeeds? That is what amassed youth believes. Let us listen to the music, says Shakespeare's Lorenzo. Let us envy music.

Perhaps what Baudelaire destines for us is audible in the last line of the threshold of *Les Fleurs du Mal,* which calls upon *"mon semblable."*

Léo Strauss, in reference to Hermann Cohen, speaks of "the discovery of humankind as my counterpart." I note that the task thus determined is poetic: similitude (being-alike) is to be discovered; the making of nearness must go by way of rapprochement; and the Claudelian phrase: "Duty is of things nearby" also concerns poetry, *poethically*—assuming there still are things, I was saying, and that is the whole question in the twentieth-century twilight. It is not true that first I am in possession of "myself" in terms of knowledge, thence proceeding to the discovery of my counterpart-brother by recognizing him starting from myself. . . . To discover the human in each of us (among the com-mutuality of mortals) as counterpart is a poetic task. The similar-to-the-counterpart, in itself similar, is to be discovered. Would that be the most important discovery yet to come? Would Baudelaire's first word be the last?

Notes

Modern Beauty versus Platonist Beauty

1. See also Cousin 1830, 1843, and 1845.

2. It will be noted that Swedenborg never concealed his debt to the Greek philosopher.

3. In this letter, Baudelaire informs his correspondent that he is preparing an essay on *"Les Peintres idéalistes,"* pilot study for *L'Art philosophique.*

4. On the impossibility for the artist to reach the beautiful, one can refer also, in *Le Spleen de Paris,* to "Chacun sa chimère" and to "Le Fou et la Vénus" (*OC* 1:282–84).

5. On this matter see also Labarthe's article (1992, especially p. 43).

6. We think notably of Jean Pommier and of Marc Eigeldinger.

7. On the interpretation of "Correspondances," see also Milner 1967, 172–78.

8. See *OC* 1:840.

9. Note that blindness for Flaubert also became a theme of derision: the beggar in *Madame Bovary* presents the decadent image of the romantic poet.

10. Quotations are taken from the annotations to pages cxviii–cxix of the "Discours extrait des différentes préfaces que les éditeurs de Shakespeare ont mises à la tête de leurs éditions," a text on which LeTourneur made a commentary and which figures in volume 1 of *Shakespeare traduit de l'anglais, dédié au roi.*

11. See Pichois 1979, 21–22. Baudelaire brings up the use of the word by Heine in the *Salon de 1846.*

12. The canvases of Elstir reveal "a kind of metamorphosis of the things depicted, analogous to what is called metaphor in poetry" (M. Proust 1987, 191).

13. Note that Gautier would also have held the same views on Courbet.

14. (*Réflexions sur quelques uns de mes contemporains. Marceline Desbordes-Valmore*). One sees again that, in such a context, *spirituel* is not to be understood in the sense of *céleste* but of *moral.*

15. The formula is Proust's.

16. See particularly the *Salon de 1859* (*OC* 2:616–17).

17. See the definition of the work of the imagination given by Baudelaire in the *Salon de 1859:* "The whole visible universe is nothing but a storehouse of images and signs to which the imagination will give a place and a relative value" (*OC* 2:627). As for the formula "exact imitation spoils the memory," it belongs to the *Salon de 1846* (*OC* 2:455).

The Linguistic Turning of the Symbol

1. The prevalence and authority of this linguistic notion of the symbol, which equates it with a sign that signifies by absence, shows up in anthropological discourse; for example, that of Claude Lévi-Strauss in "L'efficacité du symbolique": "It is a relation of symbol to thing

symbolized, or to use the vocabulary of the linguists, of signifier to signified" (218). One of the most determined and extensive theorizations of the symbol as implying essentially absence is Lacanian psycholinguistics. Entry into the symbolic stage is marked by loss of presence and plenitude in undifferentiated union with the mother's body, the symbolic per se symbolizing absence and alienation, specifically in the form of castration fears vis-à-vis the symbol of all symbols, the father's phallus. Even in as literature-oriented a version of Lacanianism as Kristeva's, the "ordre symbolique" emerges as "the yawning gap between signifier and signified" in *La Révolution du langage poétique* (45).

2. Samuel Taylor Coleridge, *The Statesman's Manual,* quoted by Angus Fletcher (16).

3. Cf. Robert Greer Cohn, "Symbolism."

4. Jena romanticism, particularly that of Schelling and Schlegel, is documented in its influence specifically on French romantics by Michel Brix in the preceding essay.

5. On the historical motivations and context for this endeavor, see Charles Taylor, chapters 22 and 23.

6. Baudelaire is actually quoting Delacroix, for example, in *Salon de 1846,* section 4.

7. This suggests why Baudelaire's poetry has lent itself so beautifully to formalist analyses such as Roman Jakobson and Claude Lévi-Strauss's "'Les Chats' de Charles Baudelaire." Henri Meschonnic's numerous writings have further developed the linguistic approach to Baudelaire.

8. Michael Hamburger, in *The Truth of Poetry: Tensions in Modern Poetry from Baudelaire to the 1960s,* argues that Baudelaire is an allegorical poet, which is true, but it does not follow that he is "not a Symbolist" (6). Basic contributions for situating Baudelaire as a symbolist include Guy Michaud, Lloyd Austin, and Henri Peyre.

9. A corrective to the idea promulgated influentially by Hugo Friedrichs that referentiality is simply eliminated and reality liquidated in symbolist poetry is persuasively argued by Paul de Man in "Lyric and Modernity."

10. Fredric Jameson describes the shift between what can be recognized as these two aspects of symbolism as a transition from production of the referent to its erasure and elimination, and he articulates these two phases in terms of a modernist and a postmodernist Baudelaire. See "Baudelaire as Modernist and Postmodernist: The Dissolution of the Referent and the Artificial 'Sublime.'" Hans-Jost Frey addresses a similar issue in discussing Baudelaire as a critic of mimetic representation and as imitating only what is immanent to his own representations.

11. In addition to de Man, Frey, and Jameson, see also Georges Poulet and Jean Starobinski.

Gautier as "Seer" of the Origins of Modernity in Baudelaire

1. Critics of our own time have often misconstrued Gautier's perception of the "bizarre" nature of Chinese art—a view which was nevertheless shared by his disciple, Baudelaire (see *OC* 2:576). Gautier's approach to Chinese art employs a mechanism similar to that seen in the case of British art where the critic steps outside the ever-pervasive classic aesthetic of his own country in order to appropriate the vision of the "other," who is operating in accordance with a different way of "seeing." Thus when Gautier uses words such as "curio," "laid" (ugly), and "le laid idéal" (ideal ugliness) in speaking about Chinese art, he is adopting the language of the outsider, who has been "blinded" by his or her automatic adherence to the dominant Greco-Roman aesthetic: "judging by our ideas of beauty, which in spite of ourselves, go back to the

Greek example, these virtuous Chinese were ugly, but their ugliness was, so to speak, pretty, gracious and spiritual," remarks Gautier upon seeing four Chinese men on a trip to London (Gautier 1849, 266). In 1855, Gautier notes apropos of the Chinese exhibit at the Exposition Universelle: "The Chinese have their own particular way of envisioning art.—Other nations, beginning with the Greeks who attained it, search for ideal beauty; the Chinese search ideal ugliness ("*le laid idéal*"); they think that art must distance itself as much as possible from nature . . . in the pure arabesque, in capricious ornamentation . . . the Chinese are art masters who cannot be imitated" (Gautier 1855e, 1: 131, 137).

2. "Charles Baudelaire né en 1821" appears in volume 4 of Eugène Crépet's anthology, *Les Poëtes français* (date recorded in the *Bibliographie de la France:* 2 August 1862). Baudelaire's obituary appears at the beginning of the theater review ("Revue des Théâtres") that Gautier wrote for *La Presse* (9 September 1867). The *Rapport sur le progrès de la poésie*, which contains the passage on Baudelaire, constitutes a part of the *Recueil de rapports sur le progrès des lettres et des sciences; Rapport sur le progrès des lettres*, by MM. Silvestre de Sacy, Féval, Théophile Gautier, and Edouard Thierry. Finally, the study which would serve as the preface for the 1868 edition of *Les Fleurs du Mal* (*Œuvres complètes* de Charles Baudelaire, Michel Lévy, 1:1–75) first appeared as a series of articles in *L'Univers illustré* (7, 14, 21, 28 March; 4, 11, 18 April 1868); the version which served as preface, referred to in this essay, contains some modifications. See *Baudelaire par Gautier* (Gautier 1986), where these four texts are reproduced and analyzed. All references to these texts will be from this edition.

3. For Gautier, it is *l'œil intérieur* (variant: *l'œil de l'esprit;* "the interior eye" or the "mind's eye"), which allows an artist like Delacroix or a writer like Homer to proceed "not by their vision of the immediate, but by intuition." Such writer-artists, instead of copying what they see in nature, select those elements from the exterior world which correspond to their artistic vision. See, among other examples in Gautier's art criticism, *L'Art moderne* (Gautier 1856c, 36, passage on Homer) and the "Salon of 1839. VII. Eugène Delacroix, Riesener" (Gautier 1839).

4. Thanks to his *œil intérieur*, Gautier brings to the transposition process both the intimate vision of the artist and the creative powers of the poet. See Hamrick 1998.

5. In addition to the example of the English painters, other instances in which "modern" elements trigger the "transfer" phenomenon for Gautier are found in the work of Edgar Allan Poe and Nathaniel Hawthorne. See Gautier 1986, 80–83, 123–30.

6. Apropos of Gautier and modernity, see Hamrick 1993, 2:521–42. For a brief review of dictionary definitions, see p. 536 n. 3. Already in 1844, Gautier was urging artists to leave off with the then worn-out classic ideal and to be more sensitive to "this ideal which is floating in the soul and in the mind of everyone" (Gautier 1844). At this time, for both Gautier and Baudelaire, the key word which conveys a preoccupation with the present is "romanticism."

The origin of the word *modernité* and its usage have been discussed by Blin, Compagnon, Jauss, Larthomas, and Froidevaux, among others.

7. Whereas contemporary French distinguishes between *la mode* ("fashion" or "custom") and *le mode* ("method" or "manner"), up until the sixteenth century, the word in all of its different meanings remained feminine (see Bloch and Wartburg 1968, 413). Ever-changing "fashion" (*la mode*) is, in the end, but an example of the ever-changing "manner" of living. Both meanings can be tied to the transitory nature of the moment.

8. See Gautier 1843, 204–6. This early text evoking the link between *la mode* and the relativity of beauty has been largely overlooked by present-day critics, who have more frequently

cited Gautier's article entitled, "De la mode," which appeared some fifteen years later in *L'Artiste*. This oversight has led to some unfortunate conclusions, including speculation that the 1858 article may owe its inspiration to Baudelaire.

9. See "De la mode," *L'Artiste*, 14 March 1858. For a more detailed analysis of the place of *la mode* in the notion of the relativity of beauty for Gautier, see Hamrick 1993.

10. The fact that Gautier's first mention of modernity predates the 1855 reviews shows that this is not a strictly British phenomenon. The key elements underlying this notion are rather its link with what is "new" ("des effets neufs") and "unexpected" ("des aspects inattendus")—that is, what is not only "modern" as opposed to classic, but also in current usage ("des effets [qui sont] neufs"), which has an effect of surprise ("aspects inattendus") on those accustomed to the traditional, academic model.

11. "Galerie du XIXe siècle: Honoré de Balzac," *L'Artiste*, 21, 28 March; 4, 18, 25 April; 2 May 1858; reprinted in *Portraits contemporains;* see 107, 109.

12. Baudelaire opens his *Salon de 1859* by paying tribute to the British painters who had exhibited in 1855 and whose absence in 1859 he deplores. This passage appears at the beginning of the first chapter entitled, "L'Artiste moderne" (*OC* 2:609–10). Later, of course, the artist in *Le Peintre de la vie moderne* would also be English.

13. "We accept each person from the point of view of his own particular ideal . . . we judge their painting as if we possessed their soul," explains Gautier in his introduction to *L'Artiste* in 1856 (Gautier 1856b, 4). Further on, referring to Delacroix and Ingres, who had opposing styles, Gautier notes: "We embrace momentarily their tastes and the phobias of these opposing natures; we judge their painting as if we possessed their soul."

14. "Who immediately grasped the varied merits, essentially brand new, of Leslie,—the two Hunts . . . ?" asks Baudelaire in his study on Théophile Gautier in 1859 (*OC* 2:123). Baudelaire was referring to the English painters who had exhibited at the Exposition Universelle in 1855.

15. "De la composition en peinture" (On Composition in Painting), *La Presse*, 22 November 1836. In this article, Gautier attacks the "expert critics sworn in by the newspapers . . . the literary hacks who write dissertations . . . the nebulous professors of transcendental aesthetics," etc. For these, "routine or education" has had the effect of pulling "thick blinders" over their pupils. Consequently, they cannot see ("Ils n'ont pas l'œil").

16. "Why deprive oneself of the delicious pleasure of being for a time another, of living in his brain, of seeing nature through his eyes as through a new prism?" (Gautier 1856b, 4).

17. See "Notes nouvelles sur Edgar Poe," *OC* 2:319–20. Gautier acknowledges his borrowing from Baudelaire in the 1862 text written for the Crépet anthology (Gautier 1986, 81). As will be seen further on, the critic gives added color and depth to this imagery when he composes the 1868 text that will become the preface to *Les Fleurs du Mal* (Gautier 1986, 123–24). Baudelaire's poem, "Le Coucher du soleil romantique," which serves as an epilogue to Charles Asselineau's volume, *Mélanges tirés d'une petite bibliothèque romantique* (Paris: René Pincebourde, 1866), accords a more nostalgic tone to the "sunset" image as symbolic of the fading Romantic era (*OC* 1:149).

18. Compare Baudelaire, who, in *Notes nouvelles sur Edgar Poe*, observes: "But what did not occur to the professors-members of the jury is that in the movement of life, complications and combinations can happen which are completely unforeseen for their schoolboy wisdom. And then their insufficient language breaks down" (*OC* 2:320).

19. Gautier 1995, 616. The grandiose, often biblical, perspectives of John Martin re- main a constant model of artistic vision for Gautier throughout his own work. Early in his journal-

istic career, Gautier devoted an entire article to the artist, "John Martynn [*sic*]," *La Presse,* 31 January 1837, as well as a lengthy passage in his review of the 1837 "Concours de sculpture" in *La Charte de 1830,* 17 September (in Gautier 1880, 164–75).

20. *OC* 1:791. Unfortunately, as a translation, the word *fusion* does not capture the succinct quality of the original term, which is *alliage.* "Son oeuvre présente un très rare et curieux alliage," observes Claude Pichois in the "Notice" to *Les Fleurs du Mal.*

21. See the letters dated 13 and 15 May 1871, which Rimbaud addresses to Georges Izambard et à Paul Demeny respectively (Rimbaud, 1972, 249–50).

22. "After having seen, our greatest pleasure was to transport into our own art, monuments, frescos, pictures, statues, bas-reliefs, often at the risk of forcing the language and changing the dictionary into an artist's palette . . ." (Gautier 1856b, 4).

23. For Gautier, the sense of the term *œil visionnaire* is close to those of "l'œil intérieur," "l'œil de l'esprit," "l'œil de l'âme," etc. See Hamrick 1998, n. 29.

24. "[J]'ai voulu . . . rendre un hommage profond à l'auteur d'*Albertus,* de *La Comédie de la Mort* et d'*España,*" wrote Baudelaire in the first version of the dedication of *Les Fleurs du Mal (OC* 1:187). It is these earlier *recueils poétiques* of Gautier—those which resonate with the eccentric "frenetic" echo of the *Jeune France*—which were particularly prized by Baudelaire.

Strangers in the Park

1. For the dating of the Manet's portraits of Baudelaire see Sandblad 1954, 64–67, and Harris 1990, 93, 149, 182–90.

2. Examples of this blindness abound. To cite but one example: Bruce Davis, in comparing the apparent style and intent of the two portraits, concludes that the *Baudelaire de face* responds to conventions of portraiture, and the *Baudelaire de profil* is more clearly a statement of caricature. While this conclusion may not be objectionable, Davis's use of the Manet letter to arrive at it plainly is:

> Manet apparently considered "Baudelaire de profil" of lesser significance and seriousness, referring in his letter to Asselineau to "Baudelaire de face"'s greater importance and appropriateness for a book of poetry. He may have considered "Baudelaire de profil" as more of a personal memento—appropriate for illustrating *Baudelaire, sa vie,* but not *Baudelaire, son œuvre,* a judgment perfectly consistent with the etching's status as a caricature rather than a pure portrait. (Davis 1983–84, 47)

3. Leo Steinberg, "Why the Visual Arts Are a Closed Book to the Literate," Modern Language Association Convention, New York, December 1983. There are, of course, individual exceptions to the general "misreading" I have referred to, both of Manet's letter and of Baudelaire's *Spleen de Paris,* but none, to my knowledge, that address the specific poetic intertext that is at issue here. Two such exceptions are Theodore Reff's article "Manet and the Paris of Haussmann and Baudelaire," in *Manet and Modern Paris,* esp. 23–28, and Therese Dolan 1997, 611–29.

4. "La Corde" (first published in 1864) is dedicated to Manet and refers to a true incident of 1859–60: the tragic suicide by hanging of the painter's model, Alexandre, the young boy in the painting *The Child with Cherries.* Manet's role in "La Corde" is double, for he serves both as the implicit model for the narrator of the episode and as the explicit addressee of the poem.

One can reasonably assume that Manet was familiar with other prose poems by Baudelaire, particularly those composed and published at the height of their friendship, before the poet's departure to Belgium in 1864.

5. Prendergast 1985, 181. The art historian Prendergast takes to task is Kathleen Adler, who in her book *Manet* "quotes from 'Les Veuves' only that passage which mentions the pleasures of the park and the concert, which, of course, gives a misleading view of a poem whose main focus is on what or who is excluded from the scene of pleasure (249 n. 78).

6. If we are to trust Antonin Proust's memory, Baudelaire was in Manet's studio the day word came that the *Buveur d'absinthe* had been rejected from the Salon of 1859. The painter angrily accused Thomas Couture of having influenced the jury members against him; it was assumed that his former teacher was shocked by the immoral subject matter of the painting. Anne Coffin Hanson has indicated the implausibility of this story (1977, 54). More likely, she suggests, it was the association of this painting with the then scandalous *Les Fleurs du Mal* that triggered Couture's disapproval, an association linked specifically to the constellation of poems entitled "Le Vin."

7. T. J. Clark, *The Painting of Modern Life: Paris in the Art of Manet and His Followers.* In a chapter surveying the impact of Haussmannization on the representation of class in the Second Empire, Clark reads *La Musique aux Tuileries* as yet another document of social fact: "hardly a picture of modernity at all, as it is sometimes supposed to be, but, rather, a description of 'society's' resilience in the face of empire. The public realm of the Jardin des Tuileries is still narrow and definite, composed of particular portraits, professions, and uniforms. It is a realm in which one recognizes friends and relations, and knows precisely how they would wish to be shown. Such knowledge depends in turn on the great protocols of class, which everyone obeys scrupulously; and it is class itself—the pure category, the disembodied order of appearances—which ends up invading every square inch between the trees" (Clark 1985, 64).

8. See Alan Bowness's suggestions that this assembly of influential and creative people may represent a direct response to Courbet's *Atelier,* subtitled a "realist allegory" ("Courbet's Early Subject Matter" in *French Nineteenth-Century Painting and Literature*).

9. Within the corpus of Baudelaire's poetry, the widow of the prose poem—and eventually the painting—represents yet another allusive incarnation of the Andromaque figure as she appears in the verse poem "Le Cygne" (1859). From a psychoanalytical point of view, I argue that the recurrent image of majestic widows and, moreover, the widow with a young child, resuscitates for Baudelaire a deep nostalgia for "le bon temps des tendresses maternelles," that he describes in the famous letter to his mother of 6 May 1861—that is, the brief period of time separating his father's death from his mother's remarriage to Jacques Aupick. This was the time during which Baudelaire's mother was a widow and, he claims, "uniquement à moi." It is significant that it is to this brief period in his life that he bitterly returns in 1861, at a time of great despondency. See Sima Godfrey 1985, 32–44. Another reading of the theme of widowhood in Baudelaire can be found in Richard Burton 1988, esp. 126–28.

10. For all its apparent pleasure, Manet's park contains the fact and the image of solitude even within its own splendid display. Nor can we dismiss that image as simply a coloristic afterthought; in the preparatory sketches for the painting (1861), a detail of the central configuration shows Eugène Manet addressing the seated woman. The figure of the widow is already there behind him, somewhat more eclipsed in this instance by the angle of his hat (Rouart and Wildenstein 1975).

11. Though concerned exclusively with the relative truth claims of any art historical

interpretation, David Carrier makes a similar point: "Interpretation seems, necessarily, a speculative activity. We interpret a given painting by attributing to the implied artist some imagined personality; and that view of him, in turn, influences how we see the remainder of his work" (1985, 322).

12. "So now, at a time when others are asleep, Monsieur G. is bending over his table, darting on to a sheet of paper the same glance that a moment ago he was directing towards external things, skirmishing with his pencil, his pen, his brush, splashing his glass of water up to the ceiling, wiping his pen on his shirt, in a ferment of violent activity, as though afraid that the image might escape him, cantankerous though alone, elbowing himself on. And the external world is reborn upon his paper, natural and more than natural, beautiful and more than beautiful, strange and endowed with an impulsive life, like the soul of its creator" (Baudelaire 1964, 12).

13. *Critical Inquiry* (1984). Aspects of the argument in the essay are reintroduced in *Manet's Modernism or The Face of Painting in the 1860s* (Fried 1996). With reference to Baudelaire, Manet, memory, and *La Musique aux Tuileries,* see especially 164–67. Elsewhere in the book, Fried argues persuasively for the influence of commedia dell'arte and puppet theater on Manet's composition of *La Musique aux Tuileries;* see 55.

The Subject of *Le Peintre de la vie moderne*

1. For a list of authors who think that Baudelaire ought to have chosen otherwise, see Carrier 1996, 50–51.

2. For a chronology of the composition of the essay, which tends to place its initial composition in 1858–60, see *OC* 2:1415–16.

3. "Beauty is made up of an eternal, invariable element, whose quantity is excessively difficult to determine, and of a relative, circumstantial element, which will be, if you like, whether severally or all at once, the age, its fashion, its morals, its emotions" (*OC* 2:685).

4. Pichois also sketches a history of this reaction: "This essay, by its date of composition, belongs to Baudelaire's last creative period, the years 1858–60; it must therefore be placed close to the Salon de 1859" (*OC* 2:1418).

5. "Recently again, when he learnt that I had in mind to write an appreciation of his mind and his talent, he begged me—very imperiously, I must admit—to suppress his name, and if I must speak of his works, to speak of them as if they were those of an anonymous artist. I will humbly comply with this singular request. The reader and I preserve the fiction that Monsieur G. does not exist" (Baudelaire 1964, 5).

6. "[T]he fact that it took Hegel thousands and thousands of pages to try to circumvent, and yet to confront, the problem would seem to indicate that something else is at stake. At that moment in the *Phenomenology,* Hegel is not speaking of language at all, let alone of writing something down, but of consciousness in general as *certainty* in its relation to the phenomenal categories of time, space and selfhood. The point is that this certainty vanishes as soon as phenomenal determination, temporal or other, is involved, as it has to be. Consciousness ('here' and 'now') is not 'false and misleading' because of language; consciousness *is* language, and nothing else, because it is false and misleading" (de Man 1989, 41).

7. In an entirely unscientific comparison of texts from Baudelaire and other writers, a dramatic difference in frequency of demonstrative adjectives and spatial markers (-ci, -là, voici, voilà, ici, and là) is evident. For three pages of *Le Peintre de la vie moderne,* I count twenty-three deictics; for three pages of Baudelaire's 1855 essay *Exposition universelle,* I count twenty-

four; for three pages of Eugène Fromentin's *Les Maîtres d'autrefois,* I count only ten; for three pages of Hugo's *William Shakespeare,* I count seventeen.

8. "What we can know is that the era whose dominant concerns were prophesied by Baudelaire, the era of modernism, is over, which is to say that his ways of thinking are now essentially of historical interest" (Carrier 1996, 171).

9. Ernst Gombrich, and later Norman Bryson, conceive of artistic evolution as a form of progress, akin to the relay structure presented by Baudelaire. Bryson, for example, rejects the "negative" relation of painter to predecessor that is typical of art critical discourse: "the interaction between the individual painter and the community of painters is once again negative: his aim is to outstrip them, to shed their formulaic legacy, to break whatever limited bond exists between that community and himself" (1983, 6). But before either Gombrich or Bryson, André Malraux modeled *Les Voix du silence* on "Les Phares." Older painters influenced younger ones who assimilated their predecessor's way of seeing only to replace it with a new way in their turn.

10. Claude Pichois summarizes the best known of the interpretations of the sequence, those of Léon Cellier and Bernard Böschenstein, in his notes to the poem. See *OC* 2:851–52.

11. "[W]hat consciousness will learn from experience in all sense-certainty is, in truth, only what we have see viz. the This as a *universal,* the very opposite of what that assertion affirmed to be universal experience" (Hegel 1977, 65).

Off the Charts

1. See Paul de Man 1989, esp. 69–70.

2. See Hans-Jost Frey's chapter entitled "Baudelaire," and especially his essay "On Presentation in Benjamin," where his remarks on Benjamin's use of the incognito are exemplary.

3. See Benjamin's formulation, "This is the nature of the lyric vocabulary in which an *allegory* appears suddenly and without preparation" ("The Paris of the Second Empire," 1983, 100); as well as Baudelaire's *Fusées* (*OC* 1:652).

"La Belle Dorothée," or Poetry and Painting

1. It was published only on 10 June 1863 in *La Revue Nationale* after "Les Tentations," before being inserted in *Le Spleen de Paris.*

Prose and Prosody

1. And this slant is an *invention.* What has to be examined with Jena romanticism is, as Philippe Lacoue-Labarthe and Jean-Luc Nancy write in *L'Absolu littéraire,* "the inauguration of the *theoretical* project in literature" (1978, 9).

2. Walter Benjamin, *Charles Baudelaire, un poète lyrique à l'apogée du capitalisme,* 143. Retranslated from the French.

3. This citation, like all those of Mallarmé in this text, is taken from "Crise de vers," in *OC* 360–68.

4. On the form this distancing takes in Baudelaire's attitude toward painting, see my "Harmony in Red and Green," in number 3 of *L'Année Baudelaire.*

5. It is at the heart of the "defect of languages" that translation works. Far from having to be thought of as the passive heir of this defect, translation, like poetry, pays for it, and very

substantially. It is even the fact of confronting this defect (that is, also the mass of all the qualities that make every language distinct and inimitable) that constitutes the essence of the translating act. On this organic connection between the translating act and poetic writing, I refer to the works of Antoine Berman, and notably to *Pour une critique des traductions: John Donne*. It must be emphasized that the question of genre—that is, the flux and flow between prose and poetry—belongs directly to what is at stake in translation; and one could even suggest that there is a connection between the invention of the prose poem and the register of choice that his translation of Poe could have imposed upon Baudelaire. Poe is completely at the center here since it is still he who comes back with the impeccable French prose writings that his poems translated by Mallarmé become.

Contingencies and Discontinuities of the Lyric *I*

1. The question of the lyric persona is articulated and addressed in a range of essays in *Figures du sujet lyrique* edited by Dominique Rabaté.

2. Pichois's comments are to be found in the *Notice* to the *Journaux intimes* in *OC* 1:1467.

3. Barthes's notion of the death of the author is predicated on the loss of origin of the voice (in language). See "The Death of the Author" (Barthes 1977, 142); Lacan makes a distinction between the "moi du sujet" and the "je du discours" in *Ecrits: A Selection*, 90; Foucault sees the subject as a function of discourse in "What Is an Author?" in *Language, Counter-Memory, Practice*, 138; and Derrida states that "Writing is other than the subject in whatever sense it is understood" in *De la Grammatologie*, 100. For an account of this with respect to Baudelaire and the fragmented self, see Nicolae Babuts, *Baudelaire at the Limits and Beyond*.

4. *Marginalia. The Complete Works of Edgar Allan Poe*, 16:128, cited in French by Claude Pichois (*OC* 1:1490).

5. Baudelaire rejects Rousseau as "model" both in the *Poème du hachisch* (*OC* 1:436) and in the *Pensées d'Album* (*OC* 1:709).

6. See Didier (1991, 135) for the relationship between the private and the public.

7. The word recurs frequently. It is significant that it refers to an experience that is remarkable and unique; one that may be strange. As its etymology (singularis = alone) suggests, it is a word that also emphasizes the individual and his isolation.

8. Indeed, Claude Pichois notes that Marcel Ruff connects this statement with Schelling's theories of knowledge and the Self, which Baudelaire may have read (*OC* 2:1378).

9. See the "Canevas de la dédicace," where Baudelaire writes: "J'ai cherché des titres. Les 66. Quoique cependant cet ouvrage tenant de la vis et du kaléidoscope pût bien être poussé jusqu'au cabalistique 666 et même 6666. . . . Cela vaut mieux qu'une intrigue de 6000 pages. Qu'on me sache donc gré de ma modération" [I have looked for titles. 66 of them. Although, this work, functioning as it does like the screw and the kaleidoscope, could easily be pushed to the cabalistic 666 or even 6666. . . . It's better than a 6000–page plot. I should, therefore, be thanked for my moderation] (*OC* 1:365).

10. Cf. Béatrice Didier (1973, 58), who writes: "The many texts about writing could easily be collected together, from *Fusées* as from *Mon cœur mis à nu*; the different styles, or 'manners,' which amount to more or less the same thing in the hands of a poet. But it is not simply a matter of reflection on style and styles; Baudelaire is, first and foremost, questioning the nature of writing itself. What does it mean to write? How to write?"

Modernity's Curse

1. *Le Livre à venir,* Gallimard 1959, 64.

2. For a discussion of the crucial events in Baudelaire's life during this period, please see "The Dandy and the Socialist" and "The Poe Translations and *Les Fleurs du Mal*" in Pichois's *Baudelaire* (Pichois and Ziegler 1989).

3. See Chambers's essay "Colère vaporisée" in *Mélancolie et opposition,* 43–48. The traumatic impact of June 1848 is analyzed at length in Oehler's *Le spleen contre l'oubli.*

4. This is very much in tune with the ideology of the July Monarchy. Guizot's motto—"Enrichissez-vous" (Enrich yourselves)—implied that social distinctions were without intrinsic content, and that anyone with enough dogged patience could pass into the ranks of the rich. Interestingly, while this attitude may characterize the "modern" economic milieu, it is antithetical to the primary attitude of aesthetic modernism.

5. Here I might make the connection with the final line of "Au lecteur"—"Hypocrite lecteur,—mon semblable,—mon frère!" [Hypocritical reader, my fellow human, my brother!]. Baudelaire is maneuvering the free will of the reader, calculating the potential reactions of the latter. The extent of the reader's reification will determine the reaction.

6. This statement seems to prefigure fragment XLVII from *Mon cœur mis à nu* (*OC* 1:707). There Baudelaire argues for the identity of freedom and fate, using the same conceptual elements that occur in *Conseils aux jeunes littérateurs* (perspectival shifts, the relationship between individual and collective instances, the role of subjective will in history). These elements persist in Baudelaire's thought across the great divide of the midcentury crisis (Pichois estimates that *Mon cœur mis à nu* was conceived around 1859).

7. Poe had used the fragment as an epigraph for his story "The Tell-Tale Heart."

8. See, for example, the careful exposition of Paul de Man's "Lyric and Modernity."

9. The poet's resistance is not really passive, at least not to begin with. Passive resistance places the burden, both of action and of cognition, outside itself. The poet's resistance begins with an action that is frustrated. The frustration forces an act of cognition that belongs first to the poet. In Baudelaire's corpus, we can trace the passage from action to cognition in poems like "Les Hiboux" and "Le Jeu." In "Le Guignon" the same passage occurs between the figure of Sisyphus and that of the poet. Sisyphus both is and is not a double for the poet, and the latter's *guignon* is defined in the space of such a suspended identification.

10. A kind of dialectical redefinition of terms is taking place in Sartre's argument. While poetry and prose at first cooperated in the critique of bourgeois society, they now have parted ways. Poetry's engagement to failure means that it is constituted by failure. The failure of instrumental language thereby becomes the failure of prose and the success of poetry.

11. Benjamin's statement is from "The Paris of the Second Empire in Baudelaire" (1983, 74). It is surprising because of the way it recasts Baudelaire's idea of "the heroism of modern life." In Baudelaire's formulation, modern life has one type of heroism, and antiquity has another. Benjamin collapses this relative notion of heroism into a universal one: we no longer have a variety of heroes, but *the* hero, whose true character is fulfilled in modernism.

(S)(m)othering Baudelaire

Many thanks to Peggy McCracken, John Ireland, and Brian Hyer for their generous help as I composed and revised this essay.

1. Baudelaire, *COR* 2:141; letter to Madame Aupick, 1 April 1861.

2. See Sartre 1975, 18; Pichois 1967; and Johnson 1998.

3. For other recent studies, with apologies to those omitted here, see Sima Godfrey, Rosemary Lloyd, Edward Kaplan, Marie Maclean, Amy Ransom, and Richard D. E. Burton. On the groundbreaking, fragmenting approach with which Proust tried to make Baudelaire readable to his (Proust's) mother, see Brigitte Mahuzier, "Profaned Memory: A Proustian Reading of 'Je n'ai pas oublié. . . .'"

4. In his editorial note on "la servante au grand cœur . . . ," Pichois cites a study published in the *Revue des Sciences Humaines* (juillet-septembre 1969): 477–80, in which William T. Bandy argues that "les pauvres morts" in line 4 include Baudelaire's deceased father (*OC* 1:1038).

5. Jérôme Thélot gives a much more detailed interpretation of "Les Dons des fées" as a "mythological narrative relating the genesis of the human world" (1993, 87–99). Although impressive in its elaboration, this reading fails, in my view, to account either for the semi-humorous tone of the text or for its opening lines, which specify that the fairies confer gifts on newborns "who have come into the world in the last twenty-four hours." This would suggest that the divine assembly is a daily, routine event rather than an inaugural scene of genesis.

6. In his detailed reading of "Les Yeux des pauvres," Christopher Prendergast explains that "'des yeux comme des portes cochères'" was a perfectly standard idiom for the wide-eyed in the nineteenth century. He then explores the irony involved in comparing the poverty-stricken eyes to the carriage entrances of elegant mansions, which poor people were never allowed to use (1985, 38–9).

Suffering and Expenditure

1. Subsequent references to Char *OC* are to his *Œuvres complètes*, 1995. No further page references will be given for "Baudelaire Irritates Nietzsche."

2. Char, in successive editions of his *Recherche de la base et du sommet*, first published in 1955, systematically developed the cult of his "grands astreignants." "Pages d'ascendants pour l'an 1964" contains a later list of "astreignants" and of "alliés," the latter term reserved for the *beaux-arts* (*OC* 711–12).

3. Prose texts in *Recherche de la base et du sommet* make it clear how central Rimbaud is to Char's view of the modern. See Char, "In 1871," "Réponses interrogatives à une question de Martin Heidegger," but especially "Arthur Rimbaud," an essay which originally served as Char's preface to the edition of Rimbaud published in the 1956 by the Club de l'Honnête Homme (*OC* 726–36). For a thorough analysis of Char's writings on and attitude toward Rimbaud, see La Charité, "The Role of Rimbaud."

4. Char states this banally in his response to a poll of contemporary poets ("Pour ou contre Baudelaire," *Les Nouvelles littéraires*): "Baudelaire's place in contemporary knowledge and sensibility is that of a very great poet whose genius and meaning have not stopped growing in the last one hundred years. Only today can we measure the degree of his undeniable sovereignty and universality."

5. *Blindness and Insight,* 148. For Char, Rimbaud remains unique, nevertheless, in that he represents life's supremacy over poetry (see Char's poem "Tu as bien fait de partir, Arthur Rimbaud," in *Fureur et mystère*). De Man ties the possibility of surpassing or abandoning literature to the concept of modernity: the "continuous appeal of modernity, the desire to break out of literature, toward the reality of the moment" is how the writer shows that literature exists in history, within time, instead of in the contradiction of endless newness (1983, 162).

6. For two more recent views on Baudelaire's modernity, see Compagnon 1990, 7–78, 177–80, and Meschonnic 1995, 469–82.

7. See Compagnon 1996 on Baudelaire's images of the good and bad seas.

8. The expressions "trois-mâts barque" and "la barque de Charon" are noted in *Heath's Standard French and English Dictionary,* 2 vols. (London: D. C. Heath, 1959).

9. *OC* 731–32, author's emphasis. The idea of a Baudelaire still enmeshed in Christianity corresponds to Breton's views in the 1930 *Second manifeste du surréalisme,* which Char signed. Char also clearly shares Breton's rejection of Claudel's Christian reading of *Illuminations* (without following Breton's shift toward a rejection of Rimbaud on the grounds, more or less, of religious ambiguities; see Breton 1988, 782–87). On Baudelaire and religion, see Ruff 1955, especially 281–366; *L'Année Baudelairie* 2 (1996), devoted to death and spirituality, but especially, in that issue, Milner, "Le paradis se gagne-t-il?," who critiques Ruff's Jansenist thesis; Lawler, *Poetry and Moral Dialectic,* who offers a balanced view of the place of the crucial section "Révolte" in *Les Fleurs du Mal* (16–25, 153–57, 182–88).

10. The broken shutter also appears in the poem "Le Ramier" (*Le Nu perdu* 1971): "Nous rallions nos pareils / Pour éteindre la dette / D'un volet qui battait / Généreux, généreux" (*OC* 448). On Char's linkage of creativity and transcendence, see Marty 1990, 159–228.

11. Char's mutilated giant also refers to another "grand astreignant," Poussin, through the figure of Orion, who is the protagonist of Char's 1975 *Aromates chasseurs* (*OC* 507–28).

12. "[J]e ne brûle pas les relais, mais je les élude," referring to his own remarks to the interviewer, but very pertinent to his poetry (*OC* 854–55). On Nietzsche and Char's aphorisms, see Aspel 1968, 168–70, 173.

13. "Réponses interrogatives à une question de Martin Heidegger," *OC* 734. See also Char's "A la question: 'Pourquoi ne croyez-vous point en Dieu?'" ("To the Question: 'Why do you not believe in God?'"): "If by some rare chance death did not end it all, we would probably find ourselves in front of something other than this God invented by men, in their image and adjusted for better or worse to their contradictions. Imagining a square of white linen, traversed by a sun ray, is nostalgically childish" (*OC* 658).

14. Veyne 1990, 318, and see for further comment his entire chapter, entitled "Héraclite, Heidegger et Nietzsche" (302–32).

15. "Faire du chemin avec . . . ," *Fenêtres dormantes et porte sur le toit,* in *OC* 580; "Peu à peu, et puis un vin silcieux," *La Nuit talismanique,* in *OC* 494. On Char's secular and metaphorical use of imagery of the gods, see Starobinski 1992.

16. Plouvier (1997) compares Nietzsche and Char as to their common rejection of history in favor of art.

17. Aspel 1968, 174, see also 179, on the "nécessité bienfaisante du hasard" in Nietzsche and Char. The article appeared before the publication of "Baudelaire Irritates Nietzsche" but is still very useful.

18. Nietzsche 1968, 126–27, author's emphasis. See also Zarathustra's speeches against suffering and pity in Nietzsche 1968, 143, 287.

19. Nietzsche 1985, 44. The English translations of the French are my own. See also Plouvier, who remarks on Nietzsche and Char's common sense of "lightness" and "marvel" in their confrontation with the world (1997, 218, 221–22).

20. See "Riche de larmes" (Rich with tears), one of Char's last poems: "Art is made of oppression and tragedy, themselves punctured occasionally by the onslaught of a joy which floods art's site, then leaves again" (*Eloge d'une soupçonnée, OC* 841).

21. See Char's "Nous avons" (*La Parole en archipel,* 1962), where a volcanic cataclysm kindles the poetic image and instills tension within freshness: "Notre parole, en archipel, vous offre, après la douleur et le désastre, des fraises qu'elle rapporte des landes de la mort, ainsi que ses doigts chauds de les avoir cherchées" [Our word, in the form of an archipelago, offers you, after pain and disaster, strawberries that it brings back from the moors of death, fingers still warm from the picking] (*OC* 409).

22. Historically, Nietzsche approved of Baudelaire in a way, as his letter to Peter Gast, dated 26 February 1888, makes clear in the context of the public reception of Wagner's music: "Wagner himself . . . surpasses a thousand times the understanding and the comprehension of the Germans. Does he surpass that of the French as well?" Nietzsche had often mused that the Frenchman most likely to appreciate Wagner "was that bizarre, three-quarters lunatic Baudelaire, the poet of *Les Fleurs du Mal.* It had disappointed me that this kindred spirit of Wagner's had not during his lifetime discovered him; I have underlined the passages in his poems in which there is a sort of *Wagnerian sensibility* which has found no form anywhere else in poetry (Baudelaire is a *libertine,* mystical, 'satanic,' but, above all, Wagnerian)" (author's emphases). Nietzsche then tells Gast of his discovery of the existence of a letter from Wagner to Baudelaire (see Nietzsche 1996, 286–88). See Delesalle, who refers in passing to this letter ("Eugène Crépet," 8 n. 16). Char seems unaware of these documents, but the thrust of "Baudelaire Irritates Nietzsche" goes to other issues.

23. Contrast "L'Etranger" with another poem in *Le Spleen de Paris,* "La Soupe et les nuages" (*OC* 1:298), where the poet becomes a useless "marchand de nuages" (cloud merchant). Remorse and self-deprecation return, like obsessions, to line the clouds.

24. See Veyne 1990, 313; Mathieu 1984–85, 1:121 n. 75, 2:90 n. 4. See also Nietzsche 1992, 63, among many other passages on the Apollonian and the Dionysian.

25. See La Charité on the crucial interplay of night and day in the collection *La Nuit talismanique:* "While light imagery may indeed tend to dominate Char's work, the creation of the active diurnal text is dependent on the order and prestige of night" (1973, 278). Some of the poems in the original edition of *La Nuit talismanique* were illustrated by Char, though not "Baudelaire Irritates Nietzsche." On the relation of image to text in this collection, see La Charité (1976), "Beyond the Poem."

26. We find an aesthetic pantheon in "Les Phares," but the notion of verse as sacrifice or defiance laid at God's feet goes against Char's impulse.

27. See de Man 1983, "Lyric and Modernity," 184.

To Spear It on the Mark, of Mystical Nature

1. Translator's note: this *incipit* subtitles Deguy's contribution, "Pour piquer dans le but, de mystique nature," in *Rue Descartes: Collège international de philosophie (Modernités esthétiques)* 10 (June 1994): 75–85 (Paris: Albin Michel). The author indicates: "An earlier draft of these pages was read at the colloquium, 'Baudelaire: Frameworks-in-Progress' (May 13–14, 1993, Lille University III)." Deguy's paper is written, as he likes to say, from "the point of the poetic view," in the style of a phenomenological *ars poetica* often verging on the prose poem. The present translation naturally adheres closely to the *meaning* of the original; however, out of deference to readers perhaps unfamiliar with the intricacies of Deguy's language, it incorporates careful rearrangement within paragraphs such that this English version represents an adaptation of Deguy's original French essay, indeed one of the richest in ramifications of his entire corpus.

Terminology inspired by semiotics appears in the passage where "reversibility" would constitute a "poieme": the coinage derives in part from "seme" and "sememe," elements in the analysis of a semantic utterance (see *Essais de sémiotique poétique* [Paris: Larousse, 1972], 13–14). Additionally, Deguy alludes throughout to two major thinkers whose influence he explicitly acknowledges in many other contexts: Heidegger and Girard. In *Being and Time* (32. et seq.), Heidegger speaks of the *Als-Struktur:* it is impossible to think through the matter of being and time without a consideration of what Deguy refers to in turn as a "structure en *comme,*" rendered here as "*like*-structure" in keeping with Deguy's critique of the *Als* in *La Poésie n'est pas seule* (Paris: Seuil, 1988), 31–37, 88–93. Deguy associates the idea of a generalized *like*-structure with the "capacity" of an artwork (its *form*), which is that of an "intrinsic analogy" whose terms are, in the example of Baudelaire's poetics: the poem is to poetry as the finite is to the infinite. Unconcealment of being and time, which Heidegger interprets as "presence," takes place through the Logos, one definition of which is analogy *of* proportion: the *like*-structure. Now, Deguy suggests, the *content* that Baudelaire conveys through poetic *capacity* or form, reaffirms "the Christian tradition of truth" as Revelation of Logos identified with the position of a sacrificial victim. For Girard, the scapegoat occupies the position of the double which in Deguy's poetics *turns into* the place where anthropomorphosis in general may occur. The play of presence/absence in the sighting of "the *very faraway very near*" (congruent with Derrida's notion of interspacing within the movement of *différance*) would be mediated by the figure of the *pharmakos* or sacrificial victim, as it were the guarantor of difference, both as Christian value and as an emblem apart from its theological meaning: hence the motif of "holy prostitution," where the oxymoron "paroxyzing a paradox" correlates to the position of the double as scapegoat /deity in Girard. The "oxymoronic existentiality of thwarted being" is equivalent to the "capacity," that of approach *and* withdrawal, at once apparition *and* erasure: the "to-be-*and*-not-to-be" that distinguishes its configuration *(Gestalt),* and to which corresponds the meaning of Christian Revelation wherein the ritual victim embodies at once finitude and the infinite.

Works Cited

Adler, Kathleen. 1986. *Manet*. London: Phaidon.

Altieri, Charles. 1973. "From Symbolist Thought to Immanence: The Ground of Postmodern American Poetics," *Boundary* 2 (Spring): 605–39.

Aspel, Paulène. 1968. "René Char et Nietzsche." *Liberté* 10.4:166–82.

Austin, Lloyd. 1956. *L'Univers poétique de Baudelaire: Symbolisme et symbolique*. Paris: Mercure de France.

Babou, Hippolyte. 1867. "Les dissidents de l'Exposition: M. Edouard Manet." *La Revue libérale* 2:284–89.

Babuts, Nicolae. 1997.*Baudelaire at the Limits and Beyond*. Newark: Delaware University Press.

Bailly, Jean-Christophe. 1997. "'Harmony in Red and Green': Un tableau de Baudelaire." *L'Année Baudelaire* 3:123–31.

Banville, Théodore de. 1978. *Petit Traité de poésie française*. Reprinted in the collection "Les Introuvables." Imprimerie de Provence, France: Editions d'Aujourd 'hui.

Barthes, Roland. 1964. "Le dernier des écrivains heureux." *Essais critiques*. 94–105. Paris: Seuil (Collection Points).

———. 1977. "The Death of the Author." In *Image, Music, Text*. Trans. Stephen Heath, 142–48. New York: Hill and Wang.

Baudelaire, Charles. 1961. *Les Fleurs du Mal*. Ed. Antoine Adam. Paris: Garnier.

———. 1964. *The Painter of Modern Life and Other Essays*. Trans. Jonathan Mayne. London: Phaidon. Distributed by New York Graphic Society, Greenwich, Conn.

———.1965. *Art in Paris, 1845–1862: Salons and Other Exhibitions*. Trans. Jonathan Mayne. London: Phaidon. Distributed by New York Graphic Society, Greenwich, Conn.

———. 1970. *Paris Spleen*. Trans. Louise Varèse. New York: New Directions.

———. 1973. *Correspondance*. 2 vols. Ed. Claude Pichois and Jean Ziegler. Paris: Gallimard (Bibliothèque de la Pléiade).

———. 1975–76. *Œuvres complètes*. 2 vols. Ed. Claude Pichois. Paris: Gallimard (Bibliothèque de la Pléiade).

———. 1991. *The Prose Poems and La Fanfarlo*. Trans. Rosemary Lloyd. Oxford: Oxford University Press.

Bays, Gwendolyn. 1964. *The Orphic Vision: Seer Poets from Novalis to Rimbaud*. Lincoln: University of Nebraska Press.

Benjamin, Walter. 1969. "Die Aufgabe des Übersetzers." Translated as "The Task of the Translator: An Introduction to the Translation of Baudelaire's *Tableaux Parisiens*." In *Illuminations*, ed. Hannah Arendt, 69–82. New York: Schocken.

———. 1977. "Über einige Motive bei Baudelaire." *Illuminationen. Ausgewählte Schriften*. Vol. 1. Pt 2. 605–54. Frankfurt a. M.: Suhrkamp.

———. 1982. *Charles Baudelaire, un poète lyrique à l'apogée du capitalisme.* Trans. Jean Lacoste. Paris: Payot.

———. 1983. "The Paris of the Second Empire in Baudelaire." In *Charles Baudelaire: A Lyric Poet in the Era of High Capitalism,*" trans. Harry Zohn, 11–106. 1973. Reprint, London: Verso.

Berman, Antoine. 1995. *Pour une critique des traductions.* Paris: Gallimard.

Blanchot, Maurice. 1959. "Rousseau." *Le Livre à venir.* 63–74. Paris: Gallimard.

Blin, Georges. 1969–70. "Littérature française moderne." *Annuaire du Collège de France.* 69e année. *Résumé des cours, 1968–1969,* 532–39.

Bloch, Oscar, and Walther von Wartburg. 1968. *Dictionnaire étymologique de la langue française.* Paris: PUF.

Bowness, Alan. 1972. "Courbet's Early Subject Matter." In *French Nineteenth-Century Painting and Literature,* ed. Ulrich Fink, 116–32. Manchester: University of Manchester Press.

Breton, André. 1988. *Œuvres complètes.* Vol. 1. Ed. Marguerite Bonnet et al. Paris: Gallimard (Bibliothèque de la Pléiade).

Brookner, Anita. 1971. *The Genius of the Future.* London: Phaidon.

Bryson, Norman. 1983. *Vision and Painting: The Logic of the Gaze.* New Haven: Yale University Press.

Burton, Richard D. E. 1988. *Baudelaire in 1859: A Study in the Sources of Poetic Creativity.* Cambridge: Cambridge University Press.

Cachin, Françoise, Charles S. Moffett, and Juliet Wilson Bareau. 1983. *Manet: 1832–83.* New York: Metropolitan Museum of Art and Harry N. Abrams.

Cargo, Robert T. 1968. *A Concordance to Baudelaire's* Les Fleurs du Mal. Chapel Hill: University of North Carolina Press.

Carrier, David. 1985. "Manet and His Interpreters." *Art History* 8 (September): 320–35.

———. 1996. *High Art. Charles Baudelaire and the Origins of Modernist Painting.* University Park: Pennsylvania State University Press.

Castex, Pierre-Georges. 1969. *Baudelaire critique d'art.* Paris: SEDES.

Chambers, Ross. 1987. "Colère vaporisée." *Mélancolie et opposition.* 39–69. Paris: J. Corti.

Char, René. 1957. "Pour ou contre Baudelaire." *Les Nouvelles littéraires* 6 (June): 1.

———. 1972. *La Nuit talismanique.* Geneva: Albert Skira.

———. 1995. *Œuvres complètes.* 2d ed. Ed. J. Roudaut et al. Paris: Gallimard (Bibliothèque de la Pléiade).

Chateaubriand, François-René de. 1978. *Essai sur les révolutions. Génie du christianisme.* Ed. Maurice Regard. Paris: Gallimard (Bibliothèque de la Pléiade).

Clark, Timothy J. 1985. *The Painting of Modern Life: Paris in the Art of Manet and His Followers.* New York: Knopf.

Compagnon, Antoine. 1990. *Les Cinq Paradoxes de la modernité.* Paris: Seuil.

———. 1993. "Baudelaire devant l'éternel." In *Dix Etudes sur Baudelaire,* ed. Martine Bercot and André Guyaux, 71–111. Paris: Champion.

———. 1996. "Le rire énorme de la mer." *L'Année Baudelaire* 2:63–74.

Cousin, Victor. 1830. *Cours de philosophie sur le fondement des idées absolues, du Vrai, du Beau et du Bien.* Paris: Hachette.

———. 1843. "Introduction." *Œuvres philosophiques du Père André.* Paris: Charpentier.

———. 1845. "Du beau et de l'art." *Revue des Deux Mondes,* n.s. 9 (11 September): 773–811.

————. 1853. *Du Vrai, du Beau et du Bien*. Paris: Didier.

Cohn, Robert Greer. 1974. "Symbolism." *Journal of Aesthetics and Art Criticism* 33 (Winter): 181–92.

Davis, Bruce. 1983–84. "Manet's Two Portraits of Baudelaire." *Print Collector's Newsletter* 14: 47–48.

Deguy, Michel. 1994. "Pour piquer dans le but, de mystique nature." *Rue Descartes* 10 (June): 75–85.

Delesalle, Jean-François. 1976. "Eugène Crépet." *Bulletin Baudelairien* 11.2: 3–10.

Delvaille, Bernard. 1971. *La Poésie symboliste: Anthologie*. Paris: Seghers.

de Man, Paul. 1983. "Literary History and Literary Modernity," "Lyric and Modernity." In *Blindness and Insight*. 2d ed. Ed. Wlad Godzich, 142–65, 166–86. Minneapolis: University of Minnesota Press.

————. 1988. "The Double Aspect of Symbolism." *Yale French Studies* 74: 3–16.

————. 1989. "Hypogram and Inscription," "Reading and History." In *The Resistance to Theory*, ed. Wlad Godzich, 27–53, 54–72. Minneapolis: University of Minnesota Press.

Derrida, Jacques. 1967. *De la Grammatologie*. Paris: Minuit.

Didier, Béatrice. 1973. "'Une économie de l'écriture,' 'Fusées' et 'Mon cœur mis à nu.'" *Littérature* 10 (May): 57–64.

————. 1991. *Le Journal intime*. Paris: PUF.

Dolan, Therese. 1997. "Skirting the Issue: Manet's Portrait of *Baudelaire's Mistress, Reclining*." *Art Bulletin* 79 (December): 611–29.

Duret, Théodore. 1906. *Histoire d'Edouard Manet et de son œuvre*. Paris: Charpentier et Fasquelle.

Eigeldinger, Marc. 1951. *Le Platonisme de Baudelaire*. Neuchâtel: A la Baconnière.

Farwell, Beatrice. 1973. "Manet and the Nude: A Study in Iconography in the Second Empire." Ph.D. diss., UCLA.

Fletcher, Angus. 1964. *Allegory: The Theory of a Symbolic Mode*. Ithaca: Cornell University Press.

Foucault, Michel. 1977. "What Is an Author?" In *Language, Counter-Memory, Practice*, ed. Donald F. Bouchard and trans. Donald F. Bouchard and Sherry Simon, 113–38. Ithaca and London: Cornell University Press.

Frey, Hans-Jost. 1986. *Studien über das Reden der Dichter*. München: Wilhelm Fink.

————. 1996a. "Baudelaire." In *Studies in Poetic Discourse*, trans. William Whobrey, 61–115. Stanford, Calif.: Stanford University Press.

————. 1996b. "On Presentation in Benjamin." In *Walter Benjamin: Theoretical Questions*, ed. David S. Ferris, 139–64. Stanford, Calif.: Stanford University Press.

Fried, Michael. 1984. "Painting Memories: On the Containment of the Past in Baudelaire and Manet." *Critical Inquiry* 10:510–42.

————. 1996. *Manet's Modernism or The Face of Painting in the 1860s*. Chicago: University of Chicago Press.

Froidevaux, Gérald. 1989. *Baudelaire. Représentation et modernité*. Paris: J. Corti.

Gautier, Théophile. 1836. "De la composition en peinture." *La Presse* (22 November).

————. 1839. "Salon de 1839. VII. Eugène Delacroix, Riesener." *La Presse* (4 April).

————. 1843. "Pochades, paradoxes et fantaisies. IV. (V.) Puchero. V. (VI.) Têtes d'anges. VI. (VII.) Parenthèse. VII. (VIII.) Orthopédie." *La Presse* (19 December). Reprinted in *Caprices*, 194–211.

————. 1844. "Salon de 1844. II." *La Presse* (27 March).

————. 1849. "En Chine." *La Presse* (25 June). Reprinted in *Caprices,* 260–76.

————. 1850. "Musée espagnol." *La Presse* (27 August).

————. 1852. "Salon de 1852. X. MM. Hébert; Cogniet; Richard; Amaury Duval; Lehmann; Dubuffe." *La Presse* (27 May).

————. 1855a. "Exposition universelle de 1855: Peinture—Sculpture (II)." *Le Moniteur universel* (19 May). Reprinted in *Les Beaux-Arts,* 1:1–9.

————. 1855b. "Exposition universelle de 1855. Peinture. Sculpture. MM. Ansdell, Maclise, Lucy, Foggo, Cross, Cope, Armitage." *Le Moniteur universel* (23 May). Reprinted in *Les Beaux-Arts* 1:9–18.

————. 1855c. "Exposition universelle de 1855. IV. M. Mulready." *Le Moniteur universel* (25 May). Reprinted in *Les Beaux-Arts,* 1:18–30.

————. 1855d. "Exposition universelle de 1855. Peinture. Sculpture. VI. MM. Webster, Grant, Frith, Frost, Egg, Hook." *Le Moniteur universel* (2 June). Reprinted in *Les Beaux-Arts,* 1:43–55.

————. 1855e. "Exposition universelle de 1855. Peinture—Sculpture. Collection chinoise." *Le Moniteur universel* (6 July). Reprinted in *Les Beaux-Arts,* 1:130–42.

————. 1855–56. *Les Beaux-Arts en Europe.* 2 vols. Paris: M. Lévy.

————. 1856a. *Caprices et zigzags.* 2d ed. Paris: Hachette.

————. 1856b. "Introduction." *L'Artiste* (14 December): 3–5.

————. 1856c. *L'Art moderne.* Paris: M. Lévy.

————. 1858a. "De la mode." *L'Artiste* (14 March): 169–71.

————. 1858b. "Galerie du XIXᵉ siècle: Honoré de Balzac." *L'Artiste* (21, 28 March; 4, 18, 25 April; 2 May). Reprinted in *Portraits contemporains,* 45–131.

————. 1874. *Portraits contemporains.* Paris: Charpentier.

————. 1880. *Fusains et eaux-fortes.* Paris: Charpentier.

————. 1978. *Histoire du romantisme.* Paris: Charpentier. 1874. Reprinted in the collection "Les Introuvables." Imprimerie de Provence, France: Editions d'Aujourd'hui.

————. 1986. *Baudelaire par Gautier.* Présentation et notes critiques par Claude-Marie Senninger avec une étude complémentaire par Lois Cassandra Hamrick. Paris: Klincksieck (Bibliothèque du XIXᵉ siècle).

————. 1995. *Œuvres. Choix de romans et de contes.* Ed. Paolo Tortonese. Paris: Laffont (Bouquins).

Godfrey, Sima. 1985. "'Mère des souvenirs': Baudelaire, Memory and Mother." *L'Esprit créateur* 25.2:32–44.

Gombrich, Ernst. 1958. *Art and Illusion.* Princeton: Princeton University Press.

Goncourt, Edmond and Jules de. 1956. *Journal. Mémoires de la vie littéraire.* Vol. 1 *1851–1863.* Ed. Robert Ricatte. Paris: Fasquelle/Flammarion,.

Gould, Evelyn. 1989. *Virtual Theater: From Diderot to Mallarmé.* Baltimore and London: John Hopkins University Press.

Grand Dictionnaire universel du XIXᵉ siècle. 1874. Vol. 11. Paris: Administration du Grand Dictionnaire Universel.

Hamburger, Michael. 1969. *The Truth of Poetry: Tensions in Modern Poetry from Baudelaire to the 1960s.* New York: Harcourt Brace Jovanovich.

Hamrick, L. Cassandra. 1993. "Gautier et la modernité de son temps." *Théophile Gautier en son temps, Bulletin de la Société Théophile Gautier* 15:521–42.

———. 1998. "Au-delà de la traduction: Baudelaire, Gautier et le dictionnaire du poète-artiste-critique." In *Langues du XIXe siècle,* ed. Graham Falconer, et al., 215–32. Coll. A la Recherche du XIXe siècle. Toronto: Centre d'études romantiques.

Hanson, Anne Coffin. 1977. *Manet and the Modern Tradition.* New Haven: Yale University Press.

Harris, Jean C. 1990. *Edouard Manet, The Graphic Work: A Catalogue Raisonné.* Ed. Joel M. Smith. San Francisco: Alan Wofsy Fine Arts.

Hegel, G. W. F. 1977. *Hegel's Phenomenology of Spirit.* Trans. A. V. Miller. Ed. J. N. Finlay. New York: Oxford University Press.

Herbert, George. 1994. *Complete Poetry.* Ed. Louis L. Martz. Oxford: Oxford University Press.

Howells, Bernard. 1996. *Baudelaire. Individualism, Dandyism and the Philosophy of History.* Oxford: European Humanities Research Center, LEGENDA.

Jackson, John E., and Claude Pichois, eds. 1996. *L'Année Baudelaire* 2.

Jameson, Fredric. 1985. "Baudelaire as Modernist and Postmodernist: The Dissolution of the Referent and the Artificial 'Sublime.'" In *Lyric Poetry: Beyond New Criticism,* ed. Chaviva Hosek and Patricia Parker, 247–63. Ithaca, N.Y.: Cornell University Press.

Jauss, Hans Robert. 1978. "La 'modernité' dans la tradition littéraire et la conscience d'aujour-d'hui." In *Pour une esthétique de la réception.* Trans. Claude Maillard, 158–209. Paris: Gallimard.

Johnson, Barbara. 1998. *The Feminist Difference: Literature, Psychoanalysis, Race, and Gender.* Cambridge, Mass.: Harvard University Press.

Kaplan, Edward. 1980. "Baudelaire's Portrait of the Poet as Widow: Three Poëmes en Prose and 'Le Cygne.'" *Symposium* 34.3:233–48.

Keats, John. 1987. *Letters.* Ed. Robert Gittings. Oxford: Oxford University Press.

Kristeva, Julia. 1974. *La Révolution du langage poétique.* Paris: Seuil.

Labarthe, Patrick. 1992. "Réel et beauté. Rencontre Stendhal-Baudelaire." *Stendhal Club* 137:37–50.

La Charité, Virginia. 1973. "René Char and the Ascendancy of Night." *French Forum* 1:269–80.

———. 1973–74. "Rimbaud and the Johannine Christ: Containment and Liberation." *Nineteenth-Century French Studies* 2.1–2 (Fall–Winter): 39–60.

———. 1974. "The Role of Rimbaud in Char's Poetry." *PMLA* 89:57–63.

———. 1976. "Beyond the Poem: René Char's *La Nuit talismanique.*" *Symposium* 30:14–26.

Lacan, Jacques. 1977. *Ecrits: A Selection.* Trans. Alan Sheridan. New York: Norton.

Lacoue-Labarthe, Philippe, and Jean-Luc Nancy (in collaboration with Anne-Marie Lang). 1978. *L'Absolu littéraire: Théorie de la littérature du romantisme allemand.* Paris: Seuil.

Laforgue, Pierre. 1996. "Baudelaire, Hugo et la royauté du poète: le romantisme en 1860." *Revue d'Histoire Littéraire de la France* 96:348–55.

Larthomas, Pierre. 1974. *Problèmes et méthodes de l'histoire littéraire.* Colloque (18 November 1972) de la Société d'histoire littéraire de la France. Paris: Armand Colin.

Lawler, James R. 1997. *Poetry and Moral Dialectic. Baudelaire's "Secret Architecture."* Cranbury, N.J.: Associated University Presses.

Lejeune, Philippe. 1977. *Le Pacte autobiographique.* Paris: Seuil.

Le Tourneur, Pierre, trans. 1776. *Shakespeare traduit de l'anglais, dédié au roi.* Vol. 1. Paris: Chez la Veuve Duchesne.

Lévi-Strauss, Claude. 1958. "L'efficacité du symbolique." In *Anthropologie structurale.* Vol. 1. 205–26. Paris: Plon.

————. 1962. "'Les Chats' de Charles Baudelaire." *L'Homme* 2 (January–April):5–21.

Littré, Emile. 1874. "Barque." *Dictionnaire de la langue française.* 4 vols. Paris: Hachette.

Lloyd, Rosemary. 1991. "Baudelaire, Marceline Desbordes-Valmore et la fraternité des poètes." *Bulletin Baudelairien* 26.2:65–74.

Maclean, Marie. 1982. "Baudelaire and the Paradox of Procreation." *Studi francesi* 26.1:87– 98.

Mahuzier, Brigitte. 1997. "Profaned Memory: A Proustian Reading of 'Je n'ai pas oublié . . .'" In *Understanding "Les Fleurs du Mal": Critical Readings,* ed. William J. Thompson, 160–75. Nashville: Vanderbilt University Press.

Mallarmé, Stéphane. 1945. *Œuvres complètes.* Ed. Henri Mondor and G. Jean-Aubry. Paris: Gallimard (Bibliothèque de la Pléiade).

————. 1969. *Correspondance.* Vol. 3. Ed. L. J. Austin. Paris: Gallimard (Bibliothèque de la Pléiade).

Malraux, André. 1951. *Les Voix du silence.* Paris: Gallimard.

Marty, Eric. 1990. *René Char.* Paris: Seuil.

Mathieu, Jean-Claude. 1984–85. *La Poésie de René Char, ou le sel de la splendeur.* 2 vols. Paris: J. Corti.

Meschonnic, Henri. 1995. "L'aujourd'hui, l'introuvable." *Politique du rythme. Politique du sujet.* Lagrasse: Verdier.

Michaud, Guy. 1947. *Message poétique du symbolisme.* 4 Vols. Paris: Nizet.

McGinnis, Reginald. 1994. *La Prostitution sacrée.* Paris: Belin (Collection "L'Extrème contemporain").

Milner, Max. 1967. *Baudelaire. Enfer ou Ciel, qu'importe!* Paris: Plon.

————. 1994. "La voyance de l'aveugle dans *L'Homme qui rit de* Victor Hugo." *VOIR* 9 (November): 26–35.

————. 1996a. "Le Paradis se gagne-t-il?" *L'Année Baudelaire* 2:11–23.

————. 1996b. "[Sur *L'Homme qui rit*]." *VOIR* 12–13 (November): 124–26.

Milner, Max, and Claude Pichois. 1985. *Littérature française.* Vol. 7. *De Chateaubriand à Baudelaire.* Paris: Arthaud.

Nietzsche, Friedrich. 1968. *Thus Spoke Zarathustra.* In *The Portable Nietzsche.* 2d ed. Ed. and trans. Walter Kaufmann. New York: Viking Press.

————. 1974. *The Gay Science.* Trans. Walter Kaufmann. New York: Vintage Books.

————. 1985. *La Naissance de la philosophie à l'époque de la tragédie grecque.* Trans. Geneviève Bianquis. 1938. Reprint, Paris: Gallimard.

————. 1992. *The Birth of Tragedy.* In *Basic Writings of Nietzsche,* 4th ed., ed. and trans. Walter Kaufmann, 1–144. New York: Random House.

————. 1996. *Selected Letters of Friedrich Nietzsche.* Ed. and trans. Christopher Middleton. 1969. Reprint, Indianapolis: Hackett Publishing.

Oehler, Dolf. 1996. *Le Spleen contre l'oubli:Juin 1848.* Trans. Guy Petitdemange. Paris: Payot.

Peyre, Henri. 1971. *Qu'est-ce que le romantisme?* Paris: PUF.

————. 1974. *Qu'est-ce que le symbolisme?* Paris: PUF.

Pichois, Claude. 1959. "Préromantiques, rousseauistes et shakespeariens (1770–1778)." *Revue de Littérature comparée* 33:348–55.

————. 1967. "Baudelaire ou la difficulté créatrice." *Baudelaire: Etudes et témoignages.* 242– 61. Neuchâtel: A la Baconnière.

————. 1979. "La Littérature française à la lumière du surnaturalisme." *Le Surnaturalisme français. Actes du colloque organisé à l'Université Vanderbilt les 31 mars et 1er avril 1978.* 9–28. Neuchâtel: A la Baconnière.

Pichois, Claude, with Jean Ziegler. 1989. *Baudelaire*. Trans. Graham Robb. London: Hamish Hamilton.

Plouvier, Paule. 1997. "Le Gai savoir ou la sagesse de René Char." In *Trois Poètes face à la crise de l'histoire: André Breton, Saint-John Perse, René Char,* ed. Paule Plouvier et al. 209–22. Paris: L'Harmattan.

Poe, Edgar Allan. 1965. *Marginalia: The Complete Works of Edgar Allan Poe*. Vol. 16. Ed. James A. Harrison. New York: AMS.

Pommier, Jean. 1967. *La Mystique de Baudelaire*. 1932. Reprint, Geneva: Slatkine.

Poulet, Georges. 1980. *La Poésie éclatée*. Paris: PUF.

Preminger, Alex, ed. 1974. *Princeton Encyclopedia of Poetry*. Princeton, N.J.: Princeton University Press.

Prendergast, Christopher. 1985. *Paris and the Nineteenth Century*. Oxford: Blackwell.

Proust, Antonin. 1913. *Edouard Manet, Souvenirs*. Paris: Renouard.

Proust, Marcel. 1987. *A la recherché du temps perdu*. Vol. 2. Ed. J.-Y. Tadié. Paris: Gallimard (Bibliothèque de la Pléiade).

Rabaté, Dominique, ed. 1996. *Figures du sujet lyrique*. Paris: PUF.

Ransom, Amy. 1993. "Mon semblable, ma mère: Woman, Subjectivity and Escape in *Les Fleurs du Mal*." *Paroles Gelées* 11:31–55.

Réau, Louis. 1958. *Iconographie de l'art chrétien*. Vol. 3. Paris: PUF.

Reff, Theodore. 1982. *Manet and Modern Paris: One Hundred Paintings, Drawings, Prints, and Photographs by Manet and His Contemporaries*. Washington: National Gallery of Art.

Richard, Jean-Pierre. 1955. "Profondeur de Baudelaire." *Poésie et profondeur*. 93–162. Paris: Seuil.

Ricœur, Paul. 1983. *Temps et récit*. Vol. 1. Paris: Seuil.

Riffaterre, Michael. 1978. *Semiotics of Poetry*. Bloomington: Indiana University Press.

Rimbaud, Arthur. 1972. *Œuvres complètes*. Ed. Antoine Adam. Paris: Gallimard (Bibliothèque de la Pléiade).

Robb, Graham. 1993. *La Poésie de Baudelaire et la poésie française, 1838–1852*. Paris: Aubier.

Rouart, Denis, and Daniel Wildenstein. 1975. *Edouard Manet, catalogue raisonné*. 2 vols. Lausanne-Paris: Bibliothèque des Arts.

Rousseau, Jean-Jacques. 1952. *Les Confessions*. Ed. Ad. Van Bever. 3 vols. Paris: Garnier.

Ruff, Marcel A. 1955. *L'Esprit du mal et l'esthétique baudelairienne*. Paris: Armand Colin.

Sandblad, Nils. 1954. *Manet: Three Studies in Artistic Conception*. Trans. Walter Nash. Lund: CWK Gleerup.

Sartre, Jean-Paul. 1948. *Qu'est-ce que la littérature?* Paris: Gallimard (Collection Folio).

———. 1975. *Baudelaire*. 1947. Reprint, Paris: Gallimard.

Seebacher, Jacques. 1993. *Victor Hugo, ou le calcul des profondeurs*. Paris: PUF.

Shiff, Richard. 1987. "Performing an Appearance: On the Surface of Abstract Expressionism." In *Abstract Expressionism: The Critical Developments*, ed. Michel Auping, 94–123. New York: Abrams.

Staël, Germaine de. 1968. *De l'Allemagne*. Vol. 1. Ed. Simone Balayé. Paris: Garnier-Flammarion.

Stendhal, Henri Beyle. 1926. *De l'Amour*. Vol. 2. Ed. Daniel Muller and Pierre Jourda. Paris: Champion.

———. 1934. *Correspondance*. Vol. 4. Ed. Henri Martineau. Paris: Le Divan.

Starobinski, Jean. 1989. *La Mélancolie au miroir: Trois lectures de Baudelaire*. Paris: Julliard.

———. 1992. "René Char et la définition du poème." In *René Char. Faire du Chemin avec . . .* by Marie-Claude Char. 305–16. Paris: Gallimard.

Tabarant, A. 1947. *Manet et ses œuvres*. Paris: Gallimard.

Taylor, Charles. 1989. *Sources of the Self: The Making of the Modern Identity*. Cambridge, Mass.: Harvard University Press.

Thélot, Jérôme. 1993. *Baudelaire: Violence et poésie*. Paris: Gallimard.

Valéry, Paul. 1957. *Œuvres*. Ed. Jean Hytier. 2 vols. Paris: Gallimard (Bibliothèque de la Pléiade).

Vegliante, Jean-Charles. 1991. *Sonnets du petit pays entraîné vers le nord*. Sens: Obsidiane.

Vendler, Helen. 1997. *The Art of Shakespeare's Sonnets*. Harvard: Belknap Press.

Verlaine, Paul. 1969. *Œuvres poétiques*. Ed. Jacques Robichez. Paris: Garnier.

———. 1977. *Les Poètes maudits*. Milan: Cisalpino-Goliardica.

Veyne, Paul. 1990. *René Char en ses poèmes*. Paris: Gallimard.

Zola, Emile. 1991. *Ecrits sur l'art*. Ed. Jean-Pierre Leduc-Adine. Paris: Gallimard (Série "Tel").

Contributors and Translators

Contributors

JEAN-CHRISTOPHE BAILLY is a dramatist, poet, and essayist. A professor at the Ecole Nationale de la Nature et du Paysage in Blois, he teaches the cultural history of the landscape. His most recent publications include *Le Propre du langage, voyage au pays des noms communs* (Seuil, 1997); *Basse continue* (Seuil, 2000); a long poem, *Panoramiques;* and a collection of essays (Christian Bourgois, 2000) reexamining the problematic broached earlier in *La Fin de l'hymne* (Bourgois, 1991).

SUSAN BLOOD is assocate professor of French at the State University of New York at Albany and the author of *Baudelaire and the Aesthetics of Bad Faith* (Stanford University Press, 1997).

YVES BONNEFOY is emeritus professor at the Collège de France, to which he was elected in 1981 to a chair in comparative poetics. Since the publication of *Du mouvement et de l'immobilité de Douve* in 1953 (Mercure de France), he has been considered a major French poet. His many publications include, as well, essays, criticism, and translations, and he is a noted translator of Shakespeare. Among his recent books are *La Pluie d'été* (La Sétérée, 1999), *Keats et Leopardi, traductions nouvelles* (Mercure, 2000), *Destins et lieux de l'image* (Seuil, 1999), *La Communauté des traducteurs* (Presses Universitaires de Strasbourg, 2000), and *Baudelaire et la tentation de l'oubli* (Bibliothèque de France, 2000), based on a series of important lectures on Baudelaire. His interest in Baudelaire is long-standing and includes his essay "Baudelaire contre Rubens," published in *Le Nuage rouge* (Mercure de France, 1977).

MICHEL BRIX is *maître de conférences* at the Université Notre-Dame de la Paix in Namur, Belgium, where he is also a scholar at the Centre d'Etudes Nervaliennes. He is the author of several works on Nerval, including *Nerval journaliste, 1826–1851. Problématiques. Méthodes d'attribution* (Namur, Presses universitaires, 1989) and *Gérard de Nerval* (Fayard, 1995), co-authored with Claude Pichois. His most recent book is *Le Romantisme français. Esthétique platonicienne et modernité littéraire* (Louvain, Peters, 1999).

MICHEL DEGUY, a major figure in contemporary French literature and thought, is emeritus professor of literature at the Université de Paris VIII and editor of the journal *PO&SIE*. He served as president of the Collège International de Philosophie from 1990 to 1992. His writings interweave the genres of poetry, poetics, autobiographical prose, and philosophical inquiry. Among his recent books are *A ce qui n'en finit pas: thrène* (Seuil, 1995), *L'Energie du désespoir* (Presses Universitaires de France, 1998), and *Gisants: Poèmes 1980–1995* (Gallimard, 1999).

WILLIAM FRANKE is associate professor of comparative literature and Italian and of religious studies at Vanderbilt University. His book, *Dante's Interpretive Journey* (University of Chicago Press, 1996), works toward defining a poetics of religious revelation in terms of contemporary hermeneutical theory.

SIMA GODFREY is director of the Institute for European Studies at the University of British Columbia, where she also teaches nineteenth-century French literature. Her numerous essays on Baudelaire include "Baudelaire and Art" in the *Oxford Encyclopedia of Aesthetics* (1998).

L. CASSANDRA HAMRICK is associate professor of Modern Languages and associate director of the Center for International Studies at Saint Louis University. A former research assistant at the W. T. Bandy Center for Baudelaire and Modern French Studies at Vanderbilt University, she was W.

T. Bandy's last Ph.D. student. After Bandy's death, Claude Pichois served as a mentor in her early career. Many of her essays center on the textual correspondences in the art criticism of Baudelaire and Gautier, and she collaborated in the preparation of the Baudelaire chapter for the Cabeen bibliography.

VAN KELLY, Cramer Associate Professor for French Teaching and Research at the University of Kansas, studied as an undergraduate at Vanderbilt University with Claude Pichois. Kelly is the author of *Pascalian Fictions* (Summa, 1992) and is coeditor of *Epic and Epoch* (Texas Tech University Press, 1994). In his essays he has explored the relationship that contemporary French poetry entertains with Baudelaire and other precursors.

ROSEMARY LLOYD is Rudy Professor of French and Italian at Indiana University, Bloomington. Her early books identified her as a Baudelaire specialist: *Baudelaire et Hoffmann: affinités et influences* (Cambridge University Press, 1979) and *Baudelaire's Literary Criticism* (Cambridge University Press, 1981). Subsequent books have ranged broadly in nineteenth-century French literature and have included translations of Baudelaire, Mallarmé, and George Sand. Among her recent writings are *Closer & Closer Apart: Jealousy in Literature* (Cornell University Press, 1995) and *Mallarmé: The Poet and His Circle* (Cornell University Press, 1999).

MARGARET MINER is associate professor of French at the University of Illinois at Chicago. She is the author of *Resonant Gaps: Between Baudelaire and Wagner* (University of Georgia Press, 1995), as well as of a number of essays on Baudelaire, Rimbaud, Mallarmé, Janin, and the interaction of music with the fantastic in French literature.

KEVIN NEWMARK is associate professor of French at Boston College and is the author of *Beyond Symbolism: Textual History and the Future of Reading* (Cornell University Press, 1991), as well as of essays on Kierkegaard, Nietzsche, Baudelaire and Mallarmé.

JAMES S. PATTY is emeritus professor of French at Vanderbilt University and a member of the editorial committee of the *Bulletin Baudelairien,* of which he was one of the founders. He is the author of *Dürer in French Letters* (Champion/Slatkine, 1989) and has coedited several volumes, including *hommages* to W. T. Bandy and Claude Pichois.

TIMOTHY RASER is associate professor of French at the University of Georgia and is the author of *A Poetics of Art Criticism: The Case of Baudelaire* (University of North Carolina Press, 1989) and additional essays on Baudelaire.

SONYA STEPHENS is senior lecturer in the Department of French at Royal Holloway, University of London. She is the author of *Baudelaire's Prose Poems. The Practice and Politics of Irony* (Oxford University Press, 1999) and is the editor of *A History of Women's Writing in France* (Cambridge University Press, 2000).

PATRICIA A. WARD is professor of French and comparative literature at Vanderbilt University, where she has served as chair of the Department of French and Italian and acting director of the W. T. Bandy Center for Baudelaire and Modern French Studies. Her publications relating to nineteenth-century French literature include *The Medievalism of Victor Hugo* (Pennsylvania State University Press, 1975), *Joseph Joubert and the Critical Tradition: Platonism and Romanticism* (Droz, 1980), and two volumes of the *Carnet bibliographique Victor Hugo* (Les Lettres Modernes, 1985 and 1992).

Translators

WILSON BALDRIDGE is associate professor of French at Wichita State University and has published numerous articles on Michel Deguy. His translations of Deguy's poetry and poetics will be collected in the complete edition of *Gisants* (Bloodaxe Books [United Kingdom]). Among Baldridge's essays is "Michel Deguy et la pensée baudelairienne du symbole."

Tony Campbell is a freelance translator. He previously was a teacher of modern languages in Ireland.

Jan Plug is assistant professor of comparative literature at the University of Wisconsin, Madison. Among his other translations is Marc Froment-Meurice's *That Is to Say: Heidegger's Poetics* (Stanford University Press, 1998).

Index